Reconstructing Afghanistan

Reconstructing Afghanistan

Prospects and Limitations

Edited by

Arpita Basu Roy

Binoda Kumar Mishra

Maulana Abul Kalam Azad Institute of Asian Studies, Kolkata

SHIPRA

ISBN: 978-81-7541-548-5

First Published in India in 2011

Reconstructing Afghanistan: Prospects and Limitations

Published by:
SHIPRA PUBLICATIONS
H.O.: LG 18-19, Pankaj Central Market, Patparganj,
I.P. Ext., Delhi-110092, Tel: 91-11-2223 5152, 2223 6152
Br.Off.: 4617/18, Ansari Road, Darya Ganj,
New Delhi-110002, Tel: 6594 6453, 9810522367
E-mail: info@shiprapublications.com
www.shiprapublications.com

Contents

Section II
Regional Approaches to Peace in Afghanistan

Section III
Mitigating War Effects Through Development Interventions

Introduction

Arpita Basu Roy and *Binoda Kumar Mishra*

The concept of peace-building is increasingly being used in order to reflect the overlapping activities in the field of conflict and peace. The term is broadly used and connotes activities that go beyond crisis intervention such as longer-term development, and building of governance structures and institutions. It was used as a form of confidence-building during the Cold War and an instrument in reducing conflict around issues of economic inequality and it gained real momentum as a policy concept within the UN's strategy for the resolution of conflict. Peace-building is a process comprising various structures and their functions. It often entails a wide range of sequential activities, proceeding from cease-fire and refugee-resettlement to the establishment of a new government and economic reconstruction.[1] Ideally, activities involved in rebuilding war-torn societies are designed to enhance public security, generate economic recovery, facilitate social healing, and promote democratic institutions. Peace-building in post-settlement phase entails both short-term and long-term frameworks. In the aftermath of a negotiated agreement, the management of humanitarian crisis situations changes to become assistance in social and economic rehabilitation. Short-term management plans are based on intense negotiations to diffuse volatile situations and respond to the immediate needs of returning refuges and other marginalized groups. In the absence of local administrative structures, essential government functions are restored by international administrators or peace-keeping forces.

The general understanding of the peace-building enterprise is largely influenced by the former UN Secretary-General Boutros Boutros-Ghali's vision and direction for peace-building in his 1992 document *An Agenda for Peace.*[2] According to this UN document, peace-building consists of a wide range of activities associated with capacity building, reconciliation, and societal transformation.[3] Peace operations were originally received with great optimism, held as a panacea for overcoming violent social orders and creating a better world. However, the experiences in various parts of the world in the mid-1990s have shown that sustained peace based on political and military stabilization is not sufficient to end a protracted conflict based on ethnic, religious and other primordially fuelled rivalries, in the absence of a long-term perspective of structural transformation.[4] Although Nigeria and the Congo had to rebuild war-torn societies in the 1960s (in the case of Congo with UN political and military intervention), more systematic attention was drawn to post-conflict reconstruction with the shift of the international focus from Cold War politics to civil wars, often arising from inter-ethnic conflicts. Since the Namibia operation in 1989, peace-building has been widely recognised as a distinctive area of policy and operations.

Moreover, the concept of the UN peace-building is characterised furthermore by long-term political, economic and social provisions to address the causes of conflict, the interdependent quality and the consequent importance of co-ordination and the 'circle of preventive peace-building'. The first defining characteristic points to the core of peace-building, which lies in the stimulus to transform society, with an economy and institutions all geared to the effective prosecution of war to a society based upon and further promoting peace. Galtung has termed this the associative feature of the peace-building process, not merely addressing the ending of hostilities ('negative peace') but also the 'root causes' of conflict (positive peace).[5] The interdependent quality refers to the notion that peace-making, peace-keeping and peace-building are not separate activities, but are either mutually supportive or mutually corrosive. Peace cannot be attained after successfully ending the hostililties and keeping it by monitoring the parties' compliance with the peace agreements that has been reached in negotiations. If aptly coordinated, peace-building can effectively contribute to the peace-making and peace-keeping process. Finally peace-building can complete the circle by ensuring against the recurrence of conflict by building capacities for, among others, labour negotiation, civil society reconciliation, fair courts, and electoral process that enable a society to resolve its conflict before violence breaks out.[6]

Some draw a distinction between post-conflict peace-building and long-term peace-building. Post-conflict peace-building is connected to peacekeeping, and often involves demobilization and reintegration programmes, as well as immediate reconstruction needs.[7] Meeting immediate needs and handling crises is no doubt crucial. But while peacemaking and peacekeeping processes are important parts of peace transitions, they are not enough in themselves to meet long-term needs and build a lasting peace. Long-term peace-building techniques are designed to fill this gap, and to address the underlying substantive issues that brought about conflict. Various transformation techniques aim to move parties away from confrontation and violence, and guide them towards political and economic participation, peaceful relationships, and social harmony.

The re-creation of political institutions is a crucial task for maintaining stability in failing states where wars have destroyed the foundations of both governmental and civic institutions. A sustainable economy and self-governance will enhance the prospects for empowerment and trust building. Thus, according to Ho-Wong Jeong, the goals of peace-building will ultimately be achieved by reconstruction and reconciliation that are geared not only towards changing behaviour and perceptions but also towards social and institutional structures that can be mobilized to prevent future conflict.

As post-conflict situations differ greatly, contextual variables such as the nature of conflict and the methods of its settlement have differing effects in particular contexts. The duration and priorities of implementation activities vary according to the divisiveness of groups, the extent of economic and social destruction and the role of external actors. More serious political and social challenges are expected where there is a combination of political rivalry, economic collapse, radical changes in ethnic boundaries, and malfunction of the central government such as in Somalia and the Balkans. A comparative analysis of South Africa, Bosnia and Rwanda suggests that the methods for ending violent conflict (through negotiated settlement or military victory) have an impact on post-conflict political configurations (such as a majority rule, carving up territorial divisions, ethnic or racial hegemony through control of military and state institutions). Thus, challenges to peace-building stem from the fact that a significant part of the constituents may not support the negotiated solutions. In fact, peace agreements do not necessarily result in an outcome that satisfies everyone's interests. Ending conflict with a military victory creates unbalanced power relations that, in turn, often lead to difficulties in democratic governance as was exemplified by Rwanda. In some post-conflict settlement processes (e.g. Liberia, Sudan, Burundi, and DRC), continued hostilities and mistrust were followed by renewed fighting, and efforts to reach another settlement needed to be undertaken. For example, an agreement between contending groups in Liberia in September 1995 did not end the chaos but was followed by the renewed war. Sudan, from its independence in 1956 to the present, has also manifested a pattern of entrenched wars and periodic efforts at peacemaking between the predominantly Muslim north and animist and Christian south. Settling Africa's longest running civil war proved to be difficult because of the persistent attempts by the minority government to impose an Islamic state on a largely non-Muslim population. The experiences of Namibia, Mozambique, and other countries suggest that demobilization and re-integration of ex-combatants into productive sectors of society are critical to the creation of a sustainable security environment. Peacekeeping in East Timor, Bosnia-Herzgovina, and Kosovo, are examples of efforts to stabilize a post-conflict situation by enhancing a security environment through maintenance of order and enforcement of rules. Political stability is not immediately brought about by elections without stable institutional relations and consensus on political values, as is suggested by the case of Liberia. In promoting the goal of peace, development programmes (e.g. land reform in El Salvador) need to address the social and economic ills that are the roots of violence. Development cannot be easily disentangled from democracy and security.[8]

Transition from conflict to peace is unlikely to be a smooth process as old conflicts like centre-province tensions continues and new ones like land conflict related to returnees are emerging. A complex, shifting geography of violence and relative peace, characterizes the present day Afghan polity. Jonathan Goodhand points out that it is an oversimplification to associate disorder with violence and return of order with peace. He cites that violent resistance may ultimately have positive social outcomes[9] – the growing assertiveness, for example, of the historically excluded groups such as the Hazaras. These, as he rightly points out, are some of the basic realities that must be factored into conflict resolution, peace building and reconstruction, otherwise peace-building efforts are unlikely to succeed.[10] Hence, one can argue that "ending the war" does not necessarily mean peace, at least not in the case of Afghanistan. It must involve the transformation of the institutions, networks and incentive systems, – nationally, regionally, and locally that caused and perpetuate the conflict system in Afghanistan.[11]

The complex tasks of peace-building involve multiple functions. Diverse operations can be characterized in terms of a balance not only between military and civilian components but also among sectors. The number and size of the international agencies involved also lead to complexities which makes it necessary for improved planning and organisational coordination for operational effectiveness. There are different levels at which peace-building in Afghanistan has to be conducted and there has to be long-term as well as short-term goals. It is quite clear that peace-building in Afghanistan cannot be achieved in a short time and seven years is too short a time to expect beneficial results. What can be sought for is a phased multi-task and multi-track peace-building policy for Afghanistan which operates at different levels which starts at the grassroots and continues up to the international level.

Lasting reconstruction and peace-building in "post-conflict" situations must be rooted in local decision-making and actions and there is a growing demand inside Afghanistan to empower local capacity. The "international" approach to reconstruction does not often take sufficient account of this factor, either for peace-building or for development and does little to strengthen local capacity at the grassroots level. Post-conflict reconstruction by the donors has privileged international agencies in allocating resources and is almost certainly not the most cost-effective in the short-term. There are no purely military solutions in Afghanistan: while the use of force will be necessary, a way forward must be rooted in political and economic processes. There has been a proliferation of initiatives, with thousands of projects run by UN agencies, Provincial Reconstruction Teams and NGOs but they are often working at cross-purposes. In the newly-constrained security environment, these initiatives have often been brought to a stand-still. As a result, many now realize that the reconstruction "system" has reached a log-jam and cannot deliver on its intended outcomes. During a 2007 survey, Afghans across the country, rural and urban, expressed the feeling of being marginalized during the reconstruction process. So it is important to understand what is needed to empower local capacity for Afghans to meet their future needs while creating the socio-economic conditions that would promote peace, stability and rehabilitation.

This book is a compilation of papers presented in an international seminar organised by the Maulana Abul Kalam Azad Institute of Asian Studies, Kolkata and the Jamia Millia Islamia University, New Delhi during March 2009. It attempted to look for answers to questions, in relation both to Afghanistan and more generally, drawing on the experience of speakers and participants. This seminar focussed on how a domestically-driven processes can be designed to work in Afghanistan and similar contexts, starting with the attributes of such an approach of

"Afghanization"; why some programmes worked and others did not in the 2001-08 period; and suggest some ways forward. The discussions revolved around the following themes:

(1) Conflict and Peace-Building in Afghanistan: The Experience So Far;
(2) Regional Approaches to Peace in Afghanistan;
(3) Mitigating war Effects through Development Interventions.

Divided into three sections, this book attempts to discuss all issues related to present Afghanistan situation. The aim is to prepare a capsule on the traditional security scenario in the country, the regional and extra-regional stakes and implications and also to have an idea about the current stage of development in Afghanistan, both progresses and challenges. Section one opens up the main debate on security. Binoda Kumar Mishra argues that the shadow of conflict has not receded on Afghanistan. The shadow is present as potential to erupt any time and also as an effect of the more than three decade long conflict. Under this shadow, he discusses the preferences and roles of all those who are directly involved in Afghanistan now. He argues that each of the actors involved in Afghanistan has his own strategic agenda in which peace of Afghanistan finds no place of priority. He supports his argument by showing the misplaced priority of the countries involved in 'so called' Afghan reconstruction. According to him, the main developmental challenge in the country is resource denial in the form of access denial to vital resources such as land, caused through mindless use of landmines. The problem of landmines is the biggest challenge and this lies at the root of the vicious circle of resource denial leading to poverty and narco-economy and supply of manpower to extremist forces. International community's commitment in creating sustainable livelihood is lacking, making the task of establishing perpetual peace difficult nay impossible.

Shahmahmood Miakhel, former Afghan Deputy Minister of Interior provides a historical account of the present problems before Afghanistan and blames the chaos, created by the fighting among the traditional war lords and their repressive rule after the Soviet exit, as the primary reason for the rise of the *Taliban*. He argues that the base of the *Taliban* is in Pakistan and not in Afghanistan. The downfall of the *Taliban* created an opportunity for Afghanistan to emerge as a viable nation but the quick fix approach of the international community made them commit more mistakes than positive actions. Among the major mistakes, Miakhel identifies the composition of the interim government, which was filled with war lords who are hated by the general public. The second flaw in the approach, according to him, is the mismanagement of the funds coming into Afghanistan for promoting development. The western controlled approach is ineffective as most of the funds that are coming into the country is going out as consultancy fees and on other administrative expenses leaving very little for the original cause. However, he concludes optimistically that recently some important corrections have been made and with their inherent resilient attitude Afghans can change their fortune for better in coming times.

The enforced governance structure is the subject matter of Sakti Sinha's paper. He identifies weak capacities, corruption and crony appointments as major drawbacks of the present government that makes the government unable to meet the expectation of the masses. Comparing with the earlier system of governance in Afghanistan, he argues that centralising efforts have never succeeded in Afghanistan. With great analytical skill Sinha discusses the lacuna in the present structure of the government and the nature of governance. He sees little prospect of the present form of government with a strong presidency and centralising tendencies if it is not connected smoothly to the local government structures. He concludes that in order to be effective, the government has to be more inclusive and urgent reforms need to be initiated at various levels of governance to increase the credibility of the Afghan government in the eyes of Afghan masses.

Jamal Rehman evaluates the Afghan reconstruction process that started after the fall of the *Taliban*. Using data he shows that there have been substantial improvements in Afghan economy and in other areas of social development. The process of democratisation is on the right path. Like others he also accepts that security is the biggest concern in the Afghan society along with narcotics. He suggests the security strategy currently employed by the international community needs to be broadened and incentive to be provided to the "good" *Taliban* to join the national mainstream which can lead to stability and further promote economic and social development.

In an extensive discussion, Sanaullah Tasal tries to identify the major challenges to peace-building in the present situation. According to him, there are both internal and external reasons for instability and lack of peace in Afghanistan. Corrupt, weak government, narcotics, warlords, religious extremism, and inability of Afghan government in addressing the human security issues are the internal challenges to Afghan peace-building. Strategic agendas of neighbouring countries such as Iran and Pakistan are main external challenges that prevent permanent peace from returning to Afghanistan. He suggests long-term economic planning, grassroots capacity building, disarming the private militia as the measures needed to be adopted with the support of international community for peace-building effort to succeed.

The role of the biggest external stakeholder in Afghanistan is the US. Sanjeev Bhadauria provides an insightful analysis of US strategic perspective and evaluates the US policy in Afghanistan. He describes Afghanistan as a strategic desert located at the confluence of four major civilisations. Due to close geographical proximity to oil rich Central Asia and having ethnic linkages with most of the neighbours, Afghanistan has been a strategic destination for all major powers in the past. US's Cold War interests in Afghanistan were clearly defined as a strategy to counter the Soviets and to contain Iranian influence. After the end of the Cold War the primary objective of the US is containing Iran and fighting the war on terror. Evaluating the counter insurgency approach, Bhadauria argues that US has hardly been successful in counter insurgency operations. This failure he attributes to the inherent militaristic approach of the US army, which may be useful in traditional wars but not in counter-insurgency operations. The final flaw he identifies with the US policy is its Pakistan appeasing policy. He suggests US to abandon short-term policy of expedience and take a long-term view of Afghan security and deal firmly with Pakistan as well, since the root of the problem (terror) lies more in Pakistan than in Afghanistan.

The US is also the focus of Jagmohan Meher's paper. Meher focuses on the US doctrine and draws parallel between the Iraq and Afghan models. Except few minor changes, the US approach towards Afghanistan, to him, is a replica of the Iraq model which brought doubtful success to the US, i.e. the 'surge first and then negotiate' policy. He identifies few basic reasons which may prove fatal for the US policy in Afghanistan. Sabotage by Pakistan, for maintaining its strategic depth in Afghanistan, is going to be the prime impediment. Increasing civilian casualty is going to diminish public support for US and NATO troops. The resurgent *Taliban* is not going to negotiate with the Afghan government. He predicts a long-term bloody involvement for the US in Afghanistan.

The second section deals with Afghanistan in the regional setting. Gulshan Sachdeva stresses on the need of rethinking the present strategy. He strongly argues for developing a regional approach where in the problem of Afghanistan can be looked in the regional context and also be solved within it. He provides an optimistic prognosis of the future of Afghanistan citing many regional organisations that Afghanistan has become party to. He further develops a case for involvement of regional countries in managing the security situation of the country as he foresees the withdrawal of International Security Assistance Forces in the near future. According to him there are two external issues that need to be solved for effectively dealing with the Afghanistan security problem namely the Iran-US and India-Pakistan problems.

In her paper, Aunohita Mojumdar raises numerous questions regarding the implications of the presence of the international forces in the region. She argues that the long-term involvement of the extra-regional forces is not going to serve the interest of the region in the long-term. Specifically, she is apprehensive of the region, with Afghanistan as the core may develop into a western base under the US. Such a development may not augur any positives for the countries of the region. She, therefore, argues for greater involvement of the regional countries like Russia and India and calls for the countries of the region to realise the spill over effects of the worsening security situation in Afghanistan and meaningfully address the Afghan issue and take positive initiatives before the west bestows uncomfortable responsibilities on them.

Some key questions are also raised by Vishal Chandra regarding the much talked about idea of reconciliation with the *Taliban*. He questions the validity of such an assumption as in the present circumstances, a weak government in Kabul and a desperate West to withdraw, presents no incentive for the *Taliban* to come to the negotiating table. He forcefully argues that negotiating with the *Taliban* at this point will only help the *Taliban*. Chandra stresses folly in the US policy that is heavily predicated on Pakistan which is playing a doubtful role in the entire equation. He further suggests that the approach needs to be revisited in the light of the interests of all the regional players and their support needs to be marshalled to effectively deal with the problem both in Afghanistan and in Pakistan.

Mondira Dutta highlights the Indian initiatives in Afghanistan to empower the Afghan population. She argues that the western countries lack in commitment to the real empowerment of the Afghan people. She emphasises that initiatives like that of India are actually directed towards capacity building of the Afghan people which India should increase in her own interest as any trouble in Afghanistan is invariably going to affect India. P. L. Dash discusses the Afghan problem in the larger regional setting. He articulates the argument that it is Pakistan that is using the uncertain situation as her strategic depth and squarely sabotages any attempt to improve the situation in Afghanistan. According to him, the role of Pakistan army particularly the ISI, is the suspect as they maintain a nebulous nexus with extremist forces like the *Taliban*. The support of these forces to the other menace, i.e. drugs is compounding the problem in Afghanistan. He identifies Central Asian countries, Pakistan and India as the serious stakeholders in the Afghan problem and calls for a wider regional approach to deal with the cauldron.

Sreemati Ganguli maps Afghanistan along with Eurasia. She identifies three links between Afghanistan and the Eurasia region namely, religious extremism, drug trafficking and energy. She is of the opinion that the Eurasian region along with Afghanistan is undergoing the process of democratisation, may be in a problematic manner. She sees a positive role for Afghanistan in the region primarily on energy security of the region.

All the four papers in the third section provide a discussion of the developmental activities that are in progress in Afghanistan and the major developmental challenges the Afghanistan society now faces. Abdul Rahman Ulfat Mahmoodi discusses all aspects of Afghanistan. In a synoptic description, he encases whole range of problems such as: poverty, narcotics, refugees, agriculture, education, and so on. He concludes that despite extreme poverty, security remains the primary concern of the Afghan society and a holistic developmental approach needs to focus on developing the basic infrastructure and accessibility to resources. The other area he advises to focus is to expand the base of modern education.

In an elaborate primary study, Sayed Muhammad Shah evaluates the Afghanistan National Development Strategy (ANDS), the biggest development strategy developed till date in modern Afghanistan. Shah elaborately discusses the various phases of strategy development that finally culminated in the formulation of ANDS. The role of various international agencies and Afghanistan government are also lucidly captured. He points out that the basic flaw of this programme is its foreign nature. According to him, the ANDS is a culmination of the agendas of the international organisations that dictated the terms in their capacity as contributors. The lack of understanding of the foreign experts involved in the drafting of ANDS and the mechanical nature of implementation of the programme has done more harm than good to the developmental process of the Afghan society. Shah concludes that better coordination among implementing agencies and regionally responsive plan of implementation may lead to the success of the spirit of ANDS.

Alef Shah Zadran gives an insider's opinion regarding one of the most important components of Afghanistan development, i.e. education.

Zadran identifies education as the basis of future Afghan development and to him a good curriculum has to be based on a blend of tradition Islamic Afghan values and modern ideas. The second major requirement, according to him, is a class of trained teachers to impart that standard of education that would help Afghanistan emerge as an useful member in the international community. He provides a detailed sketch of the academic curriculum that is being developed and the programme being implemented to train the teachers at the provincial level to impart education at all levels. In spreading education, Zadran specifically acknowledges the potential of India as a partner of Afghanistan.

Last but not the least; Farhat Akram turns attention to the structure of governance at the local levels and the contradiction created by the introduction of formal structures of governance. The crux of the paper is that there exist a pattern of governance, through *Jirgas* and *Shuras*, in the Afghan society which is deeply entrenched in their social and political systems. Introduction of formal modern system to implement reconstruction and rebuilding programmes is creating parallel structures that are not well accepted by the society. Her recommendation is to establish a bridge between the two systems of governance to take on the reconstruction challenges as in such an integrated system of governance, the Afghans would own up the developmental process as stakeholders and would not depend solely on the external agencies and their local NGO partners.

References

1. Ho-Won Jeong, *Peace-building in Post Conflict Societies: Strategy and Process,* New Delhi, Viva Books Private Limited first Indian reprint, Copyright Lynne Rienner publishers, 2006, p.1.
2. *An Agenda for Peace, preventive diplomacy and peace-keeping*, Report of the Secretary-General pursuant to the statement adopted by the Summit Meeting of the Security Council on 31 January 1992, A/47/277 - S/24111, 17 June 1992.
3. Boutros-Ghali, *An Agenda for Peace*, United Nations, New York, 1995.
4. The Peace-building experiences from Somalia, Liberia, Haiti, and Bosnia-Herzegovina reflect the same.
5. John G. Cockell, "Conceptualizing peace-building: Human Security and Sustainable Peace", in Pugh, Michael (ed.), *Regeneration of War-torn Societies*, London, Macmillan, 2000, p. 16.
6. Jeroen de Zeeuw, *Building Peace in War- Torn Societies: From Concept to Strategy*, Netherlands Institute of International Relations 'Clingendael', Conflict Research Unit, The Hague, August 2001, p. 13.

7. Michael Doyle and Nicholas Sambanis, "Building Peace: Challenges and Strategies After Civil War," The World Bank Group, 2000, *http://www.worldbank.org/research/conflict/papers/building.pdf*, p. 3.
8. Ho-Won Jeong, *Op. Cit.*
9. Jonathan Goodhand, 'Aiding violence or building peace? The role of international aid in Afghanistan', *Third World Quarterly*, Vol. 23, No. 5, October 2002, pp. 837-859.
10. *Ibid.*
11. Barnett R. Rubin, A. Ghani, W Maley, A. Rashid, and O. Roy, "Afghanistan: Reconstruction and Peacemaking in a Regional Framework," *Peacebuilding Reports 2001*, Bern, Swiss Centre for Peacebuilding (KOFF), June 2001.

Section I

Conflict and Peace-Building in Afghanistan: The Experience So Far

1

Thinking of Security in the Shadow of Conflict

Binoda Kumar Mishra

We seem to be worried about the fact that Afghanistan's population should be empowered to help themselves. But the fact is, under the current situation, the Afghan population is under a complex rule of a foreign power—trying to establish complete control over the domestic political institutions and a web of NGOs regulating their economic and social lives. The empowerment of the Afghanistan depends on the amount of space, those in charge of the fate of Afghans today allow to the Afghans to think and act for themselves. A survey conducted by the Asia Foundation in 2007 reveals that the people of Afghanistan feel that there is a general deterioration of the security situation in Afghanistan.[1] In 2006, 27 percent of the Afghan population felt security to be the biggest problem the country was facing. In 2007, the percentage has increased to 46 showing the increased dissatisfaction among the Afghan population regarding the security scenario of the country. Though the questions posed were political in nature, what comes clear out of the survey is that there had been no qualitative change in the personal security situation in the country. There is no data to compare relative increase and decrease in the sense of insecurity region wise. However, the "security" the survey takes into account is physical security such as violent attacks committed against or expected by the population. The survey, on the basis of those findings, builds a case for increased military presence in the country for increasing the sense of security among the population of the country. But, should security comprise only absence of direct violence against the population? Had it been that simple, many of the conflict-ridden societies would have regained peace and development no sooner than conflict ended or was brought to an end. It never happens since there is much more to the concept of security than just absence of violence.

Contemporary security discourse is experiencing a definitional crisis. The traditional notion of security is being strongly challenged by scholars who passionately feel that the scope of security must be enlarged and non-traditional issues such as, economic, social and environmental should also find place in the agenda of security study and policy. Non-traditionalists argue for the inclusion of these issues on the ground that security, in order to remain objective, has to take into its fold, economic, societal and environmental issues. On the other hand, the traditionalists oppose the inclusion of non-traditional issues on the ground that this would blur the focus of security and make the study of security vast and vague. The debate continues on the assumption that there is no relationship between the threats to both forms of securities. To end the argument, Afghanistan can be taken as a classic case where there exists a direct relationship between the traditional (military) security threats and the non-traditional security scenario that emerges due to management of traditional security threats.

The background of Afghan conflict is well discussed in academic circles. For the scope of this essay, the background is limited to the Soviet invasion and its aftermath. The latest game that is being played in Afghanistan is the so called "War on Terror" in which the Afghan masses have no share or say. With the intervention of the US led NATO forces and the subsequent overthrow of the *Taliban* regime, it was claimed, by the US, that conflict has come to an end in Afghanistan and the only job left to be done is reconstruction of the ravaged country. Immediately after the end of the *Taliban* regime, security of the country was taken for granted and it was thought to be a matter of time that a democratic government and a liberal market economy would be firmly in place in Afghanistan. But the prevalent conditions indicate worsening of the security condition in the country and it seems that conflict has resurfaced (if it actually ended in 2001). The latest report on the number of civilian casualties reveals an increase over the years and consistently so from 2005. The civilian deaths in 2005 was reported to be 408-478, for 2006 the figures were 653-769, for 2007 it was 1,010-1,297, and during January to September 2008 the civilian casualty was recorded to be between 628-729.[2] This shows the persistence of conflict and the potential of conflict in the country. The present level of conflict is attributed to the history of Afghanistan's society that is supposed to have a perpetual propensity towards conflict. The reason for such a characterisation is to rationalise the presence of the alien forces in Afghanistan and to present a picture that the US intervention in Afghanistan has brought the conflict to an end. However, it is essential to remember that the security condition in Afghanistan is volatile. Due to the intervention of the US and NATO forces, the spheres of security and insecurity are playing hide and seek and there is a zero-sum game in between them across the country.

In the official (US and Afghan Government) analysis, the reason for increased incidences of violence is due to the presence and increasing strength of the main opposition to "Democracy" in the country, the *Taliban*. It is more clearly now, than earlier times, being admitted by all involved in Afghanistan that the *Taliban* is growing in strength and is presenting itself as a formidable force in the country having some popular support. The concept of popular support to the *Taliban* is not accepted by the US and the West. They see the rise of the *Taliban* as a law and order problem having no local support and if there is any support towards them then it is supposed to be out of fear of reprisal from the *Taliban* if they are not supported. But in reality the situation is far from secured. On the other hand, the political situation is closer to what Robert I. Rotberg defines as a "failed state". According to Rotberg's definition, a failed state is one which is very tensed, deeply conflicted, dangerous and contested bitterly by warring factions.[3] To this, David A. Lake adds that in a failed state, the state neither possesses legitimacy nor exercises monopoly over violence.[4] The Bonn agreement provided for centralisation of coercive power with the centre but it is evident that "the means for coercion is still dispersed, with armed clashes exceeding one per day throughout the country.[5] Under these circumstances, there are efforts being made to reconstruct the country with active involvement of international forces and agencies including the United Nations. The stakes of the external actors involved are high for their own interests. The involvement of the international actors in Afghanistan is dictated more by their own interest calculations than any attitude of benevolence. In the words of Ali A. Jalali, "the Civil War in Afghanistan (1992-2001) became a multilateral competition involving internal armed factions with extensive foreign links, neighbouring states pursuing competing strategic interests, and extra-regional players with ideological, security, or economic stakes in the chaos."[6] The security situation in the country after more than seven years of intervention is no different from the so-called Civil War period. Conflict is very much present in the country. Its shadow is present as a potential and as an effect.

Shadow as Potential of Conflict

The potential of conflict is evident from the fact that there is no stable political order in the country and the attempts to disarm the warring factions have not yielded much positive results. The US along with NATO declared conflict to have ended in December 2001 and initiated the reconstruction process through the Bonn Agreement. The primary focus of the Bonn Agreement was to establish a legitimate government in Kabul and start the process of reconstruction of the war ravaged country. But the objective of establishing a legitimate government was not fulfilled. The only political objective the Bonn Agreement achieved was a constitutional unification of the country under the central authority operating form Kabul. But the control over the military power remain fragmented and the warlords of various provinces retained their private militis.[7] The increasing *Taliban* capability and activity has added to the complex of the conflict potential in the country. A recent study conducted by the United States Institute of Peace identifies five categories of actors that complicate the security scenario in the country and cast a shadow of conflict.

> The first are insurgent groups, who are motivated to overthrow the Afghan government and coerce the withdrawal of the international forces. They range from the *Taliban* to smaller groups such as the Haqqani network, Gulbuddin Hekmatyar's Hezb-i-Islami, and al Qa'ida. A second category includes criminal groups that are involved in a range of activities, such as drug trafficking and illicit timber and gem smuggling. The third includes local tribes, sub-tribes, and clans. A fourth category involves warlords and their militias, many of whom became increasingly powerful after the 2001 overthrow of the *Taliban* regime. A fifth category includes government officials and security forces in Afghanistan, Pakistan, and other neighbouring states, which have provided support to insurgent groups or become involved in criminal activity.[8]

Thus, political order in the country remains volatile and vulnerable to conflict. Another indicator of the political volatility of the country is the failure of the UN (US) backed government in obtaining disarmament of the warring factions. The first programme that was initiated to disarm the warring groups was named disarmament, demobilisation, and reintegration (DDR). Initiated in April 2003, the programme did not yield much in substance since ghost soldiers were created by groups and obsolete arms were handed over to the government in return of good money. The programme was replaced by a more ineffective programme called disarmament of illegal armed groups (DIAG). This programme is an appeal to the warring groups to surrender arms and no financial compensation were offered, thus failed to attract the fighting factions to surrender weapons. It aimed to disarm 1,800 groups with fighters numbering 150,000 but achieved nothing as the warlords prefer to keep the weapons in anticipation of the conflict erupting at any time in a volatile political situation of the country. The security situation is worsening in the country primarily because the approach of each of the actor involved in Afghanistan is determined by its own security/strategic calculations. The next section deals with the actors involved, their calculations and approaches in dealing with the situation in Afghanistan.

Who is Thinking About Security?

There are multiple stakeholders in the current Afghanistan problem. The various factions (warring and non-warring), the regional powers, such as Pakistan, and external players like the US with NATO.

The US

The first among all involved in the Afghanistan is the US. After the Soviet withdrawal from Afghanistan, The US and the international community forgot about Afghanistan. The increasing human rights violation under the strict implementation of *Sharia* law escaped the eyes of everyone. There were some domestic pressure on the US government from the human rights organisations to act pro-actively but the US administration chose to ignore these pressures. It was only after the September 11, 2001 attack on the US that the US thought seriously about Afghanistan. It demanded that the ruling *Taliban* must handover the 9/11 mastermind Osama bin Laden to the US for trial to which the *Taliban* firmly refused. The 9/11 event created a lot of anxiety in the US policy making circles. The fear of possible domestic backlash in the event of any further such attack led to an obsession with the prevention of more such attacks. It employed the seventeenth century tactic of preventive war that is build on the logic of taking out the enemy before the enemy comes close.[9] With this rationale, the US planned to intervene and intervene decisively. Thus, the primary reason for US intervention in Afghanistan is to destroy the terrorist network responsible for 9/11 attack with the objective of preventing any further attack on US soil and interests world wide. The US convinced the NATO nations about the impending danger to the West from the fundamentalist forces that have taken root in Afghanistan and the urgency of dealing with these forces if the West wants lasting peace. Naturally, it did not take the US led international forces and the Northern Alliance forces to defeat the *Taliban* militarily. The US along with the international community committed itself to secure the nation. The US adopted a two-prong strategy to deal with the situation in Afghanistan, which can be categoried as hard-power and soft-power approaches. As part of its hard power approach, US committed increasing presence of international forces (with major contributions from the US). The primary objective of the force deployment was to neutralise the threat of *Taliban* and the *Al Qaeda* and eliminate them through military engagement. As part of its soft-power approach, it pushed for the establishment of a democratic government and operationalisation of liberal market economy in the war ravaged country. The other interests that the US is mindful of are strategic in nature. The centrality of the Afghanistan can be used as a spring board to spread US influence into Central Asia, to contain Iran and possibly China. These strategic considerations are more important to the US than the actual security of the general masses of Afghanistan. Therefore, in the name of securing Afghanistan from the *Taliban* it seems that the US has convinced international community that the price of winning the global struggle against terrorism might require sacrificing fundamental human rights and freedoms of Afghan Masses.[10] We see this approach in operation in the increasing death toll of civilians in the conflict particularly in the hands of the US/international forces. A recent calculation puts the ratio of civilian casualty to every single casualty sustained by international forces between 3-4 over the last five years.[11] The other most important US objective is to ensure the triumph of its ideas of liberal democratic order.

The nature of US interest is strategic and understanding is militaristic which focuses on the elimination of the *Taliban* and Al Queda and its own prolonged presence in the country. It is not interested in understanding the nuances of Afghanistan political culture. The Afghanistan political culture has one permanent feature. No one understands it better than the US. During the Soviet occupation of Afghanistan, US played on the indomitable spirit of the Afghans to fight against the presence of alien forces on Afghan soil. Now US tries to convince every one and to itself that the Afghans would change their political culture and extend unquestionable loyalty towards the US led international forces. No need to go farther for vindication of this observation. It was on this spirit the US relied to build forces to fight the former Soviet Union in the Refugee camps in Pakistan. The spirit of Afghan population to dispel any foreign occupation was reinforced by manipulating the plight of the fleeing Afghans. It is a known fact that the US and Pakistan created forces to counter the Soviets by making relief and rehabilitation conditional to joining political organisations that were opposed to the Soviet supported regime in Kabul. The US is fighting a preventive war on the pretext of collective security against the perceived threat of terrorism. The primary interest of the US in Afghanistan currently is preventing any further attack on US soil and its interests abroad. This is purely a military objective and US does not understand any other approach than opting for military solutions. Thus, the US is more interested in engaging the *Taliban* troops all over Afghanistan while attempting to establish a democratic government and liberal market economy.

There are two structural inadequacies that stand on the way of US achieving success in either establishing a stable democracy or introducing liberal market economy. Both democracy and liberal market economy are inherently competitive and demand rational judgement on the part of the participants in such competition to understand the value of the presence of other players and the presence of rules that govern this competition. In a society where, due to long exposure to conflict, people have been habituated to resolving competition through armed violence, in the immediate aftermath of violent conflict, one cannot be sure that participants can compete even in democracy and liberal market without resorting to renewed armed conflict.[12] In such a situation, forced introduction of democratic governance and liberal market economy may seem to be operating but will not gain ground. There would be constant struggle between the intervening power with its ideas and the local culture developed over time and through conflict.

Pakistan

The role of Pakistan in the current Afghan situation is dubious. It is known and accepted that the *Taliban* received patronage from Pakistan. After 9/11, Pakistan was forced to join the US' war on terror.[13] The *Taliban* may be an anti-thesis to whatever the US stands for but for Pakistan the *Taliban* is a strategic asset for creating a client state of Afghanistan through brutal subjugation of the Afghan population.[14] The second strategic consideration that weighs heavily in Pakistani calculations is the creation of an Islamic corridor from Pakistan reaching up to Central Asian Republics through Afghanistan. The third strategic consideration is the fear of increasing Indian presence in the country by means of reconstruction which has been facilitated by the present Karzai government supported by the US. The presence of international forces, thus, is certainly not a desirable situation for Pakistan. In order to balance between its strategic desires and international pressure, Pakistan is putting up a face of cooperation with the coalition forces where as working behind the curtain to see the international forces exit from Afghanistan leaving it at the mercy of Pakistan. Thus, one finds Pakistan, at times supporting the Afghan *Taliban* not only by providing them safe shelter in Quetta but also eyewitness accounts are available to show the involvement of Pakistan soldiers in fighting alongside the *Taliban* against the US forces.[15] The role of ISI in the *Taliban* attack on Indian embassy and other targets is well exposed by Afghan authorities and even endorsed by the US. It is in the interest of Pakistan that Afghanistan remains either as a client state of Pakistan or eternally disturbed as Pakistan fears threat to its sovereignty over the territory related to Durand Line, once Afghanistan achieves stability independent of Pakistan's influence. Pakistan thus seems to be least concerned about the necessity of improved security situation in the country under the guidance of the West.

The efforts to provide security in Afghanistan primarily focus on the physical part of the security and thus try to address security through military means completely ignoring the interconnection between physical security and human security, which is equally bad and stands as an impediment to improving security situation in the country. The assumption behind the military approach to security is that once a democratically elected government is established at the centre, the grievances of the population will slowly be addressed by the central government. But this approach is bound to fail as the more than 30 years of conflict in the country has cast a shadow of conflict as an effect that makes the country ill prepared for the central government to provide governance that can ultimately lead to perpetual security in the country.

Shadow as an Effect of Conflict

In modern days, Afghanistan has witnessed conflict for over 30 years and is still reeling under conflict. Such prolonged conflict has left a long shadow on the socio-economic structure of the Afghan society that endangers the other form of security called the human security. Human security refers to the availability of opportunities for human beings to be at their human selves. The components of human security include economic, social, environment and other aspects of personal and social lives that need to be ensured for the population.

In 2007 Afghanistan ranked 174[16] in terms of Human Development Index indicating that it is one of the most impoverished nations of the world. The human security problems of Afghanistan is multi-dimensional having poverty, drought, drug and social insecurity as manifestations. Currently (by the end of 2008), an estimated seven million people are vulnerable to hunger, life expectancy is 44 years and 20 percent of the children die before reaching the age of 5.[17] The economic infrastructure of the country is completely devastated. Road and other networks are either destroyed or rendered inaccessible by the presence of landmines. Such effect of conflict makes the human security situation in the country grim. The international community now clearly acknowledges the relationship between the human security and the traditional security concerns for Afghanistan. But unfortunately the approach to improve the security situation in the country does not seem to have been given due emphasis to human security as much as it had given to the traditional security concerns. The following section tries to identify the real human security problem and discuss the roots that need to be addressed if security and governance in the country are to be improved.

Addressing the Human Security Situation in Afghanistan

There are multiple facets of the human security crisis that face the country. Along with the above discussed indicators, millions have been homeless, fled as refugees or are internally displaced for various reasons related to prolonged conflict. In terms of reconstruction of any country after prolonged conflict the basic requirement is availability of sustainable resource. In Afghanistan the real problem is lack of resources to sustain any kind of gainful licit economic activity. The most important of all resources for any country is land and this is something that has been out of bounds for fruitful use. The next section discuss the root of the human security problem in Afghanistan.

Landmines as the Longest Shadow

Every conflict casts a shadow over the society for the present and the future. The process of reconstruction depends on the length and intensity of the shadow of the past conflict(s). The effects of past conflict and disturbance in a country persist in various forms. In cases where the effect is only limited to political sphere of the society, it becomes easier for those involved in post-conflict reconstruction to re-build the country. But in some cases the behaviour of the parties to the conflict leave behind an effect that takes long time to overcome. The issue in question is a weapon that was used indiscriminately during the period of "active" conflict by all parties involved.[18] The problem of anti-personnel landmines (APMs) all over the world presents an interesting predicament for security studies. A weapon most effective in protecting traditional security and strategic interests of the warring parties has emerged as the biggest threat to human security in all forms. According to a study, anti-personnel landmines all over the world kill or maim a person every twenty minutes. Even if the production, distributions and further deployment of APMs are stopped today, it would take the full present century to get rid of the menace of APMs. Afghanistan is the worst affected of all the countries suffering from this menace. According to one report, Afghanistan by the end of 2001 was infested with 10-15 millions of anti-personnel landmines and similar number of various other kinds of Unexploded Ordinances (UXO) presently called Explosive Remnants of War (ERWs).[19] According to the latest report on the landmine situation in Afghanistan, only 3,50,000 APMs have been cleared in the last seven years.[20] On an average two persons are reported killed everyday by APMs.[21] The culprits are the Former Soviet Union, the various warring factions of the Afghanistan, the Mujahideens, the *Taliban* and the US led forces during *Operation Enduring Freedom.*[22]

Impact on Economy and Security Situation

The presence of such large quantities of APM/UXOs have far reaching economic consequences for a nation that struggles to rebuild itself after being reduced to ruins. The economic consequences have direct relationship with the security situation of the country.

Direct Impact

The intensity of the negative effect on the economy is evident from the fact that "all but one of the 32 provinces is impacted". Out of 329 districts, 259 districts are infested with APMs. Out of 32 million population, over 4.2 million are still living in APM/ERW infested areas.[23] According to the Landmine Impact Survey, till 2005, 38 percent of the flat land is mine contaminated. In terms of access to resources, the survey clearly brings out the reason for the impoverished condition of the Afghan population. The table below is rather indicative.

Sl.	*Type of Resource*	*% of Area Inaccessible*
1	Pasture	81
2	Rain-fed Cropland	32
3	Roads	33
4	Water	06
5	Housing	18
6	Irrigated Cropland	24

The figures in the table are self-explanatory in terms of their effect on the economy of the nation. An earlier study of the International Committee of the Red Cross (ICRC) had analysed if Afghanistan becomes free of landmines, the scale of economy can get boosted 200 times. The figures on the table above are to be analysed in terms of the absolute effects. Of the total landmass of Afghanistan, only 12 percent is cultivable; 10 percent pasture and only 5-6 percent considered having agricultural potential.[24] If 81 percent of the pastures, nearly one third of the rain-fed cropland, and a quarter of the irrigated cropland are inaccessible, the net result is bound to be disastrous. It is reflected in the fact that out of 22,000 farming villages 12,000 are either abandoned or deserted and 85 percent of the food and animal cultivators are dependent on imported donated food by aid agencies. To add to the existing level of access denial, new mined areas are being discovered at the rate of 12 million square meters per year. If the long period of conflict caused 1.5 million Afghan refugees and 2.25 million internally displaced persons, the shadow of the conflict (APMs/ERWs/UXOs) make their repatriation and rehabilitation impossible.

At present, mines and UXO kill or injure an average of 62 Afghans each month—approximately two persons every day.[25] 97 percent of the mine and UXO victims are male and given the religious-economic pattern of the Afghan society, this seriously affects the productivity of the households. 63 percent of the mine casualties belong to the age group of 15 to 44 and 17 percent belonging to the age group of 5 to 15. On the national economy, the effect is multi-faceted. It has, on the one hand, decreased productivity and on the other hand putting pressure on the economy by increasing the liability. According to one recent UN survey, as high as 4 percent of Afghan population are disabled due to mines and UNICEF estimates that 20-25 persons are maimed by land mines every day.[26]

Indirect Impact

The problem of landmines has other spin offs that contribute to the weakness of the Afghan economy. The first and foremost is encouraging the poppy cultivation.

In 2007, opium production climbed to a staggering 8,200 metric tons.[27] There are fluctuations in terms of opium production in the country owing primarily to weather. Currently, Afghanistan supplies more than 90 percent opium of global illicit market. The production of opium in Afghanistan broke the record in 2004 only when the cultivation was extended to all the 32 provinces of the country.[28] The country has the dubious distinction of being the largest producer of opium in the world. "Eliminating opium production in Afghanistan will only be successful if poverty and unemployment are reduced at the same time, The UN Food and Agriculture Organization (FAO) observed in 2004."[29] The Asia Foundation survey, 2007 reveals that there is high rejection of poppy cultivation among Afghans. According to the survey, nearly 80 percent of the respondent admitted that poppy cultivation is bad. General Afghan population are not addicted to opium. One needs to ponder why a society, that rejects a particular crop and does not consume it, does produce it? The historical reasons are beyond the purview of this paper but the contemporary explanation is lack of other livelihoods options. Of those who do not consider poppy cultivation a bad activity, 39 percent observe that it fetches more revenue than other crops. Since, most of the available 5-6 percent of land suitable for agriculture is inaccessible due to mines, the pressure on the residue land increases substantially and makes general agriculture unviable. This is the simple reason for which the British effort of $500 an acre offer to farmers not to cultivate opium did not work. Another angle most forgotten in explaining the increase in opium production is the availability of labour force. Poppy cultivation is highly labour intensive.[30] The refugees who live in camps in Pakistan generally constitute this workforce supplemented by internally displaced persons within Afghanistan.[31] In the event of lack of livelihoods opportunity from the scarce land made scarcer due to the presence of millions of landmines, the general population of the country find no other alternative but join the poppy cultivation to earn whatever income they can from this lucrative business run by various kinds of people with very high stakes. The drug lords take advantage of this situation and compel the farmers to cultivate poppy in place of general food crops and the farmers oblige finding no other viable livelihood options. The production of poppy keeps a thriving network of traffickers who make major profits and have taken not only insurgents like the *Taliban* but also Afghan police, tribal elites and government officials at various levels into confidence. The increase in drug production in the country can only be explained in terms of access to natural resources that can form the base of licit economy of Afghanistan.

Supply of Workforce to Insurgent Groups

The lack of livelihoods optinons and inability of the governemnt to provide alternative economic options leaves a large section of the population unemployed and vulnerable. Coupled with increasing civilian casualty due the actions of US and international forces, the unviable licit economic situation in the country caused due to denial of access to most important liveihoods resources such as land and other infrastructures, has created a condition of despire among the general population. The Afghan culture of revege against the enemy who kills the kin is supplemented by the lack of economic opportunites to create a fertile ground to grow anti-intervenor attitude. This attitude and economic vulnerability are being exploited by insurgent groups like the *Taliban* for recruiting frontline fighters. The growing strength of the *Taliban* is not only accountable to the military only approach of the intervenor(s) but also the lack of sustainable economic opportunity.

Ensuring Human Security: The Efforts

It is not to suggest that the international commuity is totally blind to the human security needs of the country. But a look at the approach of the international community and the process of addressing these needs of the Afghan masses would make it clear that the human security needs of the Afghan population do not find due prioroty in proportion to attempts of ensuing physical security. It all began in December 2001, after the US led forces assisted by Northern Allianc forces drove the ruling *Taliban* from Kabul to the south, ultimately to Pakistan. It must be remembered that it was the US who was leading the war against the *Taliban*. But shamefully or ironically the US was not ready to be part of the reconstruction process. In the first G8 meeting on security sector reform in Afghanistan, held on the sidelines of the Tokyo Conference during January 21-22, 2002, the US refused to be part of the nation-building or peacekeeing except to help build Afghanistan's national army.[32] It is beyond comprehension as to why the US, 'having vast experience in post-conflict state and nation-building,'[33] chose to stay away from similar task in Afghanisatn. There were international pressure on the US to take a lead in nation-building in Afghanistan but the task never figured in the priority list of the US foreign policy.

In the event of the US being reluctant to engage in nation-building in Afghanistan, the task was taken up by the UN. Various agencies of the UN and other International Non-Governmantal Organisations (INGOs) steped in to salvage the socio-economic situation in the country. But both the commitment and the approach were inadequate. One of the declared objectives of the international humanitarian intervention is to empower the the Afghan masses but most, if not all, of the resources are directed to relief rather than empowerment. A comparison of the expenditure on maintainnance of securtiy and all other developmental activities is revealing. Since financial year 2001 till financial year 2009, the interntinal allocation under security is estimated to be 20,966.04 million USD in comparison to 11,215.48 million USD under all other developmental activities in the country.[34] It is alleged, that of the total funds allocated towards developmental activity, a substantial amount is remitted to the western countries through salaries of the expensive western developmental workers and consultants.[35] Another major segment of the funds is channelled to meet the recurrent expenditures of the government, primarily salaries of the civil servants. The other major component of the humanitarian intervention is providing direct food to a huge number of displaced and unemployed population.

The project, empowerment of the Afghan population, cannot be effectively implemented unless sustainable resource is made availabe to the population. As discussed earlier, the presence of APM/UXOs prevents access to basic resources in the country but the international community does not seem to be enough serious about the most serious problem of the country. Though the Afghan Compact set the target to clear Afghanistan of mines completely by the year 2013, the officials do not seem too optimistic. During interactions with the present and former officialas of United Nations Mine Action Centre for Afghanistan (UNMACA) in 2007, the exact nature of the demining problem came to the fore. The task at hand is big, hazardous and multi-tasking. The primary reason for the delay in clearance is the indiscriminate nature of their use by all the warring parties, states and non-state actors, involved in this mindless activity. Use of mines needed to be careful. There are no proper information about the mine fields. No mapping of the mines were done when they were laid. To add to their problems it is found that whatever maps are available are deceptive and thus not trustworthy. There being no better effective and easy way of clearing mines, the most effective is manual clearance. It takes long time and involves high casualty. According to a former senior official of UNMACA, the incentives provided to the deminors who are Afghans are very less in comparison to the high salaries drawn by those supervisors from the western countries. Above that, the level of commitment on the part of the *de-facto* government of Afghanistan is seeriously wanting. Sufficient funds are not being made available and there have been halts in demining activites in the past due to lack of funds. Till financial year 2009, only 98 million USD[36] have been spent on demining Afghanistan resulting in lagging behind to meet the target set by the Afghan Compact of clearing the country of mines comppletely by the year 2013. High mortality among the deminors and the deminors being targetted by the warring factions are major disincentives.

Conclusion

Security in failing states like Afghanistan is more than just issues of safety to life. It involves issues of liveliohoods such as income generating opportunities, access to education, health, etc. Though physical security is important, focus on security only is not going to bring perpetual peace to the country. Even on the military/strategic front the current international stakeholders need to change their priorities. They must put the stability of Afghanistan ahead of their strategic considerations. Players like Pakistan must stop double crossing the International community and show greater commitment towards the Afghan problem. The intervening International forces must change the counter insurgency approach of indiscriminate killing as a counter strategy to cope with 4th generation warfare methods employed by the insurgent forces like the *Taliban*. For long-term security, the focus of the government (aided by the international community) must be equally if not more, on ensuring sustainable livelihoods opportunities for the Afghan masses. Thus, security in Afghanistan is deeply imbeded in governance and governance depends on resources, and if resources are inaccessible the entire chain breaks. Lack of resources restricts the income generating options and thus creates a vicious circle of, resource denial—poverty—illegal economy—conflict—insecurity. The beginning must be made with cleaning the country of APMs/UXOs, the longest and darkest shadow of past conflicts. An earlier ICRC estimate, if Afghanistan is cleared of all APM/UXOs, the economy can be boosted by 200 times. The calculation may be an exaggeration but there can be substantial increase in Afghan economy that can be the base of Afghan reconstruction from its present stage of failed or failing state to a viable state.

Notes and References

1. *Afghanistan in 2007: A Survey of the Afghan People*, Kabul: The Asia Foundation, 2007, p. 27.
2. "Afghanistan: Terror, US Style", *Frontlilne*, vol. 26, no. 6, 27, March 2009, pp. 59-65.
3. Robert I. Rotberg (ed.), *State Failure and State Weakness in a Time of Terror*, Washington DC: Brookings, 2003. Also Robert I. Rotberg (ed.), *When States Fail: Causes and Consequences*, Princeton, NJ: Princeton University Press, 2004.

4. David A. Lake, "Building a Legitimate State After Civil Wars: Order, Authority, and International Trusteeship", Unpublished Manuscript, 17 April, 2007, cited in Jan Angstrom, "Inviting the Leviathan: external forces, war, and state-building in Afghanistan," *Small Wars and Insurgencies*, vol. 19, no. 3, September 2008, p. 377.
5. Jan Angstrom, "Inviting the Leviathan: external forces, war, and state-building in Afghanistan," *Small Wars and Insurgencies*, vol. 19, no. 3, September 2008, p. 289.
6. Ali A. Jalali, "Legacy of War and Challenge of Peace Building," in Robert I. Rotberg (ed.), *Building a New Afghanistan*, Cambridge, Massachusetts: World Peace Foundation, Washington, D.C., Brookings Institution Press, 2007, p. 26.
7. *Ibid*, p. 30.
8. C. Christine Fair and Seth G. Jones, "Securing Afghanistan: Getting on Track," *United States Institute of Peace Working Paper*, January 23, 2009, p. 3. Available at, www.usip.org.
9. In his State of the Union address in January 2002, Bush argued, "I will not wait on events while dangers gather. I will not stand by as peril draws closer and closer ... [i]n the world we have entered, the only path to safety is the path of action, and this nation will act." Quoted in John Davis, "Implications of Preventive Wars for Collective Security," *Mediterranean Quarterly*, Winter 2004, pp. 112-113.
10. *Promotion and Protection of Human Rights: Protection of human rights and fundamental freedoms while countering terrorism*, U.N. ESCOR, Comm'n on Hum. Rts., U.N. Doc. E/CN.4/2005/103 at 6, 21, February 7, 2005 (prepared by Robert K. Goldman).
11. "Afghanistan: Terror, US Style", *Frontlilne*, vol. 26, no. 6, 27, March 2009, p. 60.
12. Roland Paris, *At War's End: Building Peace after Civil Conflict*, Cambridge: Cambridge University Press, 2004, cited in Jan Angstrom, "Inviting the Leviathan: external forces, war, and state-building in Afghanistan," *Small Wars and Insurgencies*, vol. 19, no. 3, September 2008, p. 375.
13. It is said that the then deputy foreign secretary of States, Mr. Richard Armitage threatened to "Bomb Pakistan to Stone Age" if it did not join the war on terror in Afghanistan.
14. Subhash Kapila, "Afghanistan: United States/NATO Strategic Fatigue Spawns Dangerous Alternatives," *South Asia Analysis Group, Paper no. 2902*, 29 October 2008. Available at, http://www.southasiaanalysis.org
15. During a 10 June 2008 firefight, US forces killed roughly a dozen Pakistani Frontier Corps soldiers who were shooting at them. One local villager located few hundred yards from the fighting on the Pakistan side remarked that "When the Americans started bombing the *Taliban*, the Frontier Corps started shooting the Americans ... They were trying to help the *Taliban*. And then the American planes bombed the Pakistani post," Reported by Dexter Filkins,

"Right at the Edge," *New York Times Magazine*, 5 September 2008, cited in C. Christine Fair and Seth G. Jones, *Op. Cit.*, p. 21. Available at, www.usip.org.

16. Afghanistan Human Development Report, 2007, available at, http://hdr.undp.org/en/reports/nationalreports/asiathepacific/afghanistan/nhdr2007.pdf
17. 161 ESC 08 E -rev 1 Economic Reconstruction in Afghanistan: Developmental and Security Implications, NATO Parliamentary Assembly, 8th Annual Session, 2008, General Rapporteur: Hugh BAYLEY (United Kingdom)
18. The period from 1979-2001 is considered the period of active conflict. Such fixation is based on the official assumption that active conflict was brought to an end by the intervention of Multinational force in November 2001.
19. "Anti-personnel landmines: the eternal sentinels", *The Third World Traveller*, http://www.thirdworldtraveler.com.
20. "UN: Afghanistan still heavily mined", *RAWA News*, April 4, 2008, http://www.rawa.org/temp/runews/2008/04/04.
21. The number of deaths due to APMs is according to reported cases of mine casualty. The real figures can be much more since most of the cases go unreported.
22. During *Operation Enduring Freedom* the US used ammunitions that left behind a large quantity of UXOs.
23. *Landmine Impact Survey: Islamic Republic of Afghanistan*, Survey Action Centre, 2005, p. 19.
24. "Landmines: Predators in the fields," *B-Flies in Action*, 2008, http://www.bp208.ca.
25. *Portfolio of Mine Action Projects*, UNMAS, 2007, p. 2.
26. UN and UNICEF figures quoted in, "Land Mines and Afghanistan," http://www.menstuff.org/issues/byissue/landmines.html
27. Un Office on Drugs and Crime (UNDOC), *Afghanistan Opium Survey*, September 2007, available at www.undoc.org/undoc/index/html.
28. Cindy Fazey, "Responding to the Opium Dilemma," in Robert I. Rotberg (ed.), *Building a New Afghanistan*, Cambridge, Massachusetts: World Peace Foundation, Washington, D.C., Brookings Institution Press, 2007, p. 180.
29. "Poppy cultivation in Afghanistan—the search for alternatives," Food for Agriculture Organisation of the United Nations, February 2, 2004.
30. Poppy cultivation needs 350 man days per acre in comparison to 135 man days for wheat per acre. UNDOC, *Strategic Study no. 4, Access to Labour: The Role of Opium in the Livelihood Strategies for Itinerant Harvesters Working in Helmand Province, Afghanistan*, Vienna, 1999. Cited in, Cindy Fazey, "Responding to the Opium Dilemma," in Robert I. Rotberg (ed.), *Building a New Afghanistan*, Cambridge, Massachusetts: World Peace Foundation, Washington, D.C., Brookings Institution Press, 2007, p. 183.
31. *Ibid.*

32. Ahmed Rashid, D*escent into Chaos: How the war against Islamic extremism is being lost in Pakistan, Afghanistan and Central Asia*, London: Allen Lane, 2008, p. 197.
33. Apart from post World War II nation-building efforts in Germany and Japan, US was involved in nation-building process in Haiti, Cambodia, East Timor and former Yugoslavia.
34. The source for the data is Office of the Special Inspector General for Afghanistan Reconstruction, Quarterly Report to the Congress, Washington DC, October 2008. A detailed Chat of Funding into Afghanistan is produced in *United States Institute of Peace Working Paper*, Appendix B, January 23, 2009, pp. 32-33. Available at, www.usip.org.
35. According to one estimate, of the total funds coming into Afghanistan, 40 percent has returned to the donor countries in the form of corporate profits and consultant salaries. *161 ESC 08 E-rev 1 Economic Reconstruction in Afghanistan: Developmental and Security Implications*, available at http://www.nato-pa.int/Default.asp?SHORTCUT=1458.
36. *United States Institute of Peace Working Paper, Op Cit.*

2

Challenges and Dilemmas of Reconstruction and Institution-Building: Social, Economic and Political Factors

Shahmahmood Miakhel

> *"The United Nations has learned that the rule of law is not a luxury and that justice is not a side issue. We have seen people lose faith in the peace process when they do not feel safe from crime. We have seen that without a credible machinery to enforce the law and resolve disputes people resorted to violence and illegal means. And we have seen that elections held when the rule of law is too fragile seldom lead to lasting democratic governance...but a one size fits all does not work. Local actors must be involved from the start. The aim is to leave behind strong local institutions when we depart."*[1]

> *"The international community has failed to get its act together on a clear plan that we pursue through unity and speaking with a single voice. The British think Afghanistan is Helmand, the Canadians think it's Kandahar, the Dutch think it's Uruzgan, the Germans think it's the Panjshir valley and the US thinks it's chasing Osama bin Laden."*[2]

After the collapse of the *Taliban* regime in 2001, the Bonn Agreement was inked very hastily with flaws and without proper consultation with all sides to ensure that social, political and economic aspects of the Afghan situation were taken into account. Even though the Bonn Agreement was not a comprehensive peace agreement, most Afghans accepted it in the hope that it would provide a starting point for peace, stability, security and prosperity.

Before one goes into details about the Bonn Agreement, two questions should be answered; 1) Why did the *Taliban* come to power? 2) Why did Osama Bin Laden and *Al Qaeda* choose to operate from Afghanistan?

To answer the first question, *Taliban* came to power because after the collapse of Dr. Najibullah's regime in 1992, the Mujahideen groups, which were based in Iran and Pakistan, had started to fight each other to have control of power in Afghanistan. As reported by the UN, in Kabul between May and August 1992, 1,800 civilians died in rocket attacks and 500,000 people fled the city.[3] The actual number is not easy to find out but according to different estimations, just in Kabul city alone, between 1992 and 1996, more than 60,000 people were killed and 80 per cent of the city was razed to ground[4].

In the regions, different warlords who were supported by some of our neighbours, had control and they were acting as warlords or mini kings and ruling their area of control with brutality. Life, property and honour of ordinary Afghans were not safe. Shooting people in the streets, playing with dead bodies for fun, rapes, mass killings, cutting the breasts of women—any crime imaginable was committed.[5] In 1994, when I used to work for the United Nations, sometimes I had to travel from Jalalabad city in east of Afghanistan to the capital of Kunar province Assadabad, about 75 km distance. In the course of that journey, one would encounter more than 150 check posts maintained by different groups. Passing each check posts was like crossing to another alien territory without visa and you were never sure what would happen to you each time you were stopped.

Unfortunately, during those years, the international community forgot post-jihad Afghanistan and left it to the hands of their neighbours to decide the destiny of the Afghans. Proxy war was going on and each neighbour supported different groups for their own national interest or to have dominance in the region. In this situation, the people of Afghanistan were waiting to welcome anyone who could disarm these warlords and criminals in order to bring peace and stability to Afghanistan. Therefore, the *Taliban* responded to common aspirations at the time by promising to rid the country of the forces that were creating chaos and misery for the people.[6]

For the above reasons, at the outset, most Afghans welcomed the *Taliban*. I do not want to go in depth here about how *Taliban* emerged and who supported them. For further details Ahmad Rashid's book "*Taliban: Militant Islam, Oil, and the Fundamentalism in Central Asia.*" can be consulted.

The *Taliban* were able to capture 95 percent of Afghanistan, disarmed almost all warlords or criminal groups under their control area and brought a level of security Afghans had not experienced for years. There was no problem in travelling to the areas of under *Taliban* control during day and night. But unfortunately, *Taliban* did not have a good agenda to rule the country. Even though Afghanistan was poor and underdeveloped, the *Taliban* became the cause of several other problems such as the expansion of poppy and drug industries, provided a safe haven for *Al Qaeda* and spread of immense poverty throughout of the country. They also deprived half the population, women and girls, from education. They converted schools into the *Madrasa* system where only Islamic subjects were taught.

To answer the second question as to why *Al Qaeda* took root in Afghanistan, the first point to make is that *Al Qaeda* wanted to be in a country without rule of law, where anarchy reigned, and where there was no regime in charge able to control their activities. Under the *Taliban*, no one could keep watch over their activities, which included planning operations throughout the world. So Afghanistan was the best choice for them. There is no need to talk about how Osama Bin Laden came to Afghanistan in the early 1980s or how again he was allowed to move from Sudan to Afghanistan. There are different interpretations which are beyond of the scope of this paper.

When I used to work as local reporter for the Voice of America in Peshawar in mid-1980s, tens of thousands of individuals from different Arab and other Muslim countries came to Pakistan and Afghanistan to fight side by side with the *Mujahideen*. Most of these Arabs and *Jihadists* were in the frontline, fighting against the communist regime in Afghanistan. In the beginning, these *Jihadists* who would eventually come under unified direction of *Al-Qaeda* were supported by different *Mujahideen* groups and later by the *Taliban*. According to several people I talked with, until the capture of Jalalabad city by the *Taliban*, there was no connection between *Taliban* and *Al Qaeda*. *Taliban* were Sunni Muslim of *Hannafi* sect, mostly, *Pashtoon*. *Al Qaeda* members were follower of *Wahabi* or *Ahle-hadith* ideology. In fact, *Al Qaeda* was very close to Peshawar based *Mujahideen* fundamentalist groups.

Al Qaeda gradually consolidated its position after the *Taliban* captured Jalalabad city, and the relationship between the *Taliban* and *Al Qaeda* grew. At the end of *Taliban* rule, its leadership in Kandahar was very close to Osama Bin Laden. In fact, Afghanistan was occupied by these Arabs and Jihadists with full support of the *Taliban*.

But the good thing was that these Arabs and Jihadists rarely mingled with local population and were only close to the top leadership of the *Mujahideen* and *Taliban*. Most of them lived in isolated areas in

Afghanistan and they had their own training centres. Therefore, they do not have bases or influence among local population in Afghanistan as they have in Pakistan because *Al Qaeda*, for long, had close links to political extremist groups in Pakistan as well as in Federally Administered Tribal Areas (FATA) region. After the collapse of the *Taliban* regime in Afghanistan in 2001, most of the *Al Qaeda* members or senior *Taliban* leaders were captured inside Pakistan rather than in Afghanistan.

Bonn Agreement and Political Consequences

After the collapse of the *Taliban* regime in 2001, from the very outset, the people of Afghanistan were watching the implementation of Bonn processes with great expectations but unfortunately due to various internal and external reasons, all components of the Bonn Agreement were not fully implemented. The focus was only on the legitimisation rather than the ability of the Afghan government to build institutions. Too much focus was on processes laid out by the Bonn Agreement itself rather than on the institutional building. Thus the focus was on:

- Holding emergency *Loya Jirga* in 2002 to approve the transitional government of President Hamid Karzai;
- Instituting second *Loya Jirga* in 2003, to approve the Constitution of Afghanistan;
- Conducting Presidential elections in 2004; and
- Running National Assembly and Provincial Councils elections in 2005.

In 2002, when I was part of election team overseeing elections for the Emergency *Loya Jirga* in four eastern provinces of Kunar, Nooristan, Nangarhar and Laghman, people were so optimistic that they participated in the election process very enthusiastically without major incidents. At that time, there were no national police, National Army or International Security Assistance Force (ISAF) forces in most part of the country but there were two things; hope and optimism.

On May 20, 2002, in very a remote district of Nooristan province, when the election team was entering the historic village of Kamdesh, where the houses and mosques are decorated with traditional wood carving, the women poured walnuts from the roof of their houses as a gesture of goodwill and welcome.[7] They were very eager to participate in an election after so many years of war and living outside of their country as refugees. But after seven years, Kamdesh and the rest of Nooristan province with exception of few towns, happened to remain outside the control of the government.

Unfortunately, the Bonn process did not prevent the return of warlords and criminal networks which were linked to international drug mafia, the very same people who had been defeated by the *Taliban* and hated by the Afghan people for their criminality and disregard of the rule of law. When I am talking about warlords, I don't only refer to those well-known figures whose names are found in the newspapers but to all warlords or illegal armed groups, whether they operate locally or nationally. Allowing these warlords to return to power is a big source of disappointment for the majority of Afghans.

When I was working in the Ministry of Interior in Afghanistan (MOI), the MOI leadership believed that in order to have good governance, peace and stability in Afghanistan, the government of Afghanistan and International community had to fight against the root causes of the problems which were the *Taliban*, the *Al Qaeda*, the warlords, the drug lords, organized criminal groups, corruption, poverty, tribal and ethnic rivalry. These elements feed and support each other, and in some cases, they are the same players and play different roles. Unfortunately, due to lack of clear strategy and political will, the government of Afghanistan and international community were reluctant to deal with the above problems. They were not willing to deal with the root causes of the problem and only seemed interested in dealing with the symptoms of the problem in Afghanistan or wanted to have quick fixes with cheap price tag.

As part of the implementation of the Bonn processes, the international community and the government of Afghanistan made a number of promises, such as initiating a new Marshall Plan for Afghanistan, which raised the expectations of the people; however, the record of fulfilled promises has been uneven at best. Consequently, after each step of the process, the confidence of the Afghan people on the government and international community has lessened. This decline of confidence of the people has provided opportunity for the drug lords, the warlords, organised criminals, the *Taliban* and the *Al Qaeda*, tribal rivalries and other spoilers including some of Afghanistan's neighbours to step in to fill the gap and develop their own strategies, which suit their interests at the cost of increased insecurity and destabilisation in Afghanistan and in the region.

The second set of component of Bonn Agreement:

- Demilitarization of Kabul and other cities which should be controlled by ISAF not by warlords;

- Adherence by members of the Interim Administration to a code of conduct elaborated in accordance with International Standards;
- Expansion of ISAF in a timely fashion;
- Provision of enough resources to build a National Army and National Police;
- Fairness and Freedom in the selection of *Loya Jirga*s membership, as well as vetting of the candidates for Parliament and Provincial Councils to ensure the non-participation of Human Rights violators as candidates or those holding on to illegal arms;
- Investigation of Human Rights violation and implementation of transitional justice action plan;
- Prevention of interference of neighbours in Afghanistan; and
- Prevention of drug cultivation and trafficking.

There has been less focus on the second set of components of the Bonn Agreement, which has a direct impact on the failure of institution building and the loss of credibility of the government, as well as by the international community. As we know, with the lack of credibility comes the lack of legitimacy of the government.

Due to the above factors, particularly in the absence of a well thought out strategy, Afghanistan, as well as neighbouring countries and international community, face a daunting challenge to deal with insurgency in Afghanistan and safe havens for terrorists outside of the country.

Current Problems: Internal and External Dimensions

After the collapse of the *Taliban* in 2001, the good points were that millions of Afghans who were living as refugees in Iran, Pakistan or other parts of the world were able to return to their homeland with great hope, energy and expectation that they would finally be able to enjoy economic, as well as physical security. I personally lived in a refugee camp in Pakistan for many years, and I knew how difficult and soul-destroying it is to live as a refugee in another country that does not recognise your status. As a refugee you do not have the opportunity to plan your family life for a better future. About six million children, boys and girls, who do not have had opportunity to study have enrolled in the education system since the end of the *Taliban* rule. But unfortunately, with all these positive starts, we are still facing a lot of challenges regarding security, governance and development in Afghanistan.

When I am talking about these problems, I do not mean to blame external or internal actors for these problems in Afghanistan but in fact both of them have shared responsibility.

External Problems: Economic Consequences

First, the international community was looking for quick fixes in Afghanistan. And mistakes were made: first the objectives were short-term; second, there was premature announcement that the *Taliban* was defeated and the war was won in Afghanistan; third, the international community did not examine very well the complexity and history of the problems in Afghanistan; fourth, much needed resources and attention was not provided to Afghanistan by all stakeholders; fifth, the Iraq war created a big diversion of attention and resources from Afghanistan; sixth, the military became involved with political, governance and reconstruction activities in Afghanistan, while little or no involvement of the civilian actors; and seventh and most important, the government of Afghanistan was not able to take the lead in aligning international assistance according to the need of Afghan people. Most of the programmes or assistance was supply-driven rather than based on the needs of the Afghan people.

As it is well known, the military when properly organised fights when it is needed, but once they become involved in political and governance issues, they create a big problem that will take many years to reverse. In our lifetime, we have seen examples of the destructive role played by the military in many countries. Internal and external intervention of military in Afghanistan as well as Pakistan provide good examples in the last few decades which have brought misery and problems to their own countries as well as to the region.

Also, in the last seven years, most of the strategies were written by foreign consultants without proper consultation with professional Afghans. We all know that most of these consultants have tendency of cut and paste ideas taken from various sources, slap them together in a 200, 300 or 400 pages documents, give it to the government and call it "Strategy". Most of these strategies are mechanical transplants of models from developed world with little understanding of realities on the ground in specific countries. In Afghanistan, there were a lot of problems in the design of most programmes as well as an absence of clear strategy of implementation. So most of the programmes, especially civil service reform and police reform, were poorly designed and badly implemented. All these reforms have created job insecurity and became exploited by people who have personal agenda.

One of our colleagues once compared consultancy in Afghanistan to a game of Afghan Buzkashi. When you discover that you are riding a dead horse, the best strategy is to dismount and find a new horse. But the aid and donor organizations in Afghanistan, instead of changing horses, set up committee to study the horse; arrange to visit other countries to see how others ride dead horses; lower the standards so that dead horses can be included; reclassify the dead horse as living "impaired"; hire outside contractors who claim they can ride the dead horses; harness several dead horses together to increase their speed; provide additional funding and/or training to increase the dead horse's performance; perform a productivity study to see if lighter riders would improve the dead horse's performance; declare that as the dead horse does not have to be fed, it is less costly, carries lower overhead, and therefore contributes substantially more to the mission of the organisations than do some other horses; rewrite the expected performance requirements for all horses; and—if all else fails—set up a workshop with paid attendants on the subject of riding dead horses in post-conflict settings. This is, of course, a joke, but it is the kind of joke that is mostly true.

Another trend that has been seen time and again is that most of the international assistance contracts, especially in the lucrative fields of security and construction, have been awarded to warlords or illegal armed groups, most of whom have earned millions of dollars from these contracts as well as from drug trafficking. I will give you specific few examples:

Eighty two or eight three percent of assistance to Afghanistan goes outside of the government budget or structure[8]. Big contracts have awarded to big companies, and most of them have been sub-contracted to smaller companies. According to one investigation, two years ago, the 29 km. roads between the capital of Zabul province, Qalat, and Arghandab district was contracted to one company for 2.9 million dollars. Then the same company sub-contracted to another local company for 928,000 dollars. Thus, just by selling the contract to another company, the original contractor was able to make 1,972,000 dollars. Of course with such kind sub-contracting, the quality of work will not be according to norms and standard expected when the contract terms were originally drawn up.

These lucrative contracts become one of the causes of increasing corruption in Afghanistan. Even Afghanistan's security sector was contracted to different companies and made millions and even billions of dollars for private individuals. So many private security companies emerged and flooded Afghanistan that a new culture of bodyguards and escorts were created. Most of these company vehicles do not have number plates, and they drive in the cities with full immunity and no one can stop them. As noted by Professor Barnett Rubin, the increase in expenditures by aid organisations outside the Afghan government budget and the disbursement of huge amounts of cash through the dozens of uncoordinated financial systems used by various aid agencies generate a tsunami of corruption, which both undermines the legitimacy of the system and prevents the assistance from achieving its objectives.[9]

According to my personal information, one international NGO operating in Afghanistan is paying 6 million US dollars per year to a security company to protect only one international staff member of that NGO. This is the reality on the ground. If the international community spent the same resources on Afghanistan's security institutions, Afghanistan would have far better institutions and security now, instead of enriching foreign companies who continue to make profits on Afghanistan's on going insecurity.

If one visits Kabul, one notice all these concrete walls on the streets and road blockades, you will get the impression that we are in highly insecure environment. All these arrangements are completely misleading and not understandable by ordinary Afghans. It seems from the perspective of ordinary Afghans that there is competition between embassies and international organisations to have more high concrete walls around their compounds. The idea here seems to be that these concrete walls will make them more secure, and the same thinking seems to have been adopted by the Afghan governments, which does not have precedent in Afghanistan during last 30 years of war or even before that of separating itself from people it is supposed to govern and represent.

Most of these security companies belong to the warlords or are their partners and they are involved in kidnapping for ransom, abduction, land grabbing, human rights violations and so many other criminal activities. Ironically, it is these very companies that are the main violators of the law which are hired to provide security. Some of these companies even make the situation appear worse than it is to ensure the continued prosperity of their businesses, such as by burning supply vehicles and so on.

Although billions of dollars have been poured into Afghanistan in the last seven years, Afghanistan is still ranked 174 out of 178 countries of the world interim of poverty and 6.6 million people do not meet their minimum food requirement (NHDR, 2007).

Internal Problems: Social Consequences

Unfortunately, despite positive start, the main problem was that in the light of Bonn Agreement of 2001, Afghanistan's transitional government was composed of warlords, technocrats and factional leaders. Each one had a different agenda and did not work collectively to bring peace and security to Afghanistan. Many experienced bureaucrats were frustrated and left the government, and instead many warlords and unqualified bureaucrats filled the gaps. After the Presidential election of 2004, it would have been better for the current government to set its own agenda and recruit its own personal and not compromise with various corrupt figures who have found place in the government system.

Also some of these warlords or human right violators have been elected to national assembly or provincial councils in order to enjoy political immunity from prosecutions. They were elected because they had local power and money to rig the election. They pressure different government departments to appoint their supporters and cronies. Currently, most of these warlords or criminal networks have executive power, economic power and legislative power. They are also able to influence judiciary process.

Now, many good and professional officers and civil servants lost their jobs or assigned to passive, unimportant positions, while corrupt or incompetent individuals who do not deserve to be in the system gained appointment by means of money and personal relationship. Therefore, the government was not able to streamline all assistance and most of the ministries were only able to spend 50 percent or less of their allocated budget. There is no respect for institutions and rule of law and corruption is endemic.[10]

Every season, the government and international community introduce new concepts or programmes that are not easy for the government machinery to digest and understand. The government is not able to prioritize their needs according to the reality on the ground, and consequently, most of the good ideas that have been introduced do not have implementation strategy that could be absorbed by government machinery and understood by ordinary Afghans.

Now, even most senior government officials do not know what is going on, and I am not talking about average Afghans who do not know what is going on at all. The government and people of Afghanistan are living in a big sea of confusion, mistrust and misunderstanding. Inability of the government and international community to meet these challenges will have long-term social consequences for the people of Afghanistan, and this can only exacerbate social and ethnic conflicts in the country. There is lack of focus on critical issue of nation building and national unity by both international community and Afghan government.

After removing the *Taliban* regime in 2001, it was the first such opportunity in the history of Afghanistan that international community have extended a lot of support to the government of Afghanistan but unfortunately, the Afghan government was not able to fully utilize this opportunity to build viable institutions to help and improve security, governance and development.

I would like to mention that recently some good steps have been taken by the government and international community to recognise the problems in Afghanistan and the downward spiral we are in. At least some within the government and international community are not living in the state of denial that has been generally the case so far. Hopefully, we will have solutions for the above problem soon.

Conclusion

The people of Afghanistan are facing immense challenges; in the city, those who have a relatively good life or salary fear kidnapping for ransom, and in the rural areas, they fear the *Taliban* and insurgents because they use very brutal tactics such as beheading and targeting those who work for the government or international community. Of course, all of these problems have social, economic and political consequences.

Failure in Afghanistan is not an option as this will have dire consequences for Afghanistan, our neighbours, as well as for the rest of the world. Insurgency can only flourish when the insurgents are protected within the community and provided save haven outside the country.

Insurgency can not be defeated simply by military means. Internally, there is a strong need for the government to lead to acquire the trust of the people in order to build strong and credible institutions. Without strong and credible institution, it will be impossible to defeat insurgency in Afghanistan. Because of the new administration in the US, a new momentum has been created to pay more attention to Afghanistan, and hopefully Afghanistan will benefit from such momentum.

There is a need for a strong regional policy which should be strongly supported by the international community to remove save haven for insurgents and terrorist groups outside of Afghanistan.

Finally, there are no quick fixes for the Afghanistan problem, and there is a need for a long-term commitment by all stakeholders to build sustainable institutions in Afghanistan. This is a very crucial time, and hopefully all stakeholders fully seize this opportunity to reverse downward spiral.

In the end, one point that needs to be made is that the Afghans are very optimistic and resilient people. During centuries and especially in the last three decades, they have been able to manage their lives under very difficult circumstances, and one can be sure that they will be able to overcome current challenges soon.

Notes and References

1. Kofi Annan, 25 September 2005, General Assembly.
2. The Times, February 3, 2009, Paddy Ashdown letter to the Special US envoy for Afghanistan and Pakistan, Richard Holbrook.
3. http://en.wikipedia.org/wiki/Civil_war_in_Afghanistan_(1992-1996) (last accessed in January 2009)
4. http://www.commondreams.org/views01/1212-01.htm
5. Gilles Dorronsoro, « Kabul at War (1992-1996): State, Ethnicity and Social Classes », *South Asia Multidisciplinary Academic Journal*, Free-Subject Articles, mis en ligne le 14 octobre 2007. URL: http://samaj.revues.org/document212.html Consulté le 20 janvier 2009.
6. *Ibid.*
7. Emergency Loya Jirga and Election Process in Eastern Provinces p-118-120 (The book is in Pashto Language and written by Shahmahmood Miakhel. Printed by Pir Printing Press, Kabul Afghanistan in 2006)
8. The Aid Relationship in Afghanistan: Struggling for Government Leadership by Clare Lockart, June 2007. (http://www.globaleconomicgovernance.org/docs/Lockhart_Afghanistan_2007-27.pdf) (accessed 26 January 2009)
9. The Transformation of the Afghan State; by Professor Barnett R. Rubin "The Future of Afghanistan, Edited by Alexander Thier, USIP, 2009 p-18"
10. Transparency International 2008 CPI report mentioned that Afghanistan is in the bottom of most corrupt nation. (176 out of 180 countries).

3

State-Building and Stabilization in Afghanistan: Design Constraints to Effectiveness

Shakti Sinha

Afghanistan's failure to stabilise continues to trouble Afghans and non-Afghans alike, since the consequences of earlier efforts led to unimaginable consequences. Researchers of many conflict ridden societies cite the failure to govern as being 'one of the main reasons for the spread of alienation, militancy and insurgency', and identify the failure to govern to include the failure to provide basic facilities. This paper takes a look at the structure of government that has emerged in post-*Taliban* Afghanistan, specifically whether its essential feature, a strong unitary state rooted in an executive presidency and a weak legislature with its unique electoral system, is conducive to establishing peace, stability and inclusive governance in the country. This would be examined with reference to the state- and nation-building experiences of modern Afghanistan, defined as the state which emerged after the second Afghan War (1878-1880), and the effect of prolonged conflict over the past three decades. The impact of foreign interference, a lot of which has been direct (Russian invasion, Pakistani support for the *Mujahideen* in the 1980s and creation of the *Taliban* later, US-led effort that overthrew the *Taliban* and continuing under UN Security Council mandate) and the Afghan reactions to these interferences has had a major impact on the internal dynamics of governance as well as on the credibility of the state, effects that are not easily captured in formal structures.[1]

Increasingly, representatives of the Afghan government and many European countries involved in Afghanistan, and lately even President Obama, are talking about the need to go in for a political settlement, particularly as they do not see the 'possibility' of a military victory.[2] This paper looks at whether the present constitutional, legal and fiscal arrangements would allow for a comprehensive political settlement that would satisfactorily involve all major political and military actors in Afghanistan. Or would the process of accommodating one set of actors create a fresh set of discontents that would not allow the Afghan State to stabilise? In this context, it would also examine a proposition recently articulated; that the best hope for those who worked to overthrow the *Taliban* was a return to power of a "moderate" *Taliban* 'still based on a strict interpretation of Islam' or of an 'acceptable dictator' who would keep the peace.[3] Such views are based on the premise that the aim of the Western intervention in Afghanistan should be limited to not allowing the problems of a dysfunctional Afghan state from spilling over to the Western world, rather than hoping to set up a Jeffersonian democracy, or what Secretary Robert Gates somewhat mischaracterised, a 'Central Asian Valhalla'.[4] This is quite a contrast to the stated goal of the intervention in 2001 that included facilitating the establishment of a functional, multi-ethnic democracy that would give the Afghan society hope that its diverse interests are a part of the new system, and that it is working in their interest. This paper hopes to add value, from a political and social perspective, to the existing debate on the inability and ineffectiveness of stabilisation efforts in Afghanistan.

Background

Increased instability in Afghanistan keeps the country in the news; news that is a source of concern to policy makers in not just in the troop-contributing countries but also in its wider neighbourhood. The surge in violence seen over the past three years (since 2006) even as news from Iraq has fallen off the headlines had lead to Obama as candidate argue for greater attention to Afghanistan, which he has followed up by agreeing to deploy another 17,000 troops even as his administration's review policy options on Afghanistan was underway.[5] (This would take the total US troops in Afghanistan to around 55,000, including 12,000 who operate outside the NATO framework; the total number of foreign troops is around 90,000.) An Iraq type of surge accompanied either by "empowering" local tribes/councils so that they are able to maintain local order and security, or by engaging 'moderate' elements of the insurgency, is seen as critical to success in Afghanistan.

The need for more effective counter-insurgency tactics is sought to be complimented with increased focus on the implementation of a broader, integrated and well coordinated strategy encompassing security, governance and development, the so-called 'civilian' surge. However, there is little evidence of key players going beyond the rhetoric of the need to obtain better governance and development outcomes into understanding why despite the billions poured into the country, "the progress of reforms has fallen short of Afghan expectations".[6] (This is not to suggest that resources going into Afghanistan are excessive, in fact they are quite low compared to the amounts of aid received by countries and regions in the Balkans, Timor, etc.) Most explanations seeking to explore links between the Constitutional and governance arrangements established in the post-*Taliban* period and the prevalent insecure environment are limited to explaining the inadequate representation of all relevant interests (read *Taliban*) at the Bonn conference that laid down the political roadmap for Afghanistan. This is a half-truth at best. Further, analysis of how improved security could be utilised to bring about better governance and much needed development is limited to using the language of counterinsurgency and advocates a policy of sequential action, namely of 'clear-hold-build'. In other words, take over and secure an area and then roll out governance and development. These explanations and causalities are both inadequate and simplistic.

What Went Wrong?

The conventional wisdom on why governance, and hence development outcomes, are inadequate or unable to meet expectations have two aspects. One, that weak capacities, corruption, crony appointments, lack of administrative restructuring, an inefficient and corrupt police force and so on have prevented the emergence of a Weberian state that would be able to deliver.[7] Two, that politics of patronage, favouring certain individuals and tribes (including sub-tribes and clans) and the inability of certain tribes who formed the backbone of the *Taliban* (the *Ghilzai* confederation of the southern *Pashtuns*) to reconcile with the post-2001 ruling elite (Durrani *Pashtuns* and their non-*Pashtun* allies) has meant that the insurgency has an increasingly larger pool of recruits to draw from.[8] And that the situation is complicated due to the large role played by the drug economy, estimated to be half as large as the licit economy.[9]

These two factors and the negative synergies they have been acting in concert are seen as primarily responsible for the current, insecure situation. Consequently, public administration reform, including that of the Afghan National Police (ANP) and political outreach to the politically excluded, as defined above, has become the centre of focus of much of international engagements with the Afghanistan government over the past year.

Public administration reform is a time-consuming, politically sensitive and an incremental process. The pervasive lack of capacity of the Afghan public sector and general lack of credibility of the government makes it is an obvious priority. An earlier attempt at public sector reform, the Priority Reform and Restructuring, was an unsatisfying initiative, which resulted in the mass migration of government staff to higher salaries with little or no reform or restructuring of line ministries in terms of revised organizational structures, weeding out of non-qualified staff, etc. The lack of a merit-based, professional and neutral civil service has definitely affected government's credibility and ability to deliver services better.

Frustration with the lack of progress on police reform is running high. The ANP is, in fact, perceived as an important cause of increased insecurity, and is identified by many as a part of problem rather than of the solution.[10] Besides, there is still the lack of clarity about whether the police should predominantly be a counter insurgency force or should it basically uphold the rule of law and public order? Further, advancing "reconstruction, development, good governance, and counter-narcotics efforts and building effective police and justice systems in Afghanistan will require many years of relative peace and security"[11] and this is a luxury that the Afghan government, the US and its allies are unlikely to obtain. And yet, without a modicum of security, it would be hard to deliver on development and governance.

The other aspect where both sections of the government and the international community are very keen on moving is what is often referred to as 'outreach', basically with the objective of connecting the government to its citizenry, especially those who feel excluded. The most important example of this is the Afghan Social Outreach Programme (ASOP), launched in late 2007 as a pilot in Wardak province by the Independent Directorate of Local Governance (IDLG), the government entity tasked with sub-national governance. ASOP is based on two fundamental premises; one, since Afghanistan has not been able to hold district and village council elections, there should be some way for the citizens at these grassroots levels to communicate to the government. The second premise is that Afghanistan has a rich history of traditional and customary mechanisms (tribal/elder leadership like *maliks*, *arbabs*, etc and consultative processes like *Jirgas* and *shuras*) and that such mechanism should be utilised to act as two-way medium between the government and the citizens. ASOP specifically seeks to create nominated district *shuras* composed of local notables, religious figures and similar persons who are seen as key to stabilisation and for extending government's authority over the districts. In other words, the establishment of these centrally nominated district *shuras* is seen by its protagonists as the solution to the governance deficit in the provinces, as well as a means of beginning a politically driven stabilisation process.

The history of the modern Afghan state established by Amir Abd al-Rahman after his understanding with the British in 1880, followed by subsequent rulers, is one of attempting to centralize the state through various means, e.g. internal colonisation by ruthlessly suppressing traditional systems/ethnic identities/rebellions, by fragmenting tribal structures and reducing them to clan identities so as to prevent powerful challenges to the ruler, using Islam as a political tool, creating a narrow non-tribal non-ethnic elite to create and run a 'modern' state, etc.[12] But such efforts have not been successful in creating a monolithic leviathan; in fact, local communities 'maintained a pragmatic distance to the state, which was regarded as a remote agency which could occasionally be useful'.[13] Therefore, in matters in which they could regulate themselves, people preferred to keep the state at arm's length.[14] However, this was not a smooth process of adjustment, and all Afghan rulers have faced formidable challenges in their state-building and centralization efforts.[15] The state was not above using violence and coercion in enforcing its writ—Amir Abd al-Rahman started the process of weakening the tribes, 'and institutionalizing the bureaucracy and the Afghan army, which he did quite extensively backed by "financial support and arms given by England to stabilise Afghanistan as a buffer state".[16] This on-off struggle resulted in the development of a centralised state that "coexisted with a fragmented, decentralised traditional society and the interplay between the two has been one of the recurrent themes in modern history".[17]

Consequently, despite all the centralising and modernising efforts of over a hundred years, and the present Constitution, Afghanistan is one of the most fragmented states where numerous power entrepreneurs exercise different levels of control over society and over state structures. The almost three decade long persistent, if low-level, conflict has only exacerbated this tendency. The gap between such informal exercise of powers and formal structures weakens the credibility of the state as the sole arbiter of power and justice. While part of the weakness can be explained by the recent conflict (temporary), far more important has been the continued inability of the modern Afghan state to obtain adequate revenues to establish a viable state (structural). The latter has forced successive rulers to rely on external patrons; the interaction between the two and the weak position rulers found themselves in has resulted in an incomplete, and distorted, process of state-building that has prevented the necessary political and economic transformation.

In such circumstances, the question to be addressed is whether within the present framework it is possible to work out a viable political solution that would end the insurgency presently raging in large parts of Afghanistan, as many commentators and representatives of troop contributing countries are increasingly arguing for? Or would a dictator acceptable to the West like Shah Amir Abd al-Rahman, funded by his external patrons, be able to establish sufficient credibility with the Afghans that would allow foreign troops to withdraw and leave behind a relatively stable and inward-looking Afghan state at peace with its neighbours, if not with its citizens? Or is it necessary to substantially revisit the basic premises of the state-citizen relationship, giving the latter a significant say in matters affecting day-to-day existence, recognizing that this is required to ensure a solid foundation of a viable Afghan state promoting social equity, political stability and economic growth. The persistence of micro-societies that enabled the vast majority of the Afghans to cope with the collapse of the state and larger social fabric over the years of conflict certainly seems to suggest that sovereign functions should be looked at much more broadly than what the present political leadership in Afghanistan and its partners are doing at the moment.

Developments in Governance

The issue of governance, and of the credibility of the government, is of critical importance to the success of the stabilization efforts. The perceived failure of the state to deliver public services, broadly defined, has constrained its abilities at establishing its credibility, despite the very high hopes it generated when it was set up as part of the Bonn process. The unprecedented voter turnout in the Presidential elections of 2004 and the significant turnout in the elections to the *Wolesi Jirga* (lower house of the National Assembly) and to the Provincial Councils in 2005 is an indicator of the popular enthusiasm that the introduction of popular democracy generated. Most surveys indicate a strong yearning for effective government on the part of the population. The lack of good governance as reflected in public perception of increased corruption is leading to loss of faith in the government.[18] Increased cynicism and a lowering of expectations is a feature of all surveys carried out by different agencies, including media and independent entities. There are various reasons for these changed perceptions.

The first limiting factor has been the lack of resources available to the state. This has crippled the government's ability to fund reconstruction and development activities adequately. The country needs substantial resources to ensure even a fairly basic level of services to the people, so this shortfall has serious consequences for the credibility of the fledging Afghan state. The modern Afghan state's ability at raising resources has been a persistent challenge since it was established in the 1870's.[19] Subsidies from the *Raj* kept it afloat during the first sixty years for most of the time.[20] This was followed in the Cold War era by the competition by the two super-powers eager to bring Afghanistan into its respective camp, with the Soviet Union emerging as its major donor. With the overthrow of the monarchy through the Daud coup, and more specifically after the Red army's invasion, Afghanistan effectively became the Soviet Union's client state.

The post-9/11 regime is critically dependent on external aid and the earliest it can even pay for its recurrent expenses, mostly salaries and office supplies, is 2013/14, a target it was supposed to meet in 2009/10.[21] As of 2008, government revenues are expected to pay for 60 percent of such expenses. The entire development and security budget is externally funded. This strengthens the perception that the writ of the government is limited to Kabul, a factually inaccurate statement but nevertheless reflecting the government's inability to dole out money to the provinces and districts. This problem of resource-scarcity is further compounded by the extremely low level of foreign aid that Afghanistan actually receives compared to other post-conflict fragile states and compared to its own requirements-Afghanistan is the fifth poorest country in the world with social indicators on par with the worst-off sub-Saharan countries. Even prior to the conflict, Afghanistan's economic and social indicators were extremely low. In recent times, the annual aid per capita to Afghanistan is dwarfed by what other, more prosperous and less-institution deficit post-conflict territories received immediately after the cessation of conflict. Bosnia tops the list at US$ 679 per capita. Comparable figures are US$ 526 for Kosovo, US$ 290 for Eastern Slavonia, US$ 233 for East Timor and US$ 206 for oil rich Iraq. Aid to Afghanistan at US$ 57 per capita lags behind even post-war Germany at US$ 129 and peaceful Namibia at US$ 132. (All figures in Year 2000 US dollars).[22]

In this age of information and globalization for a government to be seen as so dependent on the largesse of foreigners is hardly likely to help it be seen as very credible. However, this issue by itself is not as black-and-white as it appears in the Afghan context. The ability of a ruler, or even a local-level strongman to be able to extract resources from a foreign power is often seen as a virtue as it, paradoxically, demonstrates his skill at defending the national, or tribal/locality, interests.[23] What complicates the present circumstances is the knowledge that the survival of the government is contingent on the presence of foreign troops. This dual dependency allows opponents of the regime to portray it as a client state unable to adopt independent policies, which in the absence of adequate *mitigating factors*, discussed subsequently, substantially weakens its position.

The government's credibility gap is not helped by its extremely low level of ability to deliver. The government was only able to spend 39 percent of its development budget during the Afghan year 1384 (year ending March 20, 2006). Its performance has been improving, and during 1385, as much as 54 percent of a much larger budget could be spent. However, the performance since then has plateaued and even at present (2009), over 75 percent of total development expenditure is still being delivered directly by donors, bypassing government channels altogether. Further the actual mode of delivery of the government budget itself, even while highly effective, does not lend itself easily to increasing the government's profile among the population. This is not just because a lot of aid is delivered bypassing regular government channels, but by government itself using innovative delivery mechanisms such as non-state actors. This can be seen in the three sectors—health, rural development through the National Solidarity Programme and microfinance—that are seen as successes, two of which are discussed below.

In the health sector, recognising that the state system would simply not be able to expand fast enough to cover the country, the government and its international partners invited bids for the participation of non-state actors, who actually deliver health services to the population. The result has been a massive expansion in quality health care provision that is yielding good results. Health services now cover 82 percent of the districts, and it is estimated that every year, Afghanistan has managed to save the lives of around 40,000 infants due to better health coverage.[24] The government funds and regulates the performance of the service provider without having a direct role in the actual delivery.

In rural development, the Ministry of Rural Rehabilitation and Development (MRRD), a new entity, using non-government actors as facilitating partners, has established over 22,000 community development councils (CDCs) charged with planning and executing community-developed plans funded by block grants released by the government. Close to US$ 500 million has been disbursed over the last five years, with each CDC getting an average of US$ 27,000 creating substantial local assets. Here again, the government's role is removed from the direct beneficiaries by at least a couple of degrees. The MRRD contracts out to non-government implementing partners (IPs) the entire process from mobilisation to implementation. The IPs approach communities, set up CDCs, conduct their elections, prepare Community Development Plans (CDPs), get the CDPs approved (by MRRD), obtain release of block grants, report on implementation, etc. It is these NGOs, and sometimes their individual facilitators, that act as the interface between the communities and the government. Also this new ministry is insufficiently hooked into the traditionally accepted governance structure at the sub-national level. It is worth noting that while government systems may have become largely dysfunctional over the extended period of conflict and unable to deliver even basic services, they remained in place with clearly understood hierarchies and responsibilities.[25]

Further, the extensive direct delivery of aid and development projects by donors using all varieties of non-state actors—for-profit companies, NGOs, UN agencies, community groups—but bypassing government decision making processes also militates against enhancing the credibility of the government. This is not to argue for exclusive delivery of development services by the government.[26] Rather, the inability of the government to derive full advantage of the benefits of development efforts because of the reliance both by itself and by the donors on delivery through non-state actors is on account of the absence of institutionalized mechanisms that would facilitate the flow of two-way information between local communities, sub-national authorities and Kabul-based ministries. This could be largely mitigated if, besides the CDCs which work at a very micro level, there were systems in place that would allow local communities to be involved in articulating their needs and priorities, at different levels of geographical aggregations that could feed into decision making about the choice and location of development projects, or of monitoring the performance of service providers. This will be discussed in more detail in the section on the proposed structure of the government.

The next limiting factor that works against establishing the credibility of the government is one of capacity, an issue with every developing society but much more acute in the Afghan situation which has seen almost three decades of conflict. The country lacks a professional civil service and the existing system has inadequately trained and equipped staff, outdated internal systems and over-centralized decision making processes have limited the effectiveness and efficiency of the government, particularly in the provinces. Traditionally employment in the government was seen as prestigious and entry was through patronage networks. The salaries of government servants were quite low and compressed, and continue to be so.[27] The absence of systems of analyzing issues, of delegation of responsibilities and communicating decisions for example, hampers government functioning. Low levels of education among government staff, arbitrary methods of filling senior positions and lack of merit-based employment that has only partially been addressed till now neither enhances government credibility nor enables the state to deliver even basic services.[28] In the circumstances, the government and donors had little option but to use innovative measures to deliver services, even without the benefit of experience elsewhere.

In this atmosphere, it would be quite appropriate to come to the conclusion that without honest and effective administrators, police and judges, the state can do little to provide internal security—and if the government does not provide security, people will not recognise it as a government.[29]

Structure of State and Lack of Inclusion

Afghanistan is one of the most centralised and unitary states in the world in terms of its constitutional provisions, governance structures and fiscal systems, much more so than many countries with far smaller population and much greater homogeneity. There is both traditional and recent historical experiences that would explain this phenomenon. Historically, the predator nature of the state in the absence of adequate domestic revenue made its position always vulnerable to any challenger who could mobilise external support—the history of 19th century Afghanistan is full of ex-kings, challengers and pretenders who had to locate themselves in British India, Czarist Russia, Persia or the remaining Khanates of Central Asia as they plotted their next moves, initiating a tradition of neighbours' involvement in Afghan power politics that continues to this day.[30] Amir Abd al-Rahman (1880-1901) used the fiscal space that British assistance gave him to brutally suppress those who posed a challenge to his rule, resettled rebel Pashtun tribes far away from their homes, cruelly crushed rebellions and rigorously enforced his rule, launching a process of consolidation and centralisation that has continued to present times.[31] The resultant effective *Pashtunisation* of the state to the exclusion of other groups got closely identified with this process of centralisation; creating a somewhat ethnic divide in the discussions of the desirable nature of the state even today.[32] In recent times, the collapse of the Najibullah regime and the failure of the *jihadi* groups to work together combined with the easy availability of weapons led to breakdown of all attempts to form a functioning government. The resultant civil war and the *de-facto* partition even of Kabul into different sectors controlled by different groups turned a lot of opinion makers, and people, into viewing decentralisation and federalism as the inevitable first step leading to the eventual break-up of the country.

In a unitary state as Afghanistan, there is only one government with all sub-national offices being inherent components of it with no separate, local existence. Provincial authorities play no role in the formulation of their department's national budget, and are reliant for their resource allocations on decisions taken by the parent ministry in Kabul. There is absolutely no provincial discretion in desegregating expenditure at the local level, with all plans and projects required to be nationally approved. The National Assembly approves the overall budget ceilings for the government, and for each line ministry, nationally with no provincial breakdown available. In fact, the lower house of the National Assembly, the *Wolesi Jirga*, had held up the approval of the 1385 budget in March-April 2006 and again a year later as it was concerned about provincial equity issues but finally relented in the absence of factual information about the quantum of money going to individual provinces. Further, all government employees, including those appointed locally, are employees of the Government of Afghanistan.

The President, directly elected by the people for a five year term, appoints his ministers who however need parliamentary approval. The 249 member *Wolesi Jirga* is elected on single non-transferable vote treating the whole province as one electoral district (constituency) but with no party lists. Larger provinces like Kabul and Kandahar elect 33 and 29 members from a single set of candidates with each voter having only one vote. This meant that not all areas and districts are represented in the *Wolesi Jirga* or even in the Provincial Councils, and an overwhelming number of persons were elected on an extremely small minority of votes.[33] Further, since political parties were effectively not allowed to participate, all candidates were independents. The lack of effective political organisations and the lack of sufficiently localised constituencies has meant an obvious disconnect between the elector and the elected; the result is a fragmented legislature, 'disjointed and personality-driven, beholden to regional bases or strongmen rather than national interest'.[34] This has deprived the country of the option of developing democratic alternates to illegitimate power brokers.

The upper house of the National Assembly, the *Meshrano Jirga* (MJ), is partly indirectly elected and partly nominated. According to the Constitution, one-third each is to be elected from the provincial councils and district councils, with the balance being nominees of the President. However, as the district council elections did not take place, the provincial councils landed up electing two-thirds of the *Meshrano Jirga*. Of the two houses of the National Assembly, the lower house has more powers since it approves the budget, ministerial and certain other higher level appointments. Legislation is to be approved by both houses and in the event of a disagreement; a joint commission of both houses is set up to resolve them, as happened in the case of the media law where the lower house was able to have its more liberal version approved. The President's veto power can be over-ridden only by a vote supported by 60 percent of the lower house, taking effect after 15 days. However, the executive has enough 'discretion' in not complying with this constitutional provision, though more than a year has passed it has not notified the media bill into law despite the National Assembly's overriding the Presidential veto. (Counter-intuitively, it was the elected legislature that voted for a more liberal law than what the executive was able to accept). Many important appointments, like those of provincial governors, deputy ministers, provincial chiefs of police, etc lie within the sole purview of the President. The field of subordinate legislation is also a purely executive function. The National Assembly's supervisory and executive powers over the executive is extremely limited, though they do summon ministers occasionally for questioning, but they cannot enforce either such attendance or take any action to remove them.[35]

Sub-national Governance Arrangements

Since most citizens see the state only at the local level, the structures and functioning of sub-national governance arrangements are quite critical in establishing the legitimacy of the state. The *Wali*, or the Provincial Governor, heads the provincial administration, acting as an agent of the President. All line departments report to the *Wali*, and even though recent legal changes have reduced the Governor's discretionary powers, it retains many responsibilities including the authority to sign-off on expenditures of all provincial departments, participation in procurement and certain powers of appointment. The Governor is also the head of all provincial coordination mechanisms like the Provincial Development Committee (PDC), Provincial Administrative Assembly (PAA), etc and international military-run Provincial Reconstruction Teams (PRTs) work closely with them.

Elections to the Provincial Councils (PCs) were held along with elections to the *Wolesi Jirga* in late 2005, even before there was any legislation on the subject. While the law, as originally promulgated, listed among 'the duties and authorities' of the provincial council, participation in determining the development objectives of the government, consultation on the effective usage of revenues, etc, it has provided for no mechanisms through which it can actually do so.[36] The PCs complete lack of leverage with the local authorities led to obvious frustration, and after much effort by PC members and the *Meshrano Jirga*, the law was amended to give them a monitoring role over the executive. But again, there is no extant mechanism provided through which the PC and the executive wing of sub-national governance interact. The participation of PC members in governance mechanisms like the PDC remains dependant on the latitude given to them by the Provincial Governor. In any case since Provincial Councils lack both legislative and taxation powers, they are highly unlikely to emerge as credible, democratically elected power centres in the present scheme of things. This means that the pressure on the Governors and other sub-national governance functionaries to become accountable to the local people would continue to remain weak, with *Walis* intent on keeping their patrons in Kabul happy.[37]

Historically, the government's presence below the provincial headquarters level has been extremely thin, in fact till the Provisional Gazetteer of Afghanistan exercise of the late 1960's, 'the district or "*uluswali*" was defined...only in terms of district centre or "*markaz*".'[38] The head of the district, or *uluswal,* used to manage relations with the local community through the traditional power structures, e.g., *maliks* and *arbabs*. Among other functions, it was the latter's responsibility to deliver enough conscripts for the army, ensure tax collection, certify residency status in order to obtain civil registration and to hand over criminals in those cases with larger implications; how local disputes and crimes were solved did not concern the government. At present, though these formal and informal structures are in place, they have often been supplanted by new ones. For example, unless the *Uluswal* is himself a commander or is part of a powerful network, his authority is challenged by armed commanders, acting alone or locally on behalf of some powerful warlord. Similarly, the *maliks* and *arbabs* are challenged by the *mulla*h, local militia leader or by insurgency networks. Often, the parallel systems merge into one, which would ensure local stability but not necessarily the writ of the government even if the latter is not directly challenged. Elections to district councils, though mandated by the Constitution have not been held, as mentioned earlier, and are not likely to be held in the near future. This is on account of unclear roles and responsibilities of district councils, a weak appetite on the part of the executive towards creating and empowering new elected bodies, fiscal issues and disputes over district boundaries.

Way Forward

The changed, and changing, situation in Afghanistan demands appropriate institutions more in tune with present circumstances and people's expectations. Afghanistan is an extremely poor country with major developmental challenges. Globalisation and flow of information has done as much to shape people's expectations as direct exposure to the world outside; as many as a one-fifth to one-fourth of the Afghan population has lived outside the country for different periods of time and seen the functioning of normal governments. At the same time, tribal and traditional social structures have undergone major changes and distortions as "the long years of war and violence changed the fabric of the society and upset the traditional alignment of political forces in the country".[39] On the one hand, in effect, 'the state was destroyed,[40] and on the other, the logic of extensive but low-intensity conflicts led to the emergence of localised power entrepreneurs and Islamic elements, often violently and in conjunction with outside forces. Three key issues have been identified that led to this transformation, namely, "a crisis of legitimacy, a failure to substitute destroyed state institutions with new ones, and a rise of sub-state powers".[41] Any solution to the problem of incomplete state-building must keep these factors in mind, particularly that the fall of the Najibullah regime lead to a situation where the level of mistrust between the different groups and factions was so high that it proved impossible to demilitarise politics.[42]

Post-*Taliban*, people have clear expectations of what they expect from the state, and they are not willing to put up with corruption, brutality or with non-performance. Therefore, old state of affairs, "a minimum of state and a maximum of autonomy of rural institutions" will not do and that the state has to take on a stronger role.[43] This does not indicate any choice on the form of government; only what the state is expected to deliver. However, given the recent history of the past three decades, particularly the decline in levels confidence and social capital, efforts should be directed to "changing the divisive situation rather than adopting solutions solely to accommodate the existing fragmentation. Accommodation of traditional power structures and different ethnic groups has to be sought through democratic participation, political and economic integration, and the development of a civil society and private sector that mitigate the negative impacts of competing group interests".[44]

The decline in traditional social structures and hierarchies has weakened the efficacy of the policy of co-optation that Afghan rulers have applied in the past. It has been argued that the emergent local power holders, often referred to as warlords, have much weaker power-bases, so refusing to accommodate them, or dislodging them where they hold formal power, would be far less destabilising than imagined.[45] Instead, efforts to create democratic alternatives at different levels would be far more important. This would obviously be much more challenging to the establishment, which finds accommodating individuals much easier than refashioning itself to becoming accountable to representatives of citizens at large. Empowering citizens spatially and making them responsible for sorting out local governance and development challenges would go against the grain a century old centralising trend, but that does not reduce its necessity in the interest of increased participation and cohesion. On the other hand, specious arguments about bringing on-board moderate *Taliban* elements or disgruntled tribes and groups from the South and the East fail to take into consideration that in the present scheme of things, sharing of power is a zerosum game. For every new individual, assumed to be representative of a group/tribe given a high government appointment, another would be forced out. If the replacement is a genuine representative of a stronger grouping than the newly marginalized, then there could be potential gains. But there are no mechanisms for assessing the representativeness of individuals or of the strengths of groups. Far better then to look beyond individuals and create platforms that foster participation, representation and coalition building.

The desire for a strong unitary state, an expression found in the 2004 Constitution, masks the real issue of appropriateness in both what the government should be doing, and who should be doing it. In any case, the state lacks the resources and the monopoly over violence that creating a strong unitary state with a central core capable of imposing its will on the universe of micro-societies that is a characteristic feature of contemporary Afghanistan requires.[46] Federalism of the sort that the

US, Canada or Australia would be impossible to replicate in Afghanistan, due to differences in historical experience, the structure of the state and process of institution-development, etc., exacerbated by the mistrust among micro-societies that the long conflict has engendered.[47] Afghanistan obviously needs an effective national government, even if it did not face insecurity and destabilisation. However, as a perceptive observer noted, Afghanistan has always been "a territory inhospitable to the formation of states or strong government because it is very expensive to govern. It is hard to rule for the same reason it is hard to conquer: because it does not have many resources, the settlements are far apart, and there is relatively little water".[48]

Therefore, Afghanistan's historical experience and present needs suggest that rather than getting into the unitary versus federal debate, one should look at the goal of establishing "a balance between creating a strong and effective central government and ensuring a level of decentralization to secure equal distribution of resources and participation".[49] The only possible solution is to adopt what the scholar Amin Saikal has called "a centralised-decentralised process of reconstruction". Since a central core of the state has been created, it should now "act in interaction with micro-societies in order to construct a horizontal rather than vertical political order, and to constitute the kind of mode social-economic development and security building which would be conducive to re-aligning of micro-societies to one another and the core."[50] In effect, the power that this central core has gathered should be dispersed following the principles of subsidiarity,[51] so that the country can have multiple levels of governance, giving larger numbers of groups, rather than individuals, a stake in the system.

In fact in the Afghanistan context, useful guidelines on government design were suggested a few years back.

> Given the self-evident historical socio-ethnic fragility of Afghanistan, the fiscal and administrative centralisation of the state has some logic: local and regional elites have to refer to the central government for financing and the authority to deliver public activities. However, the corollary is that the central government should limit itself to a relatively minimal set of activities and functions...Overall, the ambitions of the sector ministries and their provincial and district departments must continue to be constrained by the vision of a lean, competent bureaucracy in Kabul, supporting a provincial and district administration overseeing the delivery of core services.[52]

This could form the basis for the allocation of responsibilities vertically between Kabul and the sub-national levels. In terms of accountability, there is the need to make the executive more accountable to elected representatives of the people. The 2004 Constitution created a unitary state with a strong Presidency, and a weak National Assembly. Constitutional experts have suggested that while a directly elected strong President satisfies desires for a strong leader, it is much less likely to deliver in all but the most unique of circumstances.[53] The first-past-the post system, even if qualified by necessitating a second round to ensure plurality of votes, does not guarantee majority support, and in divided societies, by having only one winner as against many potential losers, can actually become an impediment to inclusive governance.[54] On the other hand, a parliamentary executive needs to build alliances to obtain, and retain, power. While this can slow down decision-making, it has the greater good of participation, of buy-in, increased executive accountability and of creating many winners.[55] But this needs to be complemented by other structural changes in the electoral system, at sub-national levels and in the fiscal system to prevent state capture and kleptocratic tendencies.

The problems with the Afghan electoral system have been described earlier. It must be recognised that "a flawed electoral system can retard democracy's progress as much as warlords, religious fundamentalists and corrupt business leaders taken together".[56] The disadvantages of political parties participating in elections are far outweighed by their advantages, particularly its ability to bring diverse interests together for periods longer than single causes. Afghanistan's ethnic mix would force parties to reach beyond narrow, ethnic or sectarian concerns. The lack of census and political tensions preclude the formation of single-member electoral districts. However, other than in Afghanistan, closed Single Non-Transferable Vote (SNTV) system has only worked in districts with up to 4 members, not 33 (Kabul) or Kandahar (29), that too in Vanuatu, Jordan and Japan (now discarded). What Afghanistan needs is an "appropriately crafted Proportional Representation system—one that both is proportional and allows Afghans to vote for individual candidates".[57]

Nationally, the need to increase the executive's accountability at the provincial level cannot be overemphasised. Besides changes in the electoral system to make the Provincial Councils more representative and less individual-oriented, it must be empowered to exercise much greater control over the provincial level executive. At a minimum, mechanisms for improved flow of information are required to make PCs relevant in redressing citizens' grievances, and act as bridge between the executive and the citizens. Similarly, legal provisions giving the PCs a role in development decision making must be given effect to. At a maximum, they could either have a say in making the appointments of Provincial Governors or in their ability to express their confidence on the Governor's performance meaningfully.

A recent study of the World Bank established that fiscal flows to Afghan provinces were highly inequitable. Afghanistan could learn from the example of other countries and make fiscal transfers (allocations in Afghanistan's case) more normative. This is both a technical and political process, requiring both a much stronger bureaucratic system as well as a more developed polity driven much more on ideological than personality lines.

Conclusion

While the military debate is extremely important, and without minimum security, governance and development are constrained, it is time that we looked at other aspects of the situation, namely how governance arrangements have been organised on the country at national and lower levels. An inclusive system has many advantages—it better reflects people's wishes, creates incentives to participation in legitimate political processes and in enabling local political systems to take charge of the situation. Unfortunately for Afghanistan, at Bonn and beyond, there "was little sense in the aid community that the country was embarking on a comprehensive process of social and economic modernisation that was inherently conflictual".[58] To quote William Maley, the Bonn process had two main weaknesses.[59] One that "a significant number of powerful actors were unsavoury characters whose past records would not have allowed them to participate in the political process in a less destroyed state," but who were central to the Bonn process. Critically, "the Bonn process failed to engage in any appraisal of what the structures of the Afghanistan state should be and do." Instead by concentrating on ministerial appointments, it encouraged action on "the part of people who have controlled ministries to treat them as personal fiefdoms." Later, the government "tried to pacify rural areas by putting spoilers into power, which backfired."

This aversion to a discussion on systems most suitable for stabilising Afghanistan, and the continuous specious debate on who is best placed to lead the country, has significantly contributed to the deterioration in the situation, which an increase in troop deployment can temporarily hold, but not roll back substantially.

Notes and References

1. Barnett Rubin in his seminal work, *The Fragmentation of Afghanistan* (Yale University Press, 1995, updated 2002), argues quite convincingly that the Afghan society and its relations with the State are far from being static, that contemporary 'Afghanistan has been thoroughly shaped by its interactions with the modern state system.
2. See for example, 'President Barack Obama floats the idea of talks with *Taliban* moderates', The Associated Press Sunday, March 8th 2009. Further the *Financial Times* ('Reduced Insurgency best result for Afghanistan', March 6, 2009) quotes the Canadian Prime Minister, Stephen Harper that '(t)he best that NATO forces can hope for in Afghanistan is to 'push back the insurgency,' which can never be wholly defeated'.
3. See Henning, Ortwin, *An Alternate Course for Action*, Swiss Federal Institute of Technology Zurich, October 8, 2008 for the former view, and the reported remarks of the British Ambassador, Sherard Cowper-Coles talking to a French diplomat in '*A surge of pessimism*', The Economist, Oct 16, 2008 for the latter view.
4. Valhalla in Norse mythology is where the souls of the warriors who died in the battlefield went. Presumably he meant 'Utopia'.
5. This piece was written before President Obama announced his new AfPak policy on March 27th, 2009.
6. Personal discussions with an international development specialist with long experience in Afghanistan.
7. See for instance, Secretary General's report to the UN Security Council dated March 6, 2008 (A/62/722-S/2008/159)
8. Antonio, Guistozzi, *Koran, Kalashnikov and Laptop: The Neo-Taliban Insurgency in Afghanistan*, London: Hurst & Company, 2007.
9. World Bank and United Nations Office on Drugs and Crime, '*Afghanistan's Opium Economy*', Washington DC, 2006.
10. AREU (2007), *Cops or Robbers? Reforming the ANP*. Kabul: Afghanistan Research and Evaluation Unit, 2007.
11. Barnet Rubin and Ahmad Rashid, "From Great Game to Grand Bargain: Ending Chaos in Afghanistan and Pakistan", *Foreign Affairs*, November-December, 2008.
12. See for instance Shahrani, Nazif, "Resisting the *Taliban* and *Talibanism* in Afghanistan: Legacies of A Century of Internal Colonialism and Cold War Politics in A Buffer State", *Perceptions: Journal Of International Affairs,* V(4):121-140. Ankara: Center for Strategic Research, 2000; Shahrani, Nazif, "The Future of the State and the Structure of Community Governance in Afghanistan", William Maley, (ed.), *Fundamentalism Reborn Afghanistan and the Taliban*, London and New York: Hurst & Co. and Columbia University Press; pp. 212-242, 1998; Rubin, Barnett, *The Fragmentation of Afghanistan: State Formation and Collapse in the International System*, Second Edition, New Haven and London: Yale University Press, 2002.

13. Bernt Glatzer, "Afghanistan—A State in upheaval", *Agriculture and Rural Development*, 2/2006.
14. *Ibid.*
15. Ali Alfoneh, "*Hokumat* Versus *Yaghistan*: The Historical Challenge of State/Tribe Conflict to State Building in Afghanistan", in Bernard, Cheryl *et al.* (ed.), *Afghanistan: State and Society, Great Power Politics, and the Way Ahead*', Center For Middle East Public Policy, Rand, 2007.
16. *Ibid.*
17. Ali Jalali, "Afghanistan: Prospects for Nation Building", Bernard, Cheryl *et al.* (eds.), *Afghanistan: State and Society, Great Power Politics, and the Way Ahead*, Center for Middle East Public Policy, Rand, 2007.
18. According to a recent BBC poll, 50 per cent of the respondents say that corruption amongst government officials and police has increased over the past year. 63 per cent now say that corruption is a big issue, compared to 45 per cent a year ago. Not surprising, only 40 per cent agreed that the country was headed in the right direction, down from 54 per cent a year ago and 77 per cent in 2005. Other polls indicate similar trends. The BBC story can be accessed at http://www.bbc.co.uk/pressoffice/pressreleases/stories/2009/02_february/09/afghanistan.shtml
19. This phenomenon goes back to even earlier times. Ahmad Shah Durrani considered by most to be the first ruler of Afghanistan started off by intercepting a caravan carrying tribute from Delhi, loaded with gold and silver, meant for Nadir Shah, the ruler of Persia who had just died. The historian Jos J.L. Gommans (*The Rise of the Indo-Afghan Empire c.1710-1780*) makes a convincing case that with the collapse of the horse trade to India, the Afghan state lacked adequate domestic resources to support a regular state structure. This in turn led to weak taxation policies in Afghan with the state and its supporters sustaining themselves by raiding Indian territory. Once this option was denied, it led to the inevitable rise of local strong men who were left pretty free to administer their areas as long as accepted the nominal suzerainty of the Shah ('King') in Kandahar, later in Kabul.
20. Amir Amanullah Khan went from being a hero of the Third Afghan war which gave de jure independence to Afghanistan to being overthrown ten years later when his (incomplete) modernization upset many conservatives; the withdrawal of British subsidies meant that he lacked the resources to create a strong army and state structure that could carry out his policies in such circumstances. Other factors for his overthrow included an inability to build a coalition around his ideas, and the unintended consequences of new social forces generated by the reforms themselves.
21. http://www.imf.org/external/pubs/ft/scr/2008/cr08229.pdf, page 18
22. John Hodges, quoting '*The UN's Role in Nation Building*', 2005.
23. Sarah Chayes, *'The Persecution of Virtue: Inside Afghanistan after the Taliban'*, The Penguin Press. M. Hassan Kakar in his seminal work, *'A Political and Diplomatic History of Afghanistan 1863-1901*' *(2006, Brill,*

Leiden. Boston), gives many examples of many tribes accepting British cash in return for performing specific duties or accepting British suzerainty but who insisted that they remained independent. For example, the Afridis agreed to keep the road to Khyber open in return for payment, but who conveyed that they were in fact independent. For that matter, Amir 'Abd al-Rahman remained in power consolidating his rule on the strength of British subsidies and arms.

24. Praful Patel, "Bolstering the Gains in Afghan Health Care", *Washington Post*, August 4, 2007.
25. Afghanistan Research and Evaluation Unit and World Bank (2004), *A Guide to Government in Afghanistan*, IBRD/World Bank, Washington DC.
26. The World Development Report of 2004, '*Making Services Work for Poor People*', presents several ways in which different countries in different circumstances have delivered services using non-state actors, including through the market mechanism. Essentially, the state in many cases may make the citizen better off by redefining its role as a regulator rather than as a service provider itself, something Afghanistan is doing rather well in the health sector.
27. The ratio between the highest and lowest salaries in the civil services is less than 3:1, so as moving up the civil service hierarchy is mostly a matter of prestige than of incentives.
28. An attempt was made in the years immediately after the fall of the *Taliban* to reform ministries by mandating restructuring as a pre-condition for higher salaries through the Priority Restructuring and Reform (PRR) program but absent strong commitment to swallow the bitter pill meant that in practice almost wholesale migration to higher pay scales took place with little weeding out the unqualified.
29. Barnet Rubin, 'Saving Afghanistan', *Foreign Affairs*, January/February 2007.
30. Newsweek (2007), '*Afghanistan's troubled borders*', December 1, 2007
31. Barnett R. Rubin, Ashraf Ghani, William Maley, Ahmed Rashid, and Olivier Roy. '*Afghanistan: Reconstruction and Peacebuilding in a Regional Framework*', Koff Peacebuilding Reports, Report 1/2001. Bern, Switzerland: Center for Peacebuilding (KOFF), Swiss Peace Foundation (SPF), 2001. Available at http://www.swisspeace.ch/typo3/fileadmin/user_upload/pdf/KOFF/Reports/Afghanistan.pdf (pdf file).
32. For different perspectives on this, refer to Ahady (*Decline of the Pashtuns*) and Nazif Shahrani (*The Future of the State and the Structure of Community Governance in Afghanistan).* The recently formed opposition political party/alliance, United National Front, largely comprising components of the erstwhile Northern Alliance and others, is in favour of a parliamentary system of government, with provincial governors being locally elected, instead of being appointees of the President.
33. Andrew Reynolds, "Electoral Systems Today: The Curious Case of Afghanistan", *Journal of Democracy*, Volume 17, Number 2, April 2006.

34. *Ibid.*
35. Summoned by the Wolesi Jirga in October 2007, the then attorney general refused to attend on the ground that the former wanted to 'brow beat' him. Earlier in May 2007, the WJ passed a vote of no confidence in the foreign minister but the President challenged the validity of the vote; a position accepted by the Supreme Court.
36. Sarah Lister, and Hamish Nixon, '*Provincial Governance Structures in Afghanistan: From Confusion to Vision?*', AREU Briefing Paper, May 2006
37. Traditionally, the Provincial Governors looked to Kabul and often saw the local people through prejudiced eyes as illiterate and uncultured. AREU and World Bank (2004),
38. Ralph Favre, '*Interface between State and Society in Afghanistan: Discussions on Key Social Features affecting Governance, Reconciliation and Reconstruction*', AIZON, Kebele 16, House 216, Addis Ugebia, Addis Abeba, Ethiopia, 2005 also available at www.azion.com
39. Jalali, *Op. cit.*
40. Barnet Rubin's remarks at the Carnegie Council, June 25, 2002, available at http://www.cceia.org
41. Jalali, *Op. cit.*
42. William Maley, *Rescuing Afghanistan: A Balance Sheet*, presentation at Carnegie Endowment for International Peace, July 16, 2006, accessible at http://www.carnegieendowment.org
43. Glatzer, *Op. cit.*
44. Jalali, *Op. cit.*
45. Maley, *Op. cit.*
46. Amin Saikal, 'Building a Weak State amidst a String Society', presentation at ANDS secretariat, Sedarat, Kabul, November 5, 2007.
47. *Ibid.*
48. Rubin, *Op. cit.*
49. Jalali, *Op. cit.*
50. Saikal, *Op. cit.*
51. This principle stipulates that governance functions should be performed at the lowest effective level possible, e.g. communities should monitor school teachers performance but educational standards should be set t much higher levels.
52. AREU and World Bank (2004)
53. The Argentinean political scientist Guillermo O'Donnell has made a strong case for why the Presidential system has consistently led to political deadlock in South America and that importing the US model was a mistake. Essentially, it led to political outsiders being able to come to power due to their ability to excite the traditional 'disenfranchised', but who were unable to deliver as they either got corrupted or failed to build coalitions with powerful, vested interests. This led to resort to a breakdown in governance as in the fight of demagogy vs. entrenched interests; no thought was given to creating institutions that could lead to wider participation and better delivery.

54. William Maley, 'Executive, Legislative, and Electoral Options for Afghanistan', Mimeo.
55. *Ibid.*
56. Reynolds *Op. cit.*
57. *Ibid.*
58. Suhrke *Op. cit.*
59. William Maley, '*Rescuing Afghanistan: A Balance Sheet*', UNSW Press, 2007.

4

Indigenisation of Afghan Reconstruction

Jamal Rehman

The history of Afghanistan is a history of war, struggle, suffering and economic deprivation. The process of reconstruction of Afghanistan contains hopes, challenges, determination and dedication. While releasing the Report on Millennium Developments Goals incorporating vision 2020 in the Country Report 2005 for Afghanistan; Afghan President Hamid Karzai had said that "after decades of war, Afghanistan is one of the poorest and least developed countries in the world." It is a fact that years of conflict have depleted the resources of Afghanistan, necessitating the commitment of the international community to contribute to Afghanistan's development for an extended period. In the background of this historic reality; the government and the people of Afghanistan have major challenges ahead.

In the forwarding note of the Vision 2020 document for Afghanistan, Jean Arnault, Special Representative of the Secretary General noted: "the international community is working with the people of Afghanistan and the government to meet the challenge of security which still remains huge, and help in reconstruction of the country, while continuing to meet the humanitarian and rehabilitation needs. But it is now time for the people to assess the development challenges that they face and with the international community set a path for overcoming them."

No doubt Afghanistan has started its recovery from protracted violence and achieved significant gains in building democratic institutions, providing basic public services to its people, and reviving its economy. When we review the problems and prospects of reconstruction and peace-building in Afghanistan; we ought to look retrospectively on the achievements in terms of some key areas and draw an outline for the task ahead.

For having an in-depth review of the problems and prospects of indigenisation of Afghanistan we may focus on three key aspects namely: Infrastructure, Security and Corruption. However, it is agreeable that we cannot look at these three components in isolation. We need to have a brief look at related issues such as strengthening of democratic structure in Afghanistan, social security, education, health, empowerment of women and so on.

Economic Development and Reconstruction

Afghanistan remains one of the poorest countries in the world. With a per capita domestic product of only US $ 377 dollars in 2007, most Afghans live on less than a dollar a day, the World Bank measure of absolute poverty. Afghanistan was ranked the second lowest country in the world on the UNDP 2007-08 Human Development Index, and it is in the bottom five countries of the world for life expectancy (42.9 years), under-five infant mortality (257 per 1,000 live births), maternal mortality, and adult literacy (28 percent). Access to clean water and health services is extremely limited. In short, most Afghans remain desperately poor.

However, like most societies that have emerged from conflict, Afghanistan has experienced a period of rapid economic growth, averaging 8.7 percent per year since the Taliban was toppled in 2001. Per capita GDP has doubled since 2002. Economic growth has been most rapid in Kabul and other urban centres, although every part of Afghanistan has experienced higher output and incomes, with the exception of some of the most violent regions.

Other economic indicators are also positive. Inflation is in single digit. The national currency, the Afghani, has been stable against the Dollar. Reserves at the central bank are now more than $ 5 billion, enough to cover 5 months of imports. Agricultural output has been rising as refugees have returned, numerous roads have been built or repaired enabling farmers to transport crops, and urban demand for food has risen. Afghanistan has also been enjoying a construction boom triggered by rising trade (including narcotics), massive refugee return, and foreign assistance. Transport, retail and wholesale trade, and modest manufacturing gains are all contributing to growth as Afghanistan integrates into the regional economy.

Democracy in Afghanistan

Nearly 76 percent people of the country voted in the first ever presidential election held after 2004. In the elections to the National

Assembly which followed the Presidential election; women were elected for 27 percent of the total seats. The National Assembly became fully functional in 2006. New Chief Justice and other Judges were appointed for the Supreme Court the same year. New Provincial Governors were also appointed. A new Attorney General was appointed with a mandate to fight corruption. Thus, the foundation of Afghanistan's democracy was strengthened with the creation of sound legislative and judicial structure.

Rehabilitation and Development

Since the introduction of the new executive machinery; efforts were made to strengthen the democratic structure of the country. About 343,000 Afghan refugees returned from Pakistan and Iran. About 30,000 residential plots were allotted to returning refugee families.

Education

Efforts have also been made to develop the Afghan society in right perspective of gender parity. Since the take over by the new government; emphasis was laid on promoting education. The enrolment of girls has risen to 2 million which is about 40 per cent of the total enrolment at school level. About 35 per cent of the teachers appointed at school level were women.

Health

Following were the key components of the ANDS pertaining to health sector:

- By the end 2010 the basic package of health service will be extended to cover at least 90 per cent of the population.
- By end 2010 maternal mortality rate will be reduced.
- By end 2010 full immunization coverage for infants under 5 for vaccine preventable disease will be achieved and their mortality rate reduced by 22 per cent.

The country's health indicators were near the bottom of international indices and were far worse than any other country in the region. Life expectancy was low, infant under five and maternal mortality was very high and there was an extremely high prevalence of chronic malnutrition and micronutrient deficiency disease.

However, some progress has been made in health sector which can be listed as follows:

- The percentage of the population living in districts where the basic package of health services is being implemented has increased from 9 percent in 2003 to 82 percent in 2006.
- The percentage of primary health care facilities with at least one female doctor, nurse or med wife increased from 26 percent in 2004 to 81 percent in 2007.

Gains in the Period 2003-2006

Use of modern family planning methods among married women in rural Afghanistan increased from 5 percent to 16 percent.

- Receipt of skilled anti natal care by pregnant women increased from 5 per cent to 32 per cent.
- Use of skilled birth attendance for assistance with delivery increased from 6 per cent to 19 per cent.
- Coverage of BCC vaccine among children of 12-23 months of age to protect against tuberculoses increased from 57 per cent to 70 per cent and completion of the three dose oral polio vaccine increased from 30 per cent to 70 per cent.
- A 22 per cent reduction from the baseline level of 165 infant deaths per 1000 live births was recorded in infant mortality rate by 2006.

However, the government has to undertake a long journey to provide basic health facilities to common citizens of Afghanistan.

Rural Infrastructure

Efforts were made to improve the connectivity of far flung and rural areas through construction/repair of 20,000 kms of rural access roads (i.e.; all weather, village-to-village and village to district centre roads). 1800 Community Development Centres were also setup with a view to assist poorest and most vulnerables.

In the Afghanistan Compact Document, it has been resolved that Afghanistan will have a fully upgraded and maintained ring road, as well as the roads connecting the ring road to neighbouring countries by the end of 2008 and a fiscally sustainable system for road maintenance by end 2007.

Energy

On the energy front, the Compact Document resolved that by end 2010 electricity will reach at least 65 percent of households and 90 percent of non-residential establishments in major urban areas and at least 25 percent of households in rural areas; at least 75 percent of the costs will be recovered from users connected to the national power grid. A strategy for the development and the use of renewal energies will be developed by 2007.

On January 22, 2009 President Hamid Karzai, along with the External Affairs Minister of India, inaugurated the power supply line constructed by the Power Grid Corporation of India connecting Afghanistan with the power station of Uzbekistan. Through this new power supply, 70 mega watt of power is being availed for uninterrupted power supply to the city of Kabul and adjoining areas.

Urban Infrastructure

In the Compact Document it was resolved that investment in water supply and sanitation will ensure that 50 per cent of households in Kabul and 30 per cent of households in other major urban areas will have access to piped water. As against this; 31 per cent of total urban population has benefited from investment in urban water supply.

Mass Communication

The number of people connected through cellular phone services has increased from 20 thousands to more than 5 millions in less than five years.

Security

The major problem coming as a stumbling block to socio-economic development of Afghanistan is the insecurity problem. The problem of security in the whole country is a matter of major concern. In addition to the widespread poverty, the major challenge the government confronts is the continuing threat to security from extremists and terrorists, weak capacity of governance and corruption, a poor environment for private sector investment, the coercive effects of a large and growing narcotics industry, and major human capacity limitations through the public and private sectors. Meeting these challenges and rebuilding the country will take many years and require consistent international support.

One of the resolutions of the London Conference on Afghanistan on January 31 January-February 2006 was that all illegal armed groups will be disbanded by end 2007 in all provinces. However, we are still thousand miles away from the target.

One of the major threats faced by the people in large parts of the country is the threat from the landmines. Regarding mine actions and ammunitions it was resolved in the London conference that by 2010, in line with Afghanistan's Millennium Development Goals and Afghanistan's Ottawa Convention obligations, the land area contaminated by mines and unexploded ordnance will be reduced by 70 percent; all stockpiled anti-personnel mines will be located and destroyed by 2007 and by end 2010; all unsafe and unserviceable and surplus ammunitions will be destroyed.

As observed in the report of the International Crisis Group: The insurgency has gained momentum but is still not as powerful as some international and domestic actors make it out to be. The danger lies in the prospect that the growing dissatisfaction can deepen other fissures resulting from political fragmentation, the lack of government outreach at the provincial and district levels and growing lawlessness and criminality. If the international community is to retain the backing of an Afghan population increasingly dissatisfied with its government, it should focus on institution building instead of seeking quick fixes, which will further provoke disillusionment.[1]

There cannot be two opinions on the view that an unstable Afghanistan; in which extremists have a strong foothold, would again pose a serious threat to global security. Western governments need to acknowledge the importance of defeating this threat at its source and then present the case far more convincingly than they have done to publics which appear increasingly unwilling to accept casualties or long-term commitment of adequate resources.

To address the problems of current security challenges, which are critical to the issue of winning or losing Afghan hearts and minds, the following three suggestions have emerged in international quarters:

1. As a matter of policy US and NATO forces should continue to publicly reinforce their goal of minimizing civilian casualties, as well as being judicious in the frequent use of air power, erring on the side of caution when civilian casualties are probable.
2. Afghan people by and large trust their National Army. Hence Afghan forces should be involved in US and NATO military planning and operations.

3. In order to mitigate the negative effects of what is sometimes unavoidable and unintended damages; NATO should set a special compensation fund for civilian deaths, injuries or property damage resulting from its military operations in Afghanistan, to which all NATO member states should contribute.

Gender Parity

It has been resolved in the Afghan Compact Document that by end 2010 the National Action Plan for women in Afghanistan will be fully implemented; and in line with Afghanistan's Millennium Development Goals; female participation in all Afghanistan governance institutions, including elected and appointed bodies and the civil service will be strengthened.

Commitment of the Government for the vulnerable women has also been emphasised in the Compact Document where it has been resolved that "by end of 2010, the number of female-headed households that are chronically poor will be reduced by 20 percent and their employment rates will be increased by 20 percent".

Institutional Capacity Building

Capacity for Afghan Public service (C A P) Project was introduced in the year 2007 for using coaching and advisory services as a major tool to strengthen the core functions of the government in areas such as project formulation, implementation, management and service delivery, and to strengthen leadership and policy making skills. CAP is helping the Capacity Development Secretariat in developing a roster of local and regional coaches and advisers who will be available to serve the government. CAP has recruited, oriented and deployed coaches from countries in the region and from within Afghanistan's public and private sectors to increase the government's performance at national and sub-national levels. CAP has so far recruited and deployed 30 international advisers/coaches and about 35 national coaches for guiding and coaching the officials of about 25 ministries/departments of the Government of Afghanistan. CAP Project has been very effective and useful in transferring the knowledge domain and skills of office management. Efforts are being made to strengthen the role and functions of CAP at sub national levels so that maximum benefits of this project could accrue to different provinces.

Problems of Drugs and Narcotics

Narcotics is one of the major global perils which, like terrorism, seriously undermines the stability and wellbeing of the world society at large. According to the 2007 Survey Report of United Nations Office on Drugs and Crime (UNODC), the area in Afghanistan under opium cultivation rose from 165 thousand hectares to 193 thousand hectares. Some 80 percent of opium poppies were grown in a handful of provinces along the border with Pakistan, where instability is greatest. In his address to the 62nd Session of UN General Assembly on September 25, 2007; President Mr. Karzai referred to drug menace and said:

> In Afghanistan this scourage is legacy of the decades of misfortune that befell our country—from the widespread despair induced by war and oppression, to draught and climate hardships. We are working with our international partners to tackle this menace. We will prioritise the provision of alternative livelihoods to farmers, and expedite implementation of other strategies, including poppy eradication and interdiction of traffickers. However, addressing the world's drug challenge must involve focus on the far greater dimensions of drug trade that lie outside Afghanistan, such as fighting the international drug mafia, ensuring stricter border control and reduction of demand in foreign markets.

To deal with drug menace of Afghanistan it is suggested that on the pattern of Thailand; the government of Afghanistan should first introduce infrastructure and industrial development and win the confidence of farmers. After being assured of better mode of alternatives, farmers would be motivated to give up poppy cultivation for better mode of cultivation.

The Present Scenario

Although economic performance in some sectors has been positive, there are several negative trends. The government and its partners have failed in many respects to create a positive business and investment climate. The production and trade of opium is equivalent to more than a third of the licit GDP, fueling rampant corruption and diverting labour. Although opium's importance to the economy is likely to decline as other sectors grow more rapidly, opium production reached an all-time high in 2007 and there is evidence that more of the value-adding refinement of opium to heroin is taking place inside Afghanistan.[2]

As the scholars and intellectuals are observing; Afghanistan stands today at the crossroads. The progress achieved after six years of international engagement is under serious threat from resurgent violence, weakening international resolve, mounting regional challenges and a growing lack of confidence on the part of the Afghan people about the future direction of their country. In the report of an international study group it has been stated that "a recent poll in Afghanistan reflects a downward turn in attitudes towards the ability of the Afghan government and the international community to improve those conditions the Afghan people identify as the most critical problems facing the country: insecurity, weak governance, widespread corruption, a poor economy and unemployment.[3]

While talking to CNN on February 15, 2009, President Hamid Karzai stated that US forces may not leave Afghanistan so soon because the task is not yet over. They have to help Afghanistan in fighting terrorism. They need to be there till Afghanistan stands on its own feet and is able to defend itself from any possible threat.

The above statement of the President reflects the views and vision of the people of Afghanistan looking for peace and tranquillity in the country as well as the region which can be achieved by fighting terrorism with the joint efforts of international forces.

The successful transformation of Afghanistan into a secure, economically viable state that can meet the aspiration of the Afghan people to live at peace with itself and its neighbours and contribute to regional and international stability will depend on the effective utilization of all available human, natural and financial resources. This calls for an active and major role for private sector.

What should be Done?

The road ahead is rough and bumpy but the journey has to be completed. "The international community must wake up to the wider threat and summon the means and resolve to make a decisive change. Political will in capitals is needed to demonstrate that all countries are serious about sharing burdens. The priority is not simply more resources but putting them to the best use. Coordination will never be perfect, and new boards and bodies are certainly not silver bullets, but strengthened international leadership and streamlined mechanisms could help harmonise approaches. Political leadership must be at the fore, with military efforts exerted strategically as part of a border plan."[4]

An important suggestion for betterment of Afghanistan situation is that the international coalition forces need to expand their strategy beyond purely military objectives and focus attention on efforts to engage with the local population and provide security in a way that facilitates economic and development programmes and minimises civilian sufferings and casualities. Coalition troops need to develop a better understanding of the culture, politics and local customs of the areas in which they operate. An increase in Afghan civilian casualities from coalition military operations is angering the Afghans.

Friction between coalition forces and the civilians they are trying to protect is rising. As the *Taliban* refine their insurgency techniques and psychological operations aimed turning the local populace against the coalition forces, US and NATO troops will have to counter the *Taliban* tactics through increased engagement with the local population.[5]

The strategy of the international forces aiming at uprooting the *Taliban/Al Qaeda* sanctuary must take into account that the local populations in these areas are fiercely independent, adhere to conservative Muslims and entrenched tribal traditions, and hold deep ethnic loyalties and extended family connections. International officials should not overestimate their ability to influence the local tribes in this region and consider carefully the potential for blowback of providing resources to a group that one day might side with terrorists.[6]

To ameliorate the condition of Afghan people and provide better trade and market facilities; it has been suggested by an international study group that Afghanistan should be encouraged by international community to make every effort to root out the *Taliban* ideology from its own society and close down the extremist *madrassahs* (religious schools) and training camps that perpetuate the *Taliban* insurgency and cross-border activities; and encourage Pakistan to remove restrictions that inhibit the transportation of goods through Pakistan to and from Afghanistan, including from India.

A suggestion coming from some intellectuals and political experts needs strong political will and persuasion. In this model; it is suggested that the government of Afghanistan, along with international community, should develop a coordinated strategy in support of President Karzai's national political reconciliation efforts. Further, incentives should be provided to such *Taliban* that do not subscribe to extremist ideologies and agree to put down their weapons and join the political process. The international coalition partners are also being suggested to adhere to the same standards as the Afghan government while negotiating with insurgents.

It has been a general experience that in a large number of countries the governments have entered into negotiation with the rebels and ensured truce in larger public interest. The same can be tried in Afghanistan also. All those extremists, who are ready to come to negotiating table within the constitutional framework of Afghanistan may be included in negotiation in the larger and long-term interests of Afghan people.

Such a rapprochement would spare the strength and resources of the government of Afghanistan for rapid reconstruction and development and a considerable part of the aid received from international agencies which is being spent on combating terrorism and maintaining law and order; would be available for essential basic facilities such as supply of drinking water, healthcare, education and infrastructure building for the poor and needy people of the country. The will for real change of direction can be summoned if it is understood that Afghanistan is a taste not just in itself or of nation-building and conflict management, but of 21st century multilateralism. Poverty and underdevelopment, climatic hardships and above all, the menace of terrorism and narcotics; are challenges of global proportion in which Afghanistan continues to partake its share as a member of this global village.

Notes and References

1. Afghanistan: The need for International Resolve, Crisis Group Asia Report No. 145, February, 6th, 2008; page1
2. Afghanistan Study Group Report; Centre for the study of the Presidency, Jan.30, 2008; page-33.
3. Afghanistan Study Group Report, Jan 30, 2008; page-5
4. Afghanistan: The Need for International Resolve; Crisis Group Asia Report Number, 145, 6th February, 2008.
5. Afghanistan Study Group Report, p. 25.
6. Afghanistan Study Group Report, p. 24.

5

Challenges of Peace-Building in Afghanistan

Sanaullah Tasal

Introduction

Peacemaking attempts in Afghanistan dates back to June 16, 1982 with the initiation of the UN-led Geneva negotiations. Since that time there have been 'rise and fall' of hopes and expectations of the Afghan nation for peace and cessation of hostilities. These peace interventions range from high-level political negotiations by international negotiators to locally initiated peace missions, conferences/workshops direct and indirect peace building attempts by humanitarian aid organisations. But till now these attempts have failed.

After the withdrawal of Soviet forces from Afghanistan in 1989 there was a lack of external support to help Afghanistan reintegrate with the international community. The proxy wars initiated by the regional countries created a conducive environment for the expansion of conflict, terrorism, drug mafia and warlordism. All this resulted in civil war and the creation of the *Taliban* in the early 1990s, turning Afghanistan into the haven of terrorism and fundamentalism.

After 9/11 and subsequent intervention of the US led Coalition forces in Afghanistan raised high hopes among war-weary Afghan population. Afghans have made significant gains for conflict resolution, democracy, human rights, education and social justice. In fact, the Afghan people played a key role in helping the coalition forces overthrow the *Taliban* in less than two months. In the two years following the defeat of the *Taliban*, millions of Afghan refugees optimistically returned home in a show of support for international peace-building efforts and the new regime they helped establish in Afghanistan. Sadly, the increasing civilian casualties in military operations, unemployment, warlordism, lack of social security and social identity, bad governance and corruption have made people frustrated and annoyed with the state and coalition forces. Seven years after the overthrow of the *Taliban* government by US military forces, Afghanistan still remains a country mired in armed conflict. It is in danger of once again becoming a failed state, that is incapable of effectively controlling its territory or protecting its citizens or providing basic services to one of the poorest peoples of the world. The increasing level of violence in the countryside and the near complete encirclement of the capital have completely destroyed the illusion of Afghanistan on its way to peace and prosperity. The situation has reached a tipping point. In 2008, in particular, the security situation deteriorated very rapidly. The insurgency is gaining strength and much of the country is now inaccessible to the Afghan government and humanitarian and development NGOs. There is a widespread recognition that the current military strategy has failed. Despite promises of more troops to battle the increasingly confident *Taliban*, the opportunity to turn the situation around might already have been last. The insurgents have shown little inclination to engage in political negotiations, despite repeated calls for negotiations from the Afghan government. Sections of the international community have also supported calls for negotiating with the *Taliban*. The Afghan state is dependent on the outside world for virtually everything, including money, troops and most importantly legitimacy. As elsewhere, legitimacy is derived by a state's ability to protect its citizens and provide basic services. The overdependence of the Afghan state on the outside and the over-intrusiveness of the external forces in the process will have serious long-term implications for Afghanistan.

In Afghanistan, it is impossible to understand whom to turn to for justice. The Afghans are the victims of both *Taliban* and coalition forces operations, so they have become sandwiched between them. This is the most crucial factor that is increasing the disappointment among the Afghan people and threatening the peace process in Afghanistan.

People in Afghanistan have been fighting for justice, peace, democracy, freedom, progress and prosperity for a long time. They were offered many beautiful dreams by the international community, but the dreams remain unfulfilled. If we look at the nature of the present conflict in Afghanistan, there are so many actors and stakeholders beside the *Taliban* and *Al qaeda* fueling the war in Afghanistan. Warlordism, corruption among the government and international donors, poverty, weakness of the government, blind bombardments by the international coalition forces, poppy cultivation, regional and international mafias presence, lack of education, and the neighbouring countries' continuous proxy wars are the causes of ongoing conflict in Afghanistan.

The international community should understand that no peace operation will be successful without popular support. Unlike other post-conflict situations, the international community hardly attempted to win the hearts and minds of the Afghan people upon re-engagement in the country eight years ago.

Factors Contributing to Instability in Afghanistan

The following factors contribute to the increased level of disappointment and resentment among the Afghans. This resentment has contributed to the success of the *Taliban* insurgents in capturing support for their activities.

Political Factors

The Bonn Agreement

Since the Bonn Agreement of late 2001, there has been a global effort to assist the Afghan government with security, economic revival and socio-political reconstruction._The Bonn Agreement brought together various Afghan factions from within and outside Afghanistan. However, the Bonn delegation was dominated by minority ethnic Afghan groups and did not include any representatives of the *Taliban,* Hezb e Islami and the majority of Afghan Pashtoon population. A major mistakes made in the initial days of Bonn Conference supported by the US government was putting warlords and the very people who are threat to security accused of crimes against humanity in power.

Right after the collapse of the *Taliban*, the government and the international community had the opportunity to persue these warlords because they were scared and weak. Instead, the international community and the US government supported them and made them stronger. They did not bring them to justice. They waited until they committed more crimes.

After September 11, 2001, the US relied on the northern warlords and their militias to help oust the *Taliban*. Many of those leaders were given prominent positions when the new Afghan government was formed, enabling them to claw back credibility that they lost because of their behaviour in the civil war.

Weaknesses of the Afghan Government

The single most important reason for the emergence and deepening of conflict lies is the weakness of the government. Between 2001 and 2004, the basic institutions of central government were established with the full participation of the Afghan people. But law enforcement institutions, which constitute the face of any government, has been neglected from the beginning. Consequently, the security vacuum has widened in areas where law enforcement institutions are either absent or too weak to protect the people, particularly in the south and the east.

Ordinary Afghans want simple things—security, schools with competent teachers, health facilities staffed with knowledgeable doctors, and a fundamentally equitable and responsive government. The current international strategies in Afghanistan ignore the fact that in the eyes of Afghans the current Afghan government is thoroughly discredited—many officials have criminal pasts, were put in their positions early on by the US-led coalition, and are thoroughly corrupt. The Afghan people will not "bond" with a government whose officials continue to cheat and abuse them and no amount of development aid will help if it is put through corrupt channels.

The *Taliban* and *Al Qaeda* insurgents are aware of the vulnerable environment in Afghanistan where they operate. They understand that Afghanistan's weak state institutions and the slow pace of reconstruction have turned the tables in their favour. Put simply, freedom's greatest enemy in Afghanistan is not the *Taliban* or *Al Qaeda* but under-reformed and under-resourced state institutions that cannot deliver basic services to people. Thus, when left without a choice, people resort to whatever alternative is available for survival. Unfortunately, narco-terrorists have stepped in to provide that alternative by offering people protection in return for poppy cultivation and passive opposition to the government.[1]

Corruption and Loss of Credibility

The leaders in Afghanistan have shown themselves incapable as yet to develop and implement coherent strategies for addressing the needs of the Afghan people, and to overcome corruption among their ranks. For example, a significant number of politicians of all ideological affiliations are suspected to be profiting from corruption and smuggling. These suspicions have led to a significant loss of credibility of many of the democratic institutions in Afghanistan to the citizens.

Government Inability to Address Human Insecurity

The violence in Afghanistan has claimed the lives of thousand of people including national army, police officers and innocent civilians. Many have even reported US involvement in killings and the disappearance of individuals in their custody. The coalition forces have also been accused of concerted repression and discrimination against peasants and ethnic majority, whom they consider to be the *Taliban* or *Al-Qaeda* supporters. The *Taliban* have also conducted violent attacks against the civilians. The combination of the inability to contain and address the *Taliban* violence and the tendency of the coalition forces to violate human rights has done little to improve the moral standing of the authorities among the citizens.

Weakness of Afghan Army and Police Forces

At the beginning of the interim government, the US and its allies proposed an army of maximum 80,000. They opposed the proposal of the Afghan government regarding establishing 200,000 strong army for the country. The weakness of Afghan army and police forces paved the way for flourishing of the *Taliban* and currently the country faces more serious security challenges than seven years ago.

The international community should shift its focus to supporting the Afghan people first and foremost, and use its leverage to push the Afghan government to take strong measures to fight corruption and gain public trust. Failing to do so, alienates Afghans from the foreign assistance efforts—if foreign countries, providing assistance, are not going to ensure that the government is honest, responsive and accountable, many Afghans feel "they should go home." The unchecked corruption and impunity in the government also fuels a degree of nostalgia for the *Taliban*, as people remember that the *Taliban* provided security and did not take bribes.

Warlords

Warlords and local militia commanders are in many ways the real power holders in Afghanistan today. These local groups are often based on ethnic and clan allegiances, and their military power is substantial. Despite the Disarmament, Demobilization and Reintegration (DDR) programme, the warlords still have significant power. Most local leaders have relatively small armed forces standing, but have the potential of mobilizing large armies though their network of villages.

Warlords who have controlled Afghanistan with the US blessing since 2001, have no interest in either democracy or peace or human rights. The commanders, the war criminals, still have their armed groups. They are in the government and Karzai, the Americans, the British sit down with them. They have impunity and can commit whatever crimes they like.

Religious Extremism

The American strategy during the Soviet intervention in Afghanistan with support of the Saudi Arabia and Pakistan has facilitated the recruitment and training of thousand of Muslim fighters. American only recruited and trained the fundamentalist groups in Afghanistan for their own interests, and ignored the political and social parties. This caused the increasing conflict in Afghanistan and spread fundamentalism in the region. The Americans did not think that these fundamentalists will threaten the world and the region. They have engaged in the fight among the Afghan groups and used the anarchic situation in Afghanistan to create a haven for extremism and terrorism.

These Islamic fundamentalists received weapons during the war. They accumulated a lot of wealth with these weapons and are now ruling areas under their control. They have virtual control over the life and death of people. They have murdered thousands and can still kill their opponents in public or in secret. These groups and their commanders know that people are not happy with the present government in Afghanistan. Foreign hands support these Islamic parties because of their own agenda. They finance them to ensure that these groups can survive so they can influence Afghanistan to a certain extent.

In 2001, the coalition forces ousted the *Taliban* in 45 days. Collapsing like dominoes in front of the US-led advance, the *Taliban* forces gave up and crossed over into Pakistan in late 2001. From late 2001 to 2008, coalition forces focused mainly on hunting down the remaining leaders of *Al-Qaeda*, leaving thousands of former *Taliban* combatants to their fate. This effectively allowed the *Taliban* to regain strength, Regrouped and reorganised, better equipped and financed and more sophisticated tactically, they are threatening both the government of Afghanistan and the US led coalition forces on the ground.

Economic Factors

Poverty and unemployment are so prevalent that every other Afghan suffer from poverty and unemployment. The unemployment rate is estimated around 40 percent, estimated poverty incidence ranges from 34 percent around harvest season to as much as 42 percent in the lean season.

Poverty in turn forms a background for the more direct threats to peace and security that challenge the country, such as warlordism, radicalism and narcotics. Poverty forces large numbers of Afghans to serve as warlords and rely on them and not on themselves or the state for survival and protection. Poverty and underemployment also fuels resentment that helps Islamic radicalism conquer new ground. The struggle against poverty is hence the crucial element in Afghanistan's future and to that a monumental task. Economic and financial institutions have also been dogged by the same charges of corruption as political actors. The ensuing lack of confidence in financial institutions and the corresponding lack of private sector investment in Afghanistan have done little to improve Afghan's economic outlook both in the short and long term.

Regional Factors

Afghanistan—the 'Battleground' of its Neighbors' Interests

Many Afghans fear that their country has become a proxy battlefield for Iran and Pakistan, who have established intelligence services in Afghanistan. Afghanistan has been a key target for foreign intervention. Continuous foreign intervention has sustained the conflict by supporting one side against another. Afghanistan is closely attached to South Asian, Central Asian and to some extent the Middle Eastern countries through geography, history, culture, religion, economy and cross-border ethnic contiguities. Such factors have created incentives for regional and international players to intervene in Afghanistan's internal affairs to attain their own objectives. Neighboring states and other international players have often attempted to gain influence by backing one Afghan faction or another, this has created a sustained environment of political chaos and instability.

Pakistan

Pakistan has manipulated the Afghan resistance against the Soviet and used it for its own benefits. It has endeavoured to provide ingredients for the internal conflicts within the country and has supported one combatant group against another. Pakistan has three main objectives in Afghanistan. First, it is essential for Pakistan to have a friendly government in Afghanistan so that it can concentrate in its full strength over the Kashmir crisis with India. Second, Pakistan is fearful of the integration of the Pashtun tribes across its boarder, which will result in losing the claimed territory of the Durand Line. Third, Pakistan has boosted its economy by exporting its goods to Afghanistan which accounts for approximately 80 percent of Afghanistan's imports. Particularly since 1992, Afghanistan is one of the best markets for Pakistani products. Additionally, Pakistan aspires to reach Central Asian market through Afghanistan.

Iran

Iran is another country that has always tried to use religion to gain the sympathies of the Afghan *Shiites*. Although Iran in general supports Persian speaking communities in Afghanistan, they provided more support to certain *Hazara* groups who are mostly *Shiite* sharing the same sect of

Islam with Iran. Also Iran's policy towards Afghanistan was tainted by its vision of spreading its Shiite version of Islam towards the east, in particular the state form and political Islam introduced in its 1979 revolution to enhance and strengthen its role as the leader of all Shiites minorities in the Muslim World.[2] This led Afghanistan's neighbors to play proxy games in Afghanistan's internal affairs. This regional competition over the control and influence over Afghanistan leads to fuelling the war and weakening the government of Afghanistan.

Poppy Cultivation

Sustained insecurity and destruction, caused by civilian war and the *Taliban* in the early 1990s, turned Afghanistan into the world's new heroin haven. In the absence of adequate foreign aid, the only way to secure short-term financing was via participation in the drug trade. However, if opium turned Afghanistan as the world largest opium producing country it has also affected the region. Afghanistan has become a victim of this illicit cultivation, it has damaged the Afghan economy and strengthened the warlords and the *Taliban*.

The first groups of actors associated with the Afghan drug trade are the terrorists. There is a strong link between the drug business, arms purchases for conflicts and the activities of terrorists, corruption and Islamic fundamentalist groups in the region. According to a report published by United Nations Office on Drug and Crime (UNODC) in 2007, the *Taliban* gained about $100 million from opium trafficking which was the major sourcc of finance for the *Taliban* that year.[3] The international drug trafficking mafia also continues to be involved in the regional drug trade, many of their operational movements have been restricted to some extent since 2001.

In the view of the Afghan scholars, the role of opium in the current situation is seriously misunderstood and opium related corruption in the government is a much more serious problem than opium funding for the *Taliban*. The opium trade has led to the "mafiazation of the government" and many high level officials are involved, whether directly or through appointing police officers to facilitate opium routes and then collect fees for such service.

Current proposals to replace opium with wheat are not realistic, and the popular notion of licensing opium for legal markets is completely unworkable. Instead grapes, pomegranates and almonds are the real alternatives in the south and the cultivation of these crops must be enabled through infrastructure programmes and incentives that would help wean farmers from opium. Since traditional irrigation systems are completely broken down, the introduction of water conservative irrigation practices are especially critical and would enable farmers to contemplate other crops.

Civilian Causalities

Afghans have become very critical of the US because of the increasing civilian casualties in military operations. Many Afghans continue to view foreign troops on their land as a necessary evil, but even those supporting them want fundamental changes in the conditions of their presence.

President Hamid Karzai repeatedly asked the international coalition forces to coordinate their operations with the Afghan government, but the international coalition forces ignored his request. The civilian casualties will continue rising in Afghanistan, gradually giving the terrorists an upper hand. Thousand of Afghans have been killed or displaced from their native places.

US ignorance regarding the ground realities of Afghanistan is a source of major problem in Afghanistan. In 2001, the Afghans welcomed the international coalition forces to Afghanistan. The villagers handed out red roses. The elders lined up to welcome guests to their country to deliver them from the *Taliban*, but now that feeling is changing. Majority of Afghans are disappointed of the International Coalition forces. The problem of the civilian casualties in operation of foreign troops has existed from the beginning of deployment of these forces to Afghanistan in 2001 but it has intensified further. This has put a negative impact on the image of foreign troops among ordinary Afghans. There are concerns that by deployment of additional US troops to the country more civilian will lose their lives in operation of these forces. Media agencies reported that the foreign troops in Afghanistan killed more civilian than *Taliban* in the two beginning months of year 2009. *Taliban* fighters killed civilians in suicide and bomb blasts while foreign troops killed 100 Afghans in this period.

Every bomb that detonated on a wedding party led to tens, perhaps hundreds of young people—mostly young boys and many of them orphans—joining the resistance movement under the flag of the *Taliban*.

Desecration of religious texts by International Coalition Forces in Afghanistan is another impediment to peace in the country. The people of Afghanistan are Muslims and are very proud of their religion. The US troops desecrated a Koran when they had raided the mosque, rounded up worshippers and tore apart copies of the Koran in Ghazni Province. US policy toward Afghanistan will require a fundamental change in order to achieve long-term stability in that country.

Illiteracy

The majority of Afghans are illiterate, during the war educational institutions were destroyed and more than three generations of Afghans have grown up seeing just guns, tanks and bombs around them. They had little opportunity to see conflicts resolved by means other than arms.

Considering Pashtuns as Terrorists

The people of Afghanistan have never been extremists in their outlook towards religion. Even today, virtually the entire population of the country abhors the militants. There are some who believe that Pashtun culture is inherently militant, violent and aggressive and that *Talibanisation* and radicalization of the region is the expression of Pashtun nationalist sentiment. This approach assumes that all *Pashtuns* have a *Taliban* mindset ideologically. There are several causes for terrorism and religious militancy in the Pashtun belt, the prominent among them are: ideological, economic, and political economic and geostrategic. Though all the above causes may be instrumental in one way or the other, the most effective cause seems to be related to political economics.

The Terrorism and Extremism Label

Both the international as well as the national media has painted such a distorted picture of Pakhtuns that the moment you tell someone you are a Pukhtun, Pashtoon, or Pathan they visualize you as a terrorist, extremist, *Taliban* or pro-*Taliban* or some type of other irrational person who is bent on destroying humanity. Of course this label is equally used for Pakhtuns on both sides of the Durand line. These terms have become synonymous with our race and nation.[4]

Conclusion and Recommendations

The war in Afghanistan is not going well. Almost all trends are moving in the wrong direction. But we still have time to focus, improve our strategy, and calibrate our means.

In the present context of Afghanistan, people in general are expecting a strong role of international community in the conflict resolution. They even trust that they are capable to bring both state and the *Taliban* insurgents at the dialogue table. Learning from the past experiences, there should be enough home work in order to make the dialogue successful.

Re-establishing the security and rule of law, is an urgent need for peace and stability in Afghanistan. Because without rule of law and order, management in Afghanistan, the legitimacy of the state can not be established, violence cannot end, and social reconstruction and confidence building cannot begin.

Many Afghan and Western considering that solutions should be come from within Afghans not are imposed by external actors. All are concerning that any effort must be concerted and holistic, addressing in a strategic manner all of the major sources of instability.

Many Afghans believe that the core of social instability in Afghanistan lies in the inability of government to improve the living conditions of rural populations. The state should be restructured to give local communities more control over administration and the distribution of resources at the local levels by increasing the powers and decision-making functions of local governments. Donors and other international actors could have a role in working to increase the capacity of local institutions.

Government inability to provide quality education, particularly to rural children, is highlighted by the comparative success of the insurgents. To address illiteracy, the new government in Afghanistan must provide religious and modern education through Madrassas and schools to the Afghans children (boys and girls), which would prevent the Afghan children from crossing the borders in order to obtain a religious education and hence, return with a foreign ideology. They should make education the first priority and provide schools in all the remote areas of the country.

Long term economic planning is required to counter chronic underdevelopment and discourage people from resorting to violence and extremist ideologies to air their grievances. The primary thrust must be to diversify the primarily agrarian economy and further develop a manufacturing base. In addition, some have proposed efforts to map the socio-economic conditions in the *Taliban* dominated areas to predict potentially unstable regions.

Many believe that the problems raised by the *Taliban* insurgents can only be solved through the economic development of rural Afghanistan. Hunger in the regions breeds support for extreme activities among rural people. Current development efforts have been hampered by the weakness of bureaucracies, and the gap between government rhetoric and performance. The success of the international community in mobilising local people to construct roads, electric generators and bridges has convinced many that decentralised decision-making could improve the effectiveness of economic development programme. Decisions would then fall on the local people, who are most affected by these programmes, and so could better allocate the limited resources available for development. Strategies should be invented for the economic development of the regions in accordance with principles of gender equality and respect for local ecology.

The government, development agencies and civil society groups should devise strategies to decentralize decision-making on development issues and increase the capacity of local infrastructures to address the immediate needs of the local people. The communities should also become involved in monitoring and evaluating development projects in their areas. Efforts should be made to initiate programmes to encourage self-employment in deprived areas, which should be managed by local institutions.

International agencies should maintain political neutrality and focus on supporting development agenda and good governance. Development activities should continue wherever possible during the current unrest. These activities should be carried out in an atmosphere of transparency and accountability. The formation of focus groups could be considered. Members of local communities, local government and donors would assemble from time to time to discuss development strategies and ensure that the aid supports local capacities.

Meanwhile, Afghanistan's warlords are mistrustful and competitive, and their private militias are the source of their strength and threat to the stability of Afghanistan. The international community should disarm them and their militia and cut off foreign support for these armed or private militias by applying political pressure and blocking their financial sources. In fact each of the above is possible only through international support and cooperation. However, for the stabilisation of Afghanistan, political parties, government and, generally, the Afghan nation as a whole, have to work to this end.

Notes and References

1. http://afghanpenlog-en.blogspot.com/2009/01/value-of-state-building-vs-cost-of.html
2. Ahmad Wais Wardak, Master's Candidate, International Studies, University of Connecticut, U.S.A.
3. *Times*. By Carlotta Gall, February 2008 NY.
4. Khadim Hussain, Terrorism in the Pashtun belt: Analytical framework for finding solutions through people's voices, July 2008

6

The Geo-Political Dynamics of Afghanistan and the American Strategic Perspective

Sanjeev Bhadauria

The US policy has always exhibited a deep sense of insecurity and quest for materialistic gains along with its self acquired role of acting as an universal policeman—the need for which is sometimes real but most of the time imaginary, bordering on 'paranoia.' Moreover, the American engine has always needed an extraneous threat to set it in motion. Previously, it was the communist threat. Now it is the threat posed by the 'ungoverned states'. The sources of concern today are the states with large tracts of ungoverned territories like Afghanistan which offer ample opportunities to further its interests under the garb of international obligations. The situation in Afghanistan offers fertile ground for the US and the September 11, 2001 incident provided it with the reason to decipher its ambition. Afghanistan has gone from one of Washington's greatest foreign policy triumphs to one of its most profound failures. During the Cold War, the US support to the anti-Soviet Afghan resistance resulted in a debacle for Moscow, humiliating the vaunted Red Army and discrediting the Soviets throughout the Muslim world. After the Soviets withdrew, however, Afghanistan has proved to be a disaster for the US policy, especially in its second endeavour after September 11, 2001.

The geo-political dynamics of this country with a strategic location has led the policy makers in Washington to show ample interest and be involved in its affairs like it has been in the Cold War period. The American interest in Afghanistan, post-Soviet invasion in 1979, was guided initially by a purely short-term, tactical and emotive agenda to seek 'historical revenge' for Vietnam. However, once the Soviets withdrew, US interest in Central Asia suddenly revived and peaked due to the quest for the estimated 70 billion tons of oil reserves of Central Asia. The American geo-political drive also appears to be motivated by the containment/engagement of China, Iran and extracting Central Asian oil and gas for the world market, in addition to putting the NATO right there at the door-step of Russia. With 9/11 attack, it realised to its chagrin and shock that the rabidly fundamentalist *Al-Qaeda* and *Taliban*, their own creation, struck them with a vicious force that shook them beyond their imagination. It is now engaged in waging a war on terrorism with the help of an International Security Assistance Force (ISAF), mainly constituting of NATO forces and has pledged a vast sum for the reconstruction work in Afghanistan.

Afghanistan can be characterised geographically as a mountainous desert interspersed with isolated fertile valleys, river basins and oases. It extends eastward from the Iranian plateau and incorporates the foothills of the Himalayan ranges, which rise to a height of 7470 meters in the finger of land that divides Tajikistan from Pakistan and touches on Western China. To the North of this range, known as the *Hindu Kush*, begin the plains that cross the Afghan frontier at the *Amu Darya* river and stretch for thousands of miles across Central Asia and the Russian steppes to the Arctic. To the South of the *Hindu Kush* is a bleak and windswept desert that passes through Pakistan to the Indian Ocean. More importantly, Afghanistan has an important geo-strategic location, connecting Middle East, Central and South Asia.

It provides a land bridge to Central Asia's vast oil and natural gas deposits. It is completely landlocked and only 30,000 sq kms out of 6, 47,500 sq kms is irrigated land. 31.75 percent people are literate and unemployment ranges from 40-60 percent. It stands at 174 rank in terms of Human Resource Development Index in the world. In recent estimates by the United Nations Office on Drugs and Crime (UNODC), 52 percent of the nation's GDP, amounting to $2.7 billion annually, is generated by the drug trade. Some 3.3 million Afghans are involved in producing opium (90 percent of world cultivation). It has a railway network of only 24.6 km and a road network of 21,000 km most of which has been reconstructed recently. Out of 45 airports only 10 have paved runways. It is clearly one of the more under-developed countries and the only positive indicator is the growing telephone network which stood at 15,000 fixed line telephones in 2001 has now grown to 4.5 million including the cellular network due to the reconstruction effort.

The Geo-Political Dynamics

We all are aware of the role of the regional actors in Afghanistan and the resulting 'muddle' since the Soviet invasion, the consequent civil war, the Bonn Agreement and the 'Afghanistan Compact'. Some important issues that emerge which are worth taking note are:

(a) Afghanistan's strategic location at the "fault line", of four civilizations[1]—Islamic, Russian Orthodox, Chinese and Hindu—which has arguably been a significant factor for the region's instability.

(b) Afghanistan's internal political fragility and external vulnerability continues to exist due to the country's fragmented social structure and rule of warlords and their linkage to regional actors.

(c) The existence of terrorist groups in Pakistan, many of them backed by elements of the country's military and fundamentalist Islamic groups like the *Jamiat-ul-Ulema-i-Islam* which remain as the forces of instability both in Pakistan and Afghanistan—even in the face of Pakistan's apparent crackdown[2].

(d) Central Asia's huge oil and gas deposits continue to provide incentives to the regional actors including Russia who strive for their say in the region's geo-politics. That remains as an impediment in the region's political development vis-à-vis the US military presence.

(e) Afghanistan's ethnic linkages and geo-political 'susceptibility' with neighbouring countries—Pakistan, China, Tajikistan, Uzbekistan, Turkmenistan and Iran—which continue to haunt the country despite American military presence and that in turn will probably prolong the US presence.[3]

A retrospective analysis of Washington's policy towards the pre-9/11 Afghanistan shows that the US was ready to accept the fundamentalist regime of the *Taliban* to further its geo-political ambition (oil and natural resources as probable incentives) in the region. The geo-strategic argument was that since the *Taliban* was pro-Pakistani, and at the same time anti-Russian and anti-Iranian, the United States ought to accept it. As per this argument, it was not an American affair to ascertain how the *Taliban* treats its own people, or to cater to "a stable Afghanistan with an aesthetically challenged government than a convulsed Afghanistan that offers a playground for Iranian and Russian devilments." Nevertheless, the US hoped that after long years of turmoil, the *Taliban* would unite the country. A Sunni-dominated government in Kabul would serve as a bulwark against the influence of Iran in the region. There are also reports that the US is using Pakistani guerilla groups such as *Jundullah* to launch attacks on military and civilian bases in Iran[4].

The containment of Iran had become an American strategy in the region, especially, after the Teheran government declared its readiness to extend port facilities to the newly independent Central Asian Republics. American interests in Afghanistan also increased when it became clear that the Rabbani government in Kabul had been drawn closer to Teheran, after the killing of Iran-backed Shia leader Abdul Ali Mazari by the *Taliban* in early 1995. What was more alarming for the Americans and the Pakistani intelligence agencies was the Iranian diplomatic success in bringing together of the erstwhile enemies of the Afghan war, Rabbani and Hekmatyar to an agreement in June 1996.

Afghanistan, being a transport-junction and land-approach between the land-locked countries of Central Asia and the littoral states of the Indian Ocean, will remain strategically important[4]. Therefore, the competition over control of trade and pipeline routes from Central Asia to the Arabian Sea (Indian Ocean) transformed relations between Iran and Pakistan, and Teheran's initiative in this respect was openly supported by Russia and India. *Taliban*'s ability to provide security for trade, and the projected pipelines was considered strategically advantageous to both Islamabad and Washington. Significantly, around this time, in the spring of 1996, a partnership between the American company UNOCAL and the Saudi Company DELTA had concluded plans for a multimillion-dollar ($2 billion) oil and gas pipelines from Turkmenistan to Pakistani Baluchistan via Herat and Kandahar. Pakistan with the American backing (as an American company got involved) and Saudi Arabia considered the deal very lucrative since it was not just the trade route, but potential oil and gas pipelines were at stake. It was visualized that the *Taliban*'s most important function was to provide "security for roads, and potentially, oil and gas pipelines that would link the states of Central Asia to the international market through Pakistan rather than through Iran."[5]

It may be noted that the US was appeasing the *Taliban* at a time when the fundamentalist militia was training the Kashmiri, Uzbek, Tajik and Uighur radicals; thus spurring the growth of destabilising fundamentalist movements throughout the region. But the hand-in-glove relationship could not last long as the real colours of the *Taliban* came out soon. After the bombing of the American embassies in *Dar-e-Salaam* in Tanzania and Nairobi in Kenya in 1998 by *Al Qaeda*, however, Washington had to review its Afghanistan policy, while continuing its regional drive on a broad strategic setup.

US Strategic Perspective

The situation inside Afghanistan appears far from being rosy due to the current strategy being followed by the US and its NATO partners which does not inspire confidence that Afghanistan will soon do better. President Hamid Karzai or his successor will need more help from the international community to have a decent chance of avoiding future instability in his country and gradually improving the lives of Afghans. Apart from this, Pakistan (a functional anarchy) is in the grip of one of its worst political crisis in recent years. The key components of the American perspective may be analysed as under:

The Light Foot Print Policy

Lakhdar Brahimi, the first post-9/11 UN Special Representative for Afghanistan and the main architect of the Bonn Conference is the man behind the 'Light Footprint' policy. Bob Woodward reports in *Bush at War* that when the CIA analysts discussed the US options in Afghanistan in the aftermath of the 9/11 terrorist attacks, 'the general rule was to study what the Soviets had done and do the opposite'. As the Soviets had committed a large number of troops, it was decided to avoid doing that and instead rely on a small number of Special Forces, aerial bombardments and the anti-*Taliban* Afghan militias[6].

Thus, the initial 'light footprint' policy was as much owing to this fear of repeating the Soviet mistakes as to the subsequent need of personnel and equipments for the war in Iraq. Although the number of American and Allied Forces gradually increased from a few hundred in the late 2001 to a few thousand in 2002, to about 10, 000 in 2003 and to over 20, 000 in October 2004 (during the Presidential election in Afghanistan); it was never sufficient to root out remnants of the *Taliban* and *Al-Qaeda*. There is little doubt that the lack of dependable security forces around the country gave rise to 'war lordism' and problems of law and order that contributed to the resurgence of the *Taliban*. The treatment of the captured *Taliban* by the Northern Alliance, especially by General Dostum forces, added another incentive for many people to join the *Taliban*. *Taliban* prisoners of war (POWs) were treated very inhumanely[7], and it is alleged that thousands of them died while being transported in overcrowded containers from Kunduz to Dostum's headquarters in Sheberghan. The low-ranking *Taliban*, who did not attract much attention, failed to find meaningful jobs or means of livelihood either in Afghanistan or in the refugee camps. Thus, when the *Taliban* leadership reorganised itself and started recruitment, they found a fertile ground among the former members of the movement.

The trigger happy ISAF and the American troops while carrying out aerial bombardments ended up killing hundreds of civilians[8], thus alienating themselves from the local populace. Lack of understanding of the local culture and sensibilities coupled with human rights abuse and torture of the prisoners at Guantanamo Bay fuelled sympathy for the rising *Talibans*[9]. Further, the external forces and the Provincial Reconstruction Teams (PRTs) are operating without consulting or respecting the sentiments of the Kabul Government.

If we add to this the weaknesses of Karzai, viz. his own personality, factionalism within the government, questionable appointments, questionable legitimacy, rampant corruption, slow progress in reconstruction and human development, slow progress in creating an army and police force, narcotic drug problem and negative impacts of the free market economic policy have created an unacceptable situation in Afghanistan[10]. The policy of the American troops to negotiate with the local warlords while keeping the Kabul Government in dark has boosted the growth of 'war-lordism' once again and has also undermined the authority of the Karzai Government[11]. The situation has improved in Afghan capital, Kabul. But most rural parts of the country, where majority of Afghans live, remains beyond Mr. Karzai's control.

The Surge and Negotiate Policy

The "surge first, then negotiate" plan of Barrack Obama[12] is to build up security in Afghan cities with new US troop arrivals before initiating talks with the *Taliban*. For the talks to be successful, the US intends to squeeze the *Taliban* first, including by taking another page from its Iraq experiment and setting up lightly trained local militias in every provincial district. The crux of the policy is to bring down violence by cutting deals to keep the *Taliban* intact as a fighting force, with active ties with the Pakistani military. The move ignores the danger that such militias could terrorise local populations. If a resurgent *Taliban* is now on the offensive, with 2008 proving to be the deadliest year for US forces, it is primarily because of two reasons: the sustenance of the *Taliban* still draws from Pakistan; and a growing Pashtun backlash against foreign intervention. A US surge will not intimidate local *Taliban* commanders and tribal chieftains to negotiate peace deals, especially when some countries with forces in Afghanistan are exhibiting war fatigue and a desire to pull out troops. Indeed, it is naive to expect an Iraq-style surge-and-bribe experiment to work in Afghanistan, whose mountainous terrain, myriad tribes, patterns of shifting tribal and ethnic loyalties, special status as the global hub of poppy trade, and a history of internecine civil conflict set it apart from any other Muslim country.

In such a land with a long tradition of humbling foreign armies, pay-offs would not buy peace. Yet, the US champions a 21st century version of a divide-and-conquer imperial strategy. If there is any certainty, it is that the US plan will help the already-entrenched *Taliban* sharpen its claws. However, to help justify "surge and bribe"[13], a distinction is being drawn between *Al-Qaeda* and the *Taliban* to portray the former as evil and the latter as a different force with whom a compromise ought to be pursued. The blunt fact is that *Al-Qaeda* and the Pakistani military-reared organizations like the *Taliban*, *Lashkar-e-Taiba* and *Jaish-e-Muhammad* now constitute a difficult-to-separate mix of jihad-spouting soul mates with safe havens in Pakistan. A deal with any one such group will only strengthen the global-jihad syndicate, plus the Pakistani military.

"Surge and bribe" is a short-sighted approach intent on repeating the very mistakes of American policy on Afghanistan and Pakistan over the past three decades that have come to haunt US security and that of the rest of the free world. If America is to reclaim the global fight against terror, it will need to face up to the lessons from its past policies that gave rise to Frankensteins like Osama bin Laden and Mullah Omar and to "the state within the Pakistani state", the directorate of ISI, made powerful in the 1980s as a conduit of covert US aid for anti-Soviet Afghan guerrillas.

The primary lesson is to keep the focus on long-term interests and not be carried away by political expediency. Yet again, Washington is itching to give primacy to short-term considerations. Even if "in the best-case scenario" the Obama administration managed to bring down violence in Afghanistan by cutting deals that would keep the *Taliban* intact as a fighting force, with active ties to the Pakistani military, such a tactical gain would exact serious costs on regional and international security[14]. In seeking such short-term success, the Obama team is falling prey to a long-standing US policy weakness: The pursuit of narrow objectives without much regard for the security of friends[15].

At the same time, Afghanistan's neighbours have apprehensions on what they call the US grand design. They perceive that the US is now well entrenched with all its military might in the entire region and that it is not going to go back any time soon. And that the American geo-political drive is motivated by the containment of China, Iran and extracting Central Asian oil and gas to the world market, in addition to putting the NATO right there in the door-step of Russia[16]. As per this argument, American strategists believe that it would be convenient for them to deal with an unruly China and Iran while based in Pakistan, Afghanistan, and Central Asia. Washington can have a close watch on the developments of the communist China and the unruly Iran, and the position would give access to more strategic mileage to the US foreign policy interests in the geo-politics of the region. Secondly, as stated above, through its military presence and economic and political support in the Central Asian Republics, Washington hopes to get access to the regions tremendous untapped reserves of oil.

Role of Regional Powers

These strategic and geo-political ambitions of the United States have led to considerable resentment among the countries surrounding the region. Russian, Chinese, and Iranian unhappiness is particularly visible in this context. In order to keep the Americans away from their "dirty games" in the region[17], these countries will continue to support the ethnic and tribal groups through whom they consider to promote their own geo-strategic interests. For instance, Chinese will continue to be perturbed by expanding US presence on its south-western frontiers and support the anti-US forces; Russians to Tajiks and Uzbeks; and Iranians to their *Shia* minority ethnic group in the north-western part of the country. Because these countries perceive that through its military presence in the region, the US is unduly interfering in their "sphere of influence."

In this sense, the overarching American geo-political objective in the region will be kept off balance by the regional powers, and that will continue to keep Afghanistan fragile and fragmented. In the process, US might get bogged down militarily in this landlocked country that has a long history of fighting against the foreigners. Despite some high-handedness on terrorism and religious extremism, the regional actors complain that the US was not responding fully to the terrorist threat because it was not affecting the US interests directly. Leaders of Afghanistan's neighbours have pointed fingers at the US for its "selective approach" and "double standards."[18] They view that while the enduring American military presence in Afghanistan and the region is not going to eliminate the specter of terrorism and Islamic fundamentalism, the menace provided a good pretext to the US entrenching itself in the region.

US Anti-Insurgency Policy

The US does not still have an anti-insurgency policy in place primarily because like any other traditional state army, it was meant to win wars and not to fight insurgency in the first place. But then a pertinent question arises that perhaps in its exuberance to react instantly, was the US notion of dealing with insurgency flawed?

Let us examine the implications of an insurgency operation where the US army is involved. In order to undertake the challenge, the old Cold War mindset deserves a re-look. There seems to be a view that a relentless attack against Islamic insurgents wherever they surface should be waged. The view is as seemingly logical as the Cold War belief in a worldwide communist conspiracy for global domination—and just as wrong. The belief is also harmful, for four major reasons. First, as in the Cold War, the belief in a global insurgency can lead the US to make local commitments on the basis of vague overarching global principles. This commits the US to send more troops, sustain greater military casualties, and spend more money than it possibly could in multiple conflicts at times and place of the insurgents' choosing. Second, a US-led global counter-insurgency makes it more difficult for the US to defeat insurgencies. Successful counterinsurgents fight as patriots in the service of their own country—not as United States clients. Third, Americans with a mindset that places prominence on the global common features of insurgencies at the expense of fine-textured local features makes the US military less effective in combating insurgencies. Fourth, belief in a global counter-insurgency leads to mismanagement of counterinsurgency campaigns because it undercuts the leadership of governments allied with the United States and of American military commanders battling an insurgency. So, the larger lesson is to retain the clarity of a "local" versus "global" perspective and to selectively apply the lessons of previous successful campaigns in similar asymmetric conflicts.

Here, it would be interesting to analyse the politics of asymmetric conflicts and to figure out on the basis of the pre-theoretical perspective of Andrew Mack as to *Why Big Nations Lose Small Wars*?[19]

The key facets of his thesis are:

- That Conventional wisdom that military superiority prevails in this war has been destroyed as the constraints on mobilisation are political, not material. In none of the conflicts noted was more than a fraction of the total potential military resources of the external power in fact mobilised.

- The theatre of war extends beyond to encompass the polity and social institutions of the external powerful mobilisation not possible as it also increases domestic costs.
- Direct costs become of strategic importance when translated into indirect costs—psychological and political as the aim of the insurgents is not the destruction of the military capability of their opponents as an end in itself.
- Dissent permitted in 'open societies' is an obstacle. The totalitarian societies are not troubled by the domestic constraints, which the US faced on Vietnam.
- The progressively greater human, economic and political costs give rise to "war weariness". The last years of the Vietnam conflict were marked by troop mutinies, widespread drug addiction, high levels of desertion, and even the murders of over-zealous officers' intent on sending their men on dangerous patrols.

It can be appreciated that the postulates propounded by Mack are valid and applicable in all prolonged asymmetric conflicts including the ongoing one in Afghanistan. Mack concludes with a lesson for the Governments (of US and NATO countries in this case) which have committed themselves to such conflicts that they should realise that, over time, the costs of the conflict will inevitably generate widespread opposition at home. The causes of such a dissent lie in the structure of conflict itself—in the type of conflict being pursued and in the asymmetries which form its distinctive character. Henry Kissinger has correctly observed on the war in Vietnam that "we lost sight of one of the cardinal maxims of guerilla warfare that the guerilla wins if he does not lose and conventional army loses if it does not win".[20] It seems that the lessons should once again be remembered if the US and NATO extend their campaign in Afghanistan. Today, when the US is being asked to increase its level of commitment to rebuilding Afghanistan as a means of stabilising the country, even as American troops battle the resurgent Islamic extremists who operate along the Afghan-Pakistan border, the key question especially in the wake of World economic recession is no longer whether to withdraw but rather when and how.

The Road Ahead

Barrack Obama after assuming office had made a pleasing statement to the ears of Indian strategists that all aid to Pakistan will be linked to its performance in aiding and cooperating in the war against terror. Joe Biden, the Vice-President of US had made a trip to Afghanistan just before the Presidential inauguration and has also declared that it would not hesitate to hit specific targets in Pakistan especially in the safe havens in Dir, Swat valley and the region of FATA, should there be hard intelligence available. This had raised the hackles of the Pakistani establishment and they tried their level best to make the US rethink and were finally successful in extracting aid without strings—a dangerous development which has the potential to destabilise the region. Hence, 'Mission AFPAK' will need all the diplomatic, military and economic might of the US and all the regional players to succeed. Does America follow the zero-sum game or Washington re-hyphenates the relationship in such a way that Pakistan gets a 'Soft Landing' and simultaneously engages New Delhi at a much higher level than before befitting an emerging Superpower remains to be seen.

Richard Holbrooke's feedback and recommendations should help President Obama unfold his terms of engagement in future. Also there appears to be shift in the US policy towards Iran and it should be a positive change that must be welcomed by all the regional players. It is imperative that the US deals with Pakistan with an iron hand if it has to achieve success in the strife torn region. By naming Richard Holbrooke, a separate envoy for Pakistan and Afghanistan, without apparently linking the Kashmir issue, Obama seemed to follow a policy that may help its new strategic partner, viz. India follow its own game strategy in the region.

The January 2006 London Conference, attended by more than sixty countries and international agencies produced a document called "Afghanistan Compact." The document predicated on every aspect of Afghanistan's social and economic development. Some of the suggestions given by the Afghan Study Group operating under the aegis of The Centre for the Study of the Presidency[21] released in January 2008 outlined the critical issues to be addressed by the US and its NATO partners, which are related to international coordination, security, governance and the rule of law, counter-narcotics, economic development and reconstruction, Afghanistan and its neighbours.

But, on the country's security challenges, Pakistan was not even named in connection with the growing insurgency. Instead, the Compact called for "full respect of Afghanistan's sovereignty, and strengthening dialogue and cooperation between Afghanistan and its neighbours." The prime worry in Afghanistan is extremism of the kind which is continuing for a long time and these forces usually feed on political instability, which to a large extent can be attributed to forces in Pakistan.

With this background, some issues and recommendations can be outlined which should be taken into account for Stabilising Afghanistan by adoption of viable, practical and workable options: taking lessons from past counter-insurgency operations which may be enumerated as under:

- Indigenous forces eventually have to win the war on their own, they must be developed with the capacity to do so;
- Concentrate on the main aim of neutralising *Al Qaeda* and *Taliban*—countering sanctuary in Pakistan;
- Increase funds for rebuilding infrastructure—'Reconstruction light';
- Restrained use of force in Civilian areas-not "Clear by Fire" tactics;
- Understand the local culture-family, clan, and tribal ties with concepts such as revenge and honour with less attachment and respect for the centralised state government;
- Establish a regional approach to Afghanistan with the aid of UN and neighbouring countries, encourage Pak-Afghan border to be settled.

Conclusion

Bringing about a normal situation in this war-ravaged country will depend on how the US acts in the coming days. The present trend does not look conducive to permanent peace in the country. The American peace efforts so far appear fragile, and the country is passing through a thin edge of instability as it is still being haunted by so many divisive and centrifugal forces. Afghanistan remains critical to the future of its neighbours, as instability in this land-locked country has the potential to destabilise the whole region. A potent combination of drugs, weapons, and militants traverse Afghanistan and cross into its neighbours and beyond, and hence, the seeds of instability remain intact[22]. The Bonn Process, reconstruction of the country and its national security are not intrinsic to Afghan situation alone. It is in fact, heavily loaded with regional geopolitics. And within this geo-political entanglement, the regional actors look at the US presence with suspicion. As stated above, many believe that the geo-political factors such as Central Asia/Caspian energy resources; China's Xinjiang, Iran, etc. are the reasons for US interest in Afghanistan. And, if that is the case, and the US remains bogged down in a growing insurgency in the country, and if the US missiles take more innocent lives, Washington's strategy could well backfire[23].

This is the centre of gravity of the problem and unless a suitable 'end game' is played out, the desired end state where the regional aspirations are fulfilled satisfactorily, may remain elusive. Within this geo-political entanglement, the regional and non-regional actors, especially the US, have to play their parts decisively, proactively and positively. We must be optimistic about Afghanistan, Afghans want security and hope which they deserve after about 30 years of near-constant war but realism says it will take time.

Notes and References

1. Samuel P. Huntington, *The Clash of Civilizations and Remaking of the World Order*, Delhi: Viking Penguin Books India, 1996.
2. *Koran* Giustozzi, *Kalashnikov, and Laptop: The Neo-Taliban Insurgency in Afghanistan*, New York: Columbia University Press, 2008.
3. *Ibid.*
4. Barnett R. Rubin, *The Fragmentation of Afghanistan: State Formation and Collapse in the International System*, New Haven and London: Yale University Press, 1995.
5. Barnett R Rubin, "Still Ours to Lose: Afghanistan on the Brink", *Council on Foreign Relations*, September 21, 2006.
6. Najibullah Lafraie, *Resurgence of the Taliban insurgency in Afghanistan: How and why*?, New Zealand: Department of Politics, University of Otago.
7. D. Rohde and D.E. Sanger, "How a 'good war' in Afghanistan went bad", *The New York Times*, August 12, 2007.
8. Najibullah Lafraie, *Op. cit.*
9. *Ibid.*
10. T.H. Johnson, "On the Edge of the Big Muddy: The *Taliban* Resurgence in Afghanistan", *China and Eurasia Forum Quarterly*, Vol. 5, No. 2, 2007.
11. Najibullah Lafraie, *Op. cit.*
12. Brahma Chellaney, *Times of India*, January 2, 2009.
13. *Ibid.*
14. www.crisisgroups.org
15. Brahma Chellaney, *Op. cit.*
16. www.cfr.org (Council on Foreign Relations-Washington)
17. Barnett R. Rubin, "Still Ours to Lose: Afghanistan on the Brink", *Council on Foreign Relations*, September 21, 2006.
18. *www.cfr.org* (Council on Foreign Relations—Washington)
19. Andrew Mack, "Why Big Nations Lose Small Wars: The Politics of Asymmetric Conflict", Klaus Knorr (ed.), *Power, Strategy and Security*, New Delhi: Asian Books, 1983, p. 126.
20. Henry A. Kissinger, "The Vietnam Negotiations", *Foreign Affairs*, XLVIII, January, 1996, p. 214 Afghanistan Study Group Report (Centre for the Study of the Presidency), Second Edition, January 30, 2008.

21. Afghanistan Study Group Report (Centre for the Study of the Presidency), Second Edition, January 30, 2008.
22. E. Sky, "Increasing ISAF's Impact on Stability in Afghanistan", *Defense and Security Analysis*, Vol. 23, No. 1, 2007.
23. *Afghanistan Study Group Report*, Centre for the Study of the Presidency, Second Edition, January 30, 2008.

7

America's Coming War in Afghanistan: The "Bloody" Iraq Model

Jagmohan Meher

In its tumultuous history, today's Afghanistan is again "a bleeding wound." But this time around, the wound is not bleeding for any outside powers (at least not yet for the US and its European allies); it is bleeding for its own people, society, and government. The Afghan state is clearly at its cross-roads. The conflict in Afghanistan has entered a dangerous phase, and the next few years could prove crucial in determining whether the US and NATO can suppress a revitalised enemy—or be dragged in to another fight with the Islamic insurgency. The *Taliban* insurgency is on the move once again to takeover the hapless country. More than seventy percent of the Afghan territory has been already engulfed by the fundamentalist militia and its footprints are visible in the rest of the country. The gun-trotting terrorists are knocking at the very door-steps of the country's capital, Kabul. Countless lives and property have been lost since the 2001 US invasion, and the country is increasingly witnessing a Hobbesian state of nature. *Al-Qaeda* and *Taliban* have established a new safe haven in the tribal agencies of Pakistan, where it is defended by a new organization called the Pakistani *Taliban.*[1] President Obama has rightly said that the future of Afghanistan is inextricably linked to the future of its neighbour, Pakistan, and called Pakistan's northwest frontier region "an international security challenge of the highest order" and "the most dangerous place in the world."[2] Today's *Taliban* force is well trained, well armed, well organized, and well fed (financed).

Who is behind these horrifying monsters? What are the sources of their survival? How to track their roots? Should the United States negotiate with them? Or should it try to eliminate them in the battlefield? Confronting these questions is a tough task. But the new US administration seems to have a plan: (with some cosmetic changes though) the Iraq Model, which is often described as "surge first, then negotiate" formula. In order to do so, the United States proposes deployment of some 30,000 more troops in Afghanistan (i.e. in addition to its already deployed 36,000 troops and a combined 32,000 troops operating under NATO command) and along with the Afghan National Army, the US plans to turn the tide of war in favour of the allied forces. At the same time, American Generals hope to negotiate with the warlords, local commanders and tribal chieftains—the mainstay of the *Taliban*. The new Obama administration has also indicated the need for a strategic partnership with all the parties in the region — Pakistan and India and the Afghan government — to stamp out terrorist base camps in the region. In a greater strategic context, the United States also plans a détente with Russia and Iran, and seeks their assistance in resolving the Afghanistan problem. It does not see Afghanistan as an isolated conflict zone; rather rightly looks at it as a problem which is deeply rooted in a complex web of regional conflicts spread over the whole region. The US plan also includes billions of dollars worth economic aid and reconstruction efforts in Afghanistan and Pakistan.

But the US plan of "surge first" is going to be "bloody," while the suitable time for "negotiation" may not come; putting the country on a next round of civil war leading to more deaths and destructions. America's Iraq policy will not work in Afghanistan because of the Pashtun's tradition of *jihad*, the porous Pak-Afghan border, Afghanistan's complex patterns of shifting tribal and ethnic loyalties, Pakistani strategic obsession, etc. Negotiating with the terrorists and warlords also means terrorizing local people that will lead to more resentments and resistance against the "foreigners."

For some kind of peace and stability in Afghanistan, the United States would have to be audacious both militarily and diplomatically in going against its own past policies in both Afghanistan and Pakistan, which created Frankensteins under the complete protection of the Pakistani intelligence agency (ISI).

This paper aims to look at the genesis and evolution of US military strategy in Afghanistan which could be emerging shortly as the Obama Doctrine and analyze its strategic value vis-à-vis the Iraq model. The study aims to highlight the reasons for American optimism in this war-ravaged country and hopes to underline the perceptions of regional actors on the US's new regional approach. Finally the study peeps at drawing certain conclusions as to where do the US strategy stand in terms of making peace or war in this land-locked country.

The Doctrine Takes Shape

In fact, the idea of a 'surge' policy in Afghanistan goes back to the closing months of the former Bush administration. With the "military success" in Iraq through such a policy, some Bush administration officials became tempted to replicate the same formula in Afghanistan which was increasingly going out of hand despite the US and NATO military presence in the country.

On September 9, 2008, President Bush in a speech at the National Defense University in Washington said, "*Al-Qaeda*'s leaders have repeatedly declared that Iraq is the central front of their war with America, but it is not the only front. As *Al-Qaeda* faces increased pressure in Iraq, the terrorists are stepping up their efforts on the front where this struggle first began — the nation of Afghanistan." The President also announced that he would send 5,000 additional troops to Afghanistan.[3]

Reacting on the President's Afghanistan policy, Barak Obama, the then Senator and Presidential hopeful, who has long called for more US troops in Afghanistan, said at a news conference that Bush "is moving in the direction of the policy that I have advocated for years." But he also criticised the Bush's policy saying that the plan also "comes up short" because "it is not enough troops and not enough resources, with not enough urgency." In a bold electoral move the Democratic nominee emphasised: "What President Bush... doesn't understand is that the central front in the war on terror is not in Iraq, and it never was. The central front is in Afghanistan and Pakistan, where the terrorists who hit us on 9/11 are still plotting attacks seven years later."[4]

On February 17, 2009, President Obama ordered 17,000 more American troops to Afghanistan saying the increase was "necessary to stabilise a deteriorating situation in Afghanistan, which has not received the strategic attention, direction and resources it urgently requires."[5] The new deployments, beginning in May, increase the US forces in Afghanistan by nearly 50 percent, bringing it to 55,000 by mid-summer of 2008, along with 32,000 non-US NATO troops. In a statement issued by the White House, Obama said that "urgent attention and swift action" were required because "the *Taliban* is resurgent in Afghanistan, and *Al-Qaeda*... threatens America from its safe-haven along the Pakistani border."[6] A White House spokesman, Robert Gibbs, latter said that the deployment decision "does not prejudge the outcome of the review process but... allows us instead to meet an urgent need for more troops."[7]

One leading advocate of the new policy is General David Petraeus, the Central Command chief who believes that more troops can create the conditions for enhanced reconstruction efforts and increase America's leverage for the political solution. One special feature about the new policy is that General Petraeus is openly looking for ways to win over local commanders and warlords. The General wants to explore truces and alliances with local tribal chieftains and guerrilla leaders to take them off the battlefield. That is precisely what he did as the US military Commander in Iraq during the surge. Similarly, US defence secretary Robert Gates has endorsed efforts in the recent past to reach out to members of the *Taliban* or other militants in Afghanistan who may be considered reconcilable, much like what has happened in Iraq. "That is one of the key long-term solutions in Afghanistan, just as it has been in Iraq," Gates has said.[8]

The "surge first, then negotiate" plan is to build up security in Afghan cities with new US troops arrivals before initiating talks with the *Taliban*. The aim is not to militarily rout the *Taliban* but to strike a political deal with the enemy from a position of strength. For the talks to be successful, the US intends to squeeze the *Taliban* first including setting up lightly trained local militias in every provincial district. A senior US commander has warned recently that it is going to get worse before it gets better.

Clearly, the Obama administration is trying to "press the reset button" in its relations with Afghanistan. It has been quite clear that Pakistan-Afghanistan has superseded Iraq as the new flash point in the US administration list of crisis. The US President has announced a "thorough-going review" of what it calls Af-Pak policy, which was drafted under complete leadership of General Petraeus, the CENTCOM chief, in concert with Richard Holbrooke, special ambassador for Afghanistan and Pakistan[9] "to evaluate a regional approach." The new policy clearly indicates that the consensus in Washington is that Pakistan now poses a greater threat to the world, let alone the region, than any other country and that the core issue is getting Pakistan to close down the safe haven it provides to terrorists in its tribal region bordering Afghanistan.[10] As expected, the new policy essentially included a strong military component, and hopes to explore the possibility of an eventual deal with some version of the *Taliban*.

Obama has set benchmarks for progress in fighting *Al-Qaeda* and the *Taliban* in both countries. "The United States of America did not choose to fight a war in Afghanistan," he said in announcing his decision.

"Nearly 3,000 of our people were killed on September 11, 2001, for doing nothing more than going about their daily lives." "So let me be clear: *Al-Qaeda* and its allies—the terrorists who planned and supported the 9/11 attacks—are in Pakistan and Afghanistan,". The President emphasised that the United States has a clear and focused goal to "disrupt, dismantle and defeat" *Al-Qaeda* in Pakistan and Afghanistan, and to prevent their return to either country in the future.[11]

For quite some time, Obama has been insisting that the central front of war on terror is not Iraq, but Afghanistan and that only in Afghanistan that the war should be brought to a close. Secondly, Obama rightly argued that the problem in Afghanistan cannot be solved without addressing the sources of support for extremism and terrorism in Pakistan. Thirdly, Obama has defined a more specific mission saying that the United States is not in Afghanistan to control that country or dictate its future. The administration announced that the primary goal in the region is narrow, i.e. disrupting terrorist networks in Afghanistan and especially Pakistan to degrade any ability they have to plan and launch international terrorist attacks.

President Obama has recently said that as the US Commander-in-chief, he wanted to make sure that he has a well thought out strategy, clear goals and that they are achievable. He summarised the US strategy as: "the key, though, is to understand that we are not going to win in Afghanistan or get an acceptable outcome in Afghanistan if we're only dependent on our military…" "…If we do not have an Afghan government that can deliver for its people; if we do not have an economic development strategy where farmers do not have to grow heroin poppy but instead can grow other crops so that they're not feeding narco-terrorism… then this isn't going to work."[12] The President seems determined to turn around the war in Afghanistan with a regional approach recognising that stability of neighbouring Pakistan is increasingly at risk. He is trying to fashion an efficient counter-insurgency strategy, as in Iraq, with a comprehensive surge of military and civilian reinforcements.

Pakistan has emerged as the focus of the Obama doctrine although at the heart of the strategy is the idea of treating both sides of the Afghanistan-Pakistan border as a "single theatre." The US administration has declared Pakistan of being a safe haven for *Al-Qaeda* and its leadership, but at the same time it supports the people and government of Afghanistan. The US President has warned: "Make no mistake: *Al-Qaeda* and its extremist allies are a cancer that risks killing Pakistan from within."[13] Given the emphasis of the new US administration, Afghanistan has now become the frontline state for a war in Pakistan. It is no longer the other way around. Both countries are in the same wave length as far as the terrorist threat perception is concerned. The critical Af-Pak policy, therefore, hopes to save both the countries from implosion from within.

As a part of its expanded assistance, the US has decided to give aid to Pakistan to a tune of $1.5 billion annually over the next five years. However, in a clear message to Islamabad that it has to shape up and deliver, the US President warned that it would be held accountable for the generous aid he is requesting from the US. "After years of mixed results, we will not provide a blank cheque. Pakistan must demonstrate its commitment to rooting out *Al-Qaeda* and the violent extremists within its borders. And we will insist that action be taken—one way or another—when we have intelligence about high-level terrorist targets," he said.[14]

The new US doctrine lacks specifics, and hence, it is yet to be seen how exactly the new American strategy will be implemented in the coming months and years. Obama will also have to grapple with a series of very difficult questions starting with how he will define success in Afghanistan. Most importantly, the success or failure of the Obama doctrine will be judged on how the US administration chooses to engage Pakistani military and its intelligence agency. In Afghanistan, the president will have to consider whether to keep supporting a central government in Kabul or focus more on cultivating local leaders. How the US will handle President Hamid Karzai in coming days and months also remains a conundrum as the rampant corruption of his government has driven far too many Afghans back to the extremists.

The American Optimism

American optimism in Afghanistan is based on certain raison d'être experienced from the Cold War era which convinces the American generals and field commanders that the war is "winnable." Unlike the anti-Soviet *Mujahideen* of the 1980s, they argue, the *Taliban/Al-Qaeda* do not have the support of a superpower. Additional advantage for the US is that America has broad international backing for its actions, and still enjoys good measure of support among ordinary Afghans.

Secondly, American strategic analysts and defence experts are of the view that the newly trained (or being trained) Afghan Air Force and Afghan National Army will eventually be in a position to control and check the insurgency in the country. As per this argument, the experts believe, American pilots and their Afghan charges dominate the sky, with little fear of being shot at with anti-aircraft missiles of the kind Americans once gave the *mujaheedin*. Helicopters are allowing troops to move with less risk of ambush or bombs throughout the country. Under American tutelage, the Afghan Air Force has grown from four aircraft that had somehow survived the civil war of the 1990s and American air strikes in 2001 into a modest fleet of Antonov transport planes, Mi-17 transport helicopters and Mi-35 attack helicopters. It has been estimated that by 2016, the Afghan Air Force is expected to grow to more than 120 aircrafts, perhaps including some light attack jets. In such air power, it is argued, it is possible to control the insurgency. The programme, which is projected to cost American taxpayers $5 billion into 2016, is aimed at giving Afghanistan the ability to defend itself from the skies and one day allowing the Americans to leave. The Afghan programme is modeled after an earlier American effort to build up the Iraqi Air Force, which also includes some Mi-17s. Similarly, the Afghan National Army is being trained, expanding from the current 80,000 troops to 134,000 (plus embedded Western troops) by 2011.[15] Afghan soldiers are known as tough fighters, and are well-liked by most Afghans as members of one of the few functioning national institutions. They are also respected by many Afghans as a symbol of national unity and integrity.

Thirdly, the US hopes that with more American troops and extra-Afghan units in addition to NATO deployments, it is perhaps possible to improve security in the provinces and establish greater control of the border with Pakistan. The new deployments will seek to interdict fighters and weapons being smuggled into Afghanistan and drugs being taken out of it. Field commanders argue that with more troops on the ground, they will have less reason to use the air power which has contributed to a sharp rise in civilian casualties[16] and has raised tensions with the Afghan government and created public resentment against the "foreign troops." From this perspective, it is argued, more troops will help minimize the death toll and ultimately stabilise the country.

The US officials are optimistic that the planned addition of up to 30,000 troops, combined with a new strategy to support local governance and development aimed at weaning villagers away from *Taliban* influence, will show significant results within the year. They believe that the reinforcements would help change the dynamics of the security situation in rural areas and that the improved cooperation from the army in neighboring Pakistan and better performance by the Afghan national army would change the existing situation.

Given such a prospect, many American generals and military

strategists who have witnessed a "successful" "surge and negotiate" policy in Iraq, predict an Iraq-style improvement in security. Defence Secretary Robert Gates has spoken openly about the possibility of reconciliation, saying, "at the end of the day, that is how most wars end.... That is ultimately the exit strategy for all of us."[17]

Perceptions on Regional Approach

The most significant part of the Obama doctrine is that the President is actually focusing on this war and placing it in the broader regional framework that was missing from the American policy under President Bush. From the regional strategic view points, Washington's efforts to mend fences with Moscow and begin negotiations with Teheran are the positive developments, because neither Russia nor Iran would want to see the triumph of the *Taliban* in Afghanistan. It is not in Russia's interests to allow the *Taliban* to control the Afghanistan-Pakistan area. Given how things are spiraling out of control in Pakistan, the US is in a better position to impress upon Russia the vital role Moscow could play in aiding NATO and US troops on their mission in the region. Similarly, in order to engage Iran on the Af-Pak problem, Russia could play a very constructive role. India, on the other hand, is contributing in a variety of ways to stabilise Afghanistan. From large-scale training of armed forces to assistance in the creation of the Afghan air force, from supplying non-lethal military equipment to sending volunteers for local reconstruction in Afghan provinces, New Delhi's contribution is strategically, economically and politically of great significance to Afghanistan.[18]

China, India, Iran and Russia might cooperate with Washington simply because there is no motivation greater than the nightmare of extremists controlling Pakistan's nuclear weapons. They should also be more willing to help in this anti-*Taliban* effort as the American military presence on their sensitive borders restricts their freedom of maneuver. The recent Russian overtures particularly indicate a mild rapprochement. Consider the recent American expulsion from the military base in Kyrgyzstan which was used for the Afghan war effort. That the decision was not the local Bakiyev leadership's alone, but that of the Kremlin was a behind the scene. But then Russia offered NATO a transit route through its own territory. This unprecedented gesture has enormous implications: a cooperative Russia could alter NATO's make-up tremendously.

However, the most difficult regional task is about ending the Pakistan army's power to define its national security objectives towards Afghanistan and India and its more than three decade old alliance with extremist groups to achieve its aims. The stability of Afghanistan is intrinsically connected to the stability of its southern neighbour Pakistan which itself is reeling through *Talibanization* of some 170 million people and the country that happens to possess a nuclear arsenal. There is growing unease in Washington that the military and its spy agency ISI, with their close ties to jihadis, still call the shots in Pakistan. So long as the "semi-autonomous" badlands of Pakistan's tribal areas provide refuge for terrorists—*Taliban/ Al-Qaeda*—Afghanistan will never know security. If the Obama doctrine helps drive the US foreign policy in South and Southwest Asia in that direction, Washington might find the regional actors more than enthusiastic on the US game plan.

Iran, on Afghanistan's western border, has played a mixed role over the years, at times indirectly cooperating with US objectives and at times assisting the extremists. While Teheran had proved very helpful at Bonn,[19] the US excluded it from regional efforts at building peace rather than pursuing cooperation. The Bush administration had kept Tehran at arm's length. But the Obama administration must feel that it would be helpful to have an interlocutor to explore shared objectives on regional strategic issues with Teheran. The Iranians do not want Sunni extremists in charge of Afghanistan any more. Tehran has also announced that despite its dislike of the "ineffective" foreign forces in Afghanistan, it was "fully prepared" to help fight drugs-trafficking and rebuild Afghanistan. Therefore, dialogue between Washington and Teheran is essential to ensure that Iran does not feel threatened by the presence of the US troops in Afghanistan and that it plays a responsible role in stabilising Afghanistan.

Obama also announced that together with the United Nations, Washington will forge a new Contact Group for Afghanistan and Pakistan "that brings together all countries who should have a stake in the security of the region," including India, Iran, Russia, China, Gulf Nations, Central Asian States, and NATO allies. "None of these nations benefit from a base for *Al-Qaeda* terrorists, and a region that descends into chaos. All have a stake in the promise of lasting peace and security and development".[20]

The US President acknowledged in passing Pakistan's insistence that its troublesome security outlook was tied to disputes with India, saying "to lessen tensions between the two nuclear-armed nations that too often teeter on the edge of escalation and confrontation, we (US) must pursue constructive diplomacy with both India and Pakistan."[21] It seems that the

Obama team is not naming Kashmir as part of its regional approach to avoid Indian apprehensions on this sensitive issue. It only indicates that it will stick only to building trust and confidence between New Delhi and Islamabad to allow them to resolve the matter bilaterally.

In a significant development, the US Congress has proposed that Pakistan will have to provide guarantee that it will not support terror against India before Washington doles out billions in fresh civil and military assistance to Islamabad. It says, among other things, that the US expects Pakistan "not to support any person or group that conducts violence, sabotage, or other activities meant to instil fear or terror in India."[22] If passed into a law, it will put a lot of pressure on Pakistani establishment to ensure the flow of dollar from Washington to Islamabad. It will also help revive the stalled peace talks between India and Pakistan.

The Iraq Model

After the 2003 US invasion, Iraq started burning with sectarian and insurgent violence which appeared to be spiraling out of control by the end of 2006. President Bush knew he needed to change course, but he refused to, as he put it, "give up the goal of winning." So rather than acquiesce to calls for withdrawal, he decided to ramp up US efforts. With a "surge" in troops, a new emphasis on counterinsurgency strategy, and new commanders overseeing that strategy, Bush declared, the deteriorating situation could be turned around.[23]

Within a year or so, it was estimated that the policy of 'surge' paid off well. The rate of US casualties took a down ward turn, and the level of violence in the country became lower than what it was in previous three years. The backers of such a policy argued that the Iraq war was over and that the complete victory for Washington was at the door-step. Significantly, the surge changed the situation when it came along with several other developments including a series of deals between the US forces and Sunni tribes that constituted a new "bottom-up" approach.[24] Through such a strategy the Sunni Arab tribes were made to put them against the central government and against one another. Using mainly Sunni Muslim community leaders to employ locals to patrol their own neighborhoods has been credited as one of the main reasons behind sharp falls in violence in Iraq. It has been estimated that more than 100,000 Sunni gunmen, many of them former insurgents, were placed on the government payroll. A key to the success of the surge was the way the

US military worked together with Sunni tribal leaders in Al-Anbar Governorate against *Al-Qaeda* militants.

Replicating this Iraq formula, President Obama declared that the US was not winning the war in Afghanistan only through military means. So he opened the door to a reconciliation process in which the American military would reach out to moderate elements of the *Taliban*, much as it did with Sunni militias in Iraq. The President said that "there may be comparable opportunities in Afghanistan to employ the strategies used in Iraq;" although he warned that the Afghan crisis was possibly even more complex.[25] He signaled that reconciliation could emerge as an important initiative mirroring the strategy used by General David H. Petraeus in Iraq. "If you talk to General Petraeus, I think he would argue that part of the success in Iraq involved reaching out to people that we would consider to be Islamic fundamentalists, but who were willing to work with us because they had been completely alienated by the tactics of *Al-Qaeda* in Iraq," President Obama said.[26] Similarly, Vice-President Joe Biden has found the mathematical coordinates of this oxymoron: only 5 percent of the *Taliban* (in Afghanistan) are "extremists."

The *Taliban*, who have turned down similar overtures from Karzai in the past, have said that there are no 'moderates' in its rank and that Obama's tactics of adopting a strategy similar to that of Iraq is 'illogical.'[27] However, despite this reaction, there are unconfirmed reports that the *Taliban* leader Mullah Omar is now willing to talk peace with the US.[28]

It appears that both the insurgents in Afghanistan and the US policy makers are trying to replicate the Iraq model. The difference is that for insurgents seems to be succeeding in their goal: a formidable resistance against the "foreign troops," "capture of more territory," and more deaths and destructions. On the other hand, the US and allied forces have failed so far. The insurgents in Afghanistan are a fresh new generation who are coping the skills and ways of the armed resistance groups in Iraq.

President Obama's national security team has given a dire assessment of the war in Afghanistan, with one official calling it a challenge "much tougher than Iraq" and others hinting that it could take years to turn around. They have remarked that "NATO's future is on the line here," and "It is going to be a long, difficult struggle.... it is going to be much tougher than Iraq."[29]

Why Obama Doctrine Will Not Work

Today's *Taliban* is resurgent, offensive with 2008 proving as the deadliest year for the US forces. It is primarily because of four factors. Firstly,

Pakistan's strategic obsession of gaining "strategic depth" in Afghanistan[30] and its complain that with its presence in Afghanistan, India is encircling Pakistan with its consulates and commandos and is financing anti-Pakistan militant organisations within that country.[31] That is the main reason for which even at the cost of national security, some rogue elements of Pakistan Army and ISI are still supporting the *Taliban* and *Al-Qaeda* in search of a satellite state in Afghanistan. It is possible that the Pakistan Army/ISI, whose strategic objectives in Afghanistan will fail if the US surge is successful, may be tempted to step up their support for the Afghan *Taliban* and increase the pressure on US/NATO supply lines. Secondly, the porous border between Pakistan and Afghanistan is also a great impediment on the way to check infiltration. The Pak-Afghan border is 2400 kilometers (1500 miles) long and is mountainous and rugged, making it difficult to guard and search. The natural geography and the area's traditional autonomy makes it difficult for outside forces to pin point the *Al Qaeda* and the *Taliban* leaderships believed to be hiding in this mountainous terrain. Thirdly, the burgeoning narcotics trade presents a fundamental challenge to the future of Afghanistan. Today, Afghanistan risks degenerating into a state controlled by "narco-terrorists" and "drug cartels." Undoubtedly, the proceeds from the rampant narcotics trade are fueling insurgency, with the *Taliban* insurgents making common cause with heroin traffickers. Clearly, drug has domino effects in Afghanistan: "... when fighting drugs weakens the Afghan polity, the anti-narcotics fight fails; when fighting terrorism allows drugs to flourish, the anti-terror fight fails too."[32] Fourthly, the Afghan tradition of jehad against foreigners is also increasingly playing a very significant role in moulding people in favour of insurgency. As Louis Dupree, one of the leading authorities on Afghanistan noted, "the two Pushtun tribes might fight each other to the death for control of Herat, Farah, and Qandahar, but any external invader welded them together in a common cause."[33] In the recent history, these facts have been painfully discovered by the British in the 19th century and the Soviets in the 20th century.[34] It was Lord Lawrence, the Viceroy of British-India, on the eve of the Second Anglo-Afghan War (1878-80) said: "The Afghan will put up with poverty and even insecurity of life but he will never tolerate being governed by foreigners."[35] Under such circumstances, the new US policy will not intimidate local *Taliban* commanders, tribal chieftains and warlords to negotiate peace deals.

There is a traditional saying in Afghanistan: "Kill one Pashtun, create ten enemies." So the "successful" American air raids in Pashtun lands are bound to be counter-productive because a generation of poor young Muslims growing up in Pakistan in these 'badlands' feels bombarded by American bombs on one side and by fanatical Islamist propaganda on the other. The situation is naturally going from bad to worse.

The recent overtures of the Afghan government to persuade "moderate *Taliban*" fighters to lay down their weapons and participate in the elections have met with horrible consequences. For instance, a *Taliban* commander in Wardak province accepted an offer of reconciliation from the government was shot dead three days later in March 2009. According to Afghan officials, the order to kill him had come from the *Taliban* authorities.[36] Under such circumstances, finding "moderate *Taliban*" is also difficult, and equally complex is bringing them to national mainstream.

The new US military strategy will also not work in Afghanistan whose mountainous terrain, myriad tribes, special status as the global hub of poppy trade and a history of internecine civil conflict set it apart from any other Muslim countries in the world. In such a landmass with a long tradition of humbling foreign armies, it is only naïve to expect an Iraq style surge-and-bribe experiment to work.

Unlike the troop "surge" in Iraq, the doubling of the US military presence on the ground in Afghanistan does not seem temporary. Rather, troops will maintain a protracted presence focused on securing and holding villages currently dominated by the *Taliban*. One conundrum, US military officials say, is that the expanded forces will have to come in with heavy firepower and aggressive military tactics—likely to create more civilian casualties and public animosity—in order to secure rural districts so that they can bring in services, aid and governance aimed at winning over the local populace.

It seems that while implementing the new policy, the US administration is trying to differentiate between *Al-Qaeda* and the *Taliban* to portray the former as evil and the latter as a different force with whom a compromise ought to be pursued. But the blunt fact is that *Al-Qaeda*, Afghan-*Taliban*, Pakistan-*Taliban*, Lashkar-e-Taiba and Jaish-e-Muhammad, all work under complete guidance and support of the elements of the Pakistani Army and ISI.[37] The US military "surge" planned for Afghanistan has reportedly brought the Afghan and Pakistan *Taliban* into closer alliance and strengthened the links between the *Taliban* and *Al-Qaeda* and other terrorists groups.[38] Hence a deal with any one group will only strengthen the others.

Creating local militias would be a disaster. Past experiences show that the local militias often fight among themselves which lead to war-like situation in their controlled territory. It also undermines central authority, and civilian life comes under threat. The growth of warlordism ultimately becomes the consequence of the surge. By empowering the tribes and other networks without regulating their relationship to the state, the United States will enable them to compete with one another for local control, mostly through criminal revenue.[39]

The indigenous ties of the insurgents perhaps present the most difficult challenge to the new US strategy. Whereas Westerners tend to view the *Taliban* as a source of cruelty and terror, for many Afghans they are simply another option in a fluid power struggle. Even former Afghan soldiers and police officers have joined the insurgents, who pay cash wages, share their religion and traditions and are often from the same tribe.

There is possibility that with the arrival of more foreign troops, there will be more suicide bombings and the violence will get worse. It has been reported that the *Taliban* fighters based in the border region are preparing for the anticipated influx of American troops to "greet them" with roadside bombings and suicide attacks and that the Pakistani and the Afghan *Taliban* are negotiating among themselves to meet such a situation.[40] Many Afghans appreciate America's help, but they feel that the US should send its troops to the borders near Pakistan, where the trouble is from. When American bombs hurt civilians, it creates more hatred.

Roads Ahead

Afghanistan is not Iraq, and the US should not expect the same results from a troop increase as occurred in Iraq. There, a broad Sunni tribal awakening was crucial. In Afghanistan, decades of war have weakened tribal structures, and the *Taliban*—unlike the brutal foreigners who comprise *Al-Qaeda* in Iraq—have deep roots in Pashtun society. More troops, however, can create the conditions for enhanced reconstruction efforts and increase little more leverage for the political solution as sought by the Obama administration. However, over the years, increasing the number of reliable Afghan forces would be vital to maintaining security. In the sidelines of the 'surge,' the United States and other countries involved on Afghanistan conflict must understand the sensitivities of dynamics and patterns of Afghan society and its ethos.

First, recent opinion polls suggest that most Afghans prefer a negotiated settlement with the insurgents rather than an intensified military campaign. Several of them point out that the *Taliban* fighters are fellow Afghans and Muslims, and that the country has traditionally settled conflicts through community and tribal meetings. One big step for the Afghan peace could be negotiating and bringing the *Taliban* to the national mainstream as a political party which could participate in the country's elections.[41]

Second, Obama administration rightly figures out that there is no military solution to the Afghanistan problem. Foreign troops alone will certainly not bring any victory. America's military commitment must be matched with realistic goals, beginning with a comprehensive "bottom-up strategy" acknowledging Afghanistan's history of decentralised governance and recognising the capabilities of NATO and the Afghan forces.

Third, many suggest that one way of reversing the course is to identify the masterminds of all terror attacks in Pakistan and Afghanistan, and put them on trial, and their sponsors in the Pakistani military-intelligence establishment are indicted in The Hague for war crimes. The Obama administration must understand that the core of any Af-Pak strategy should be to get the Pakistani military-intelligence complex to reverse their support to the *Taliban* and *Al-Qaeda*. Until there is a definite strategy for that to happen, the "cancer" is unlikely to be eradicated. But the US is reluctant to apply such an approach because of its close connections with the Pakistani institution that reared the forces of jihad. In any case, America's ability to influence events in Pakistan directly appears to be limited.

Fourth, through its intelligence networking and diplomatic channels, the Obama administration must do what the Bush team inexplicably never seemed to succeed in doing—stop the flow of funds to the *Taliban*/*Al-Qaeda* that comes mainly through the Arab Gulf states including Saudi Arabia. Although there is no involvement of any superpower in the current Afghan crisis, the flow of Gulf money plays a vital role in sustaining the *Taliban*.

Fifth, there is Pakistan, both the heart of the problem and the key to its solution. The peaceful future of the region depends on the resolve and ability of Pakistan's secular and moderate religious leaders to provide decent government to their people. Pakistani journalist Ahmed Rashid, an expert on militancy in South and Central Asia, says that the biggest problem is the militants trained on Pakistani soil.

"These groups that are operating openly on Pakistani soil have to be shut down and put away. The point is that many of these groups are deeply involved with *Al-Qaeda*. They are involved with the Pakistani *Taliban* and the Afghan *Taliban*. They are creating mayhem in India, in Iraq and around the world," "And these groups have had it very easy so far. They have to be put away. But also, at the same time, what is needed is a strategic rethink by [Pakistan's] military as to how it looks at national security."[42] The US must persuade the Pakistani intelligence service to stop underwriting the *Taliban* and *Al-Qaeda* elements.

Sixth, any future American disengagement will have to involve a negotiated accord with the Afghanistan government, a dialogue with Afghanistan's neighbours, and new diplomatic initiatives throughout the region. Through the dialogue process, the US will also have to develop resilient institutions in the Afghan state that will, in turn, help establish democratic norms and rule of law. If the US does all this, it can minimise the strategic costs of its failure in Afghanistan.

Seventh, Afghanistan's army needs to be much bigger than the planned 134,000. International community should understand that Iraq, smaller than Afghanistan in terms of land area and population, has over 267,000 troops. Money should not be a constraint on the way to enhancing the Afghan National Army. After all, building, equipping and training the Afghan Army is much more economical than the deployment of foreign troops. Compared to Iraq, Afghanistan has also been allocated minimal resources for its reconstruction.[43]

Eighth, the US and the regional actors should have shared strategic objectives in Afghanistan and Pakistan: defeating the *Taliban*, addressing the aspirations of the Pashtuns across the Durand Line, eliminating the sources of extremism in Pakistan, strengthening civilian control over military in Islamabad and providing secure and legitimate borders to Pakistan.

Afghanistan has been known over the years as the graveyard of empires. Critics argue that America is repeating the errors of the Soviet Union. Like the Soviet empire (and the British one before it), it has failed to understand that controlling Afghanistan is much harder than invading it. In that sense, critics say, President Barak Obama is now reinforcing failure by sending thousands of more troops to confront an insurgency that cannot be won. Former President Bill Clinton has already cautioned that if the US President attempts to do what the British and the Russian did, Afghanistan could become "Barak Obama's Vietnam."[44]

Notes and References

1. Violence in Pakistan has spread well beyond the dangerous Afghan border region, and one wing of the Pakistani *Taliban* has vowed to carry out at least two suicide attacks per week in Pakistan. In what will deepen fears about

Pakistan's capacity to tackle *Al-Qaeda—Taliban*, North-West Frontier Province police chief Malik Navid has told the Pakistan National Assembly's standing committee that the *Taliban* was present in every city and town and hoped to launch more 9/11-type strikes against the West. See "*Taliban* in every city and town of Pakistan," *The Times of India,* 06 April 2009, p. 13. The extremist organizations are spreading so rapidly through out the country that one expert on the issue has predicted that Pakistan could collapse within six months in the face of snowballing insurgency. Given an unprecedented upswing in terrorist strikes, some analysts are even putting forward apocalyptic timetables for the country. See "Pak could collapse in 6 months: Expert," *The Times of India,* April 07, 2009, p. 1.

2. For details, see the text: "Obama on New Strategy for Afghanistan and Pakistan," The White House, Office of the Press Secretary, Washington DC, Distributed by the Bureau of International Information Programs, US Department of State, http://www.america.gov, March 27, 2009.
3. Dan Eggen, "Focus Is on Afghanistan As Bush Lays Out Plans," *The Washington Post,* September 10, 2008, p. A11.
4. *Ibid.*
5. As quoted in Charlie Savage, "Obama's war on terror may resemble Bush's" *The Indian Express,* February 19, 2009, p. 13.
6. Koren De Young, "More Troops Headed to Afghanistan," *The Washington Post,* February 18, 2009, p.A01.
7. *Ibid.*
8. As quoted in "US backs *Taliban* return to power," *The Times of India,* October 8, 2008, p. 15.
9. The present special Ambassador for AF-Pak is a former UN Ambassador who helped write the peace deal that ended Bosnia's 1992-95 war.
10. For details, see the text: "Obama on New Strategy for Afghanistan and Pakistan," The White House, Office of the Press Secretary, Washington DC, Distributed by the Bureau of International Information Programs, US Department of State, http://www.america.gov, March 27, 2009.
11. *Ibid,* also see Helene Cooper and Eric Schmitt, "White House Debate Led to Plan to Widen Afghan Effort," *The New York Times,* March 28, 2009.
12. As quoted in Lalit K Jha, "Redefine Afghan goals: Obama," *The Indian Express,* March 02, 2009, p. 13. Also see the text of President Obama's Remarks on New Strategy for Afghanistan and Pakistan, *ibid.*
13. See the text: "Obama on New Strategy for Afghanistan and Pakistan," *Ibid.* Also see Chidanand Rajghatta, "Pak still safe haven for Qaida: Obama," *The Times of India,* March 28, 2009, p. 15.
14. "Obama on New Strategy for Afghanistan and Pakistan," *Ibid.*
15. The new goal, according to American military planners, is to produce an Afghan army of some 220,000 troops and an enlarged police force of 180,000.
16. The United Nations has recorded the deaths of 2,118 civilians in the conflict in 2008, 39 percent higher than in 2007 and highest yearly toll since the fall of the *Taliban*.

17. Karen DeYoung, "Obama to Explore New Approach in Afghanistan War," *The Washington Post,* November 11, 2008.
18. India has contributed more than $1.2 billion for Afghanistan's reconstruction.
19. James Dobbins, *After the Taliban: Nation Building in Afghanistan,* Washington, 2008, pp. 74-92.
20. See the text: "Obama on New Strategy for Afghanistan and Pakistan," The White House, Office of the Press Secretary, Washington DC, Distributed by the Bureau of International Information Programs, US Department of State, http://www.america.gov, March 27, 2009.
21. *Ibid.*
22. Chidanand Rajghatta, "US to enforce PEACE on Pak," *The Times of India,* April 05, 2009, p. 11.
23. Steven Simon, "The Price of the Surge," *Foreign Affairs,* May/June 2008.
24. *Ibid.*
25. Helene Cooper and Sheryl Gay Stolberg, "Obama Ponders Outreach to Elements of the *Taliban*," *The New York Times,* March 8, 2009.
26. *Ibid.*
27. "*Taliban* tells Obama there are no 'moderates' in its ranks," *The Times of India,* March 11, 2009, p. 11. Also see, M.J. Akbar, "There is nothing called the 'Moderate *Taliban*', *The Times of India,* April 12, 2009, p. 12.
28. "Mullah Omar willing to talk peace with US," *The Times of India,* March 16, 2009, p. 1.
29. Craig Whitlock, "National Security Team Delivers Grim Appraisal of Afghanistan War," *The Washington Post,* February 9, 2009, P.A13.
30. For a background to the Pakistani search of strategic depth in Afghanistan, see V.R. Raghavan, "Strategic depth in Afghanistan," *The Hindu,* November 7, 2001.
31. Amin Tarzi, "Islamabad Anxious as Kabul gets chummy with New Delhi," *eurasianet.org,* April 16, 2006.
32. As cited in Paul R. Newberg, "A Drug-Free Afghanistan Not So Easy," *Yale Global,* March 7, 2005, seehttp://yaleglobal.yale.edu/article.print?id=5385
33. Louis Dupree, *Afghanistan,* Princeton, NJ: Princeton University Press, 1973, p. 330.
34. For scholarly works on the subject, see Ralph H. Magnus and Eden Naby, *Afghanistan: Mullah, Marx, and Mujahid,* Boulder: Westview Press, 1998, p. 274. Also see, Martin Ewans, *Afghanistan: A New History*, Richmond: Curzon Press, 2001, p. 239.
35. For a comprehensive study on the subject, see Jagmohan Meher, "Understanding the Dynamics of Afghan Instability," *Contemporary Central Asia,* Vol. 10, No. 3, December 2006, pp. 1-31.
36. Pamela Constable, "Splintered *Taliban* Thwarts Afghan Peace," *The Washington Post,* April 03, 2009, p.A08. Also see Dexter Filkins "In Recruiting an Afghan Militia, US Faces a Test," *The New York Times,* April 15, 2009.

37. Baitullah Mehsud, the chief of Pakistani *Taliban*, who claimed credit for so many recent attacks in Pakistan, has links with the ISI. Based in lawless border between Pakistan and Afghanistan, Mehsud was tipped off by ISI, to enable him escape attempts to capture or kill him in last two years. See "Mehsud has links with ISI: Report," *The Times of India,* April 12, 2009, p. 13.
38. "Afghan and Pakistani *Taliban* join hands," *The Times of India,* March 28, 2009, p. 15.
39. See Jagmohan Meher, "Dealing with the Devils: The Other Side of Bush's Afghanistan," *Icfai Journal of International Relations,* Vol. 2, No. 1, January 2008, pp. 23-43.
40. "Afghan and Pakistani *Taliban* join hands," *The Times of India,* March 28, 2009, p. 15.
41. One of the *Taliban*'s leading supporters in Pakistan, Maulana Fazlur Rahman has publicly stated that *Taliban* could participate as a party in elections in Afghanistan, just as his party did in Pakistan, so long as they were not labeled as terrorists. For a comprehensive study on the reconciliation process in Afghanistan, see, Barnett R. Rubin and Ahmed Rashid, "From Great Game to Grand Bargain: Ending Chaos in Afghanistan and Pakistan," *Foreign Affairs,* November/December 2008.
42. Quoted in Ron Synovitz, "2008 In Review: Pakistan Under Pressure As War On Terror Focuses On South Asia," *Radio Free Europe/Radio Liberty,* December 28, 2008.
43. For a comparison of the resourcing of Iraq and Afghanistan, see Anthony H. Cordesman, "Follow the Money: Why The US Is Losing the War in Afghanistan," *Centre for Strategic and International Studies (CSIS),* September 22, 2008.
44. As quoted in "Afghanistan Could be Obama's Vietnam," *The Times of India,* February 19, 2009, p. 17.

[illegible] Report.

Section II

Regional Approaches to Peace in Afghanistan

8

Developing a Regional Approach to Development and Security in Afghanistan

Gulshan Sachdeva

Introduction

In the last four decades, Afghanistan has witnessed diverse projects of nation building and socio-political transformation. The Soviet project of building communism in Afghanistan resulted in over a million dead and five million Afghan refugees, mainly in the neighbourhoods. Similarly, when Pakistan pushed backward theocracy in Afghanistan, the world faced disastrous consequences, including the 9/11. The current international project of building democracy and market economy is mandated by the United Nations but it is openly led by the US. So far, this endeavour has produced mixed results. Apart from installing a democratic government, the country has made achievements in infrastructure, education and the economy in the last eight years. After reaching record levels in 2007, opium cultivation and production have somewhat moderated in the last two years. Despite significant success in many areas, however, the *Taliban* insurgency is gaining strength in some parts of the country and security situation has deteriorated. There is also an alarming rise in suicide bombings. Most analysts believe that there is a need to rethink the present strategy.[1] Within six months of announcing a 'comprehensive new strategy for Afghanistan and Pakistan' in which the new US President Barack Obama aimed "to disrupt, dismantle and defeat *Al Qaeda* in Pakistan and Afghanistan, and to prevent their return to either country in the future,"[2] he is again considering for a strategy shift[3]. This paper tries to understand the current economic and security situation in Afghanistan. It also suggests that that to tackle the problems of security, development and opium production, Afghanistan needs a regional approach. In the new approach, regional countries, viz. China, Pakistan, Central Asian republics, Iran, India, Turkey, and Russia will have to play a much bigger role than hitherto.

Background

Decades of war, followed by the *Taliban* regime, destroyed the core institution of Afghan state. The war torn economy faced high levels of absolute poverty, ill health, large scale illiteracy and complete marginalisation of female population. In addition, millions of Afghans left the country and became refugees mainly in the neighbouring countries.

After the Soviet withdrawal in early 1989, the Nazibullah regime was able to last few more years till 1992. In 1992, different *Mujahideen* groups established the Islamic Republic of Afghanistan with the introduction of rotating presidency. Between 1992 and 1996 Afghanistan saw one of the worst periods in its history. Different parts of the country were controlled by different warlords. During this period, much of the infrastructure in Afghanistan was destroyed. In this chaotic situation, a new *Taliban* movement emerged in the south, seizing control first of Kandahar and surrounded areas and later Kabul in 1996. The *Taliban* had strong backing from Pakistan's Inter Services Intelligence (ISI), which assisted in recruitment, provided weapons, training and technical assistance. In the beginning, the *Taliban* were well received and quickly they established new political and social order in the country. The world was horrified when it learned the way the *Taliban* were treating the women or blasting Buddha's of Bamyan. However, it was still a forgotten place for most western countries as larger strategic objective of defeating Soviets was achieved. Still, some of the regional countries (Iran, Russia, India and Tajikistan) were helping the Northern Alliance which was fighting the *Taliban* regime in Afghanistan. In the hindsight it seems these regional countries had better understanding of the dangers of the *Taliban* than many western capitals. The US became active only when *Taliban*'s links to Osama Bin Laden became clear. Finally, when 9/11 happened, President Bush delivered an ultimatum to the *Taliban* to extradite Osama. Later at a press conference in Pakistan, *Taliban* ambassador to Pakistan asked proof and refused to extradite Osama to the US. Consequently, on October 7, 2001, "Operation Enduring Freedom" was launched with the initial objectives of (a) destruction of terrorist training camps and infrastructure within Afghanistan; (b) capturing of *Al Qaeda* leaders; and (c) cessation of terrorist activities in

Afghanistan.[4] Initially, the US and the UK led the aerial bombing campaign, with ground forces supplied primarily by the Northern Alliance. In 2002, US, British and Canadian infantry along with some special forces from other allied nations also joined. Later, the North Atlantic Treaty Organization (NATO) troops were also added.

After the fall of the *Taliban*, all Afghan factions who were opposed to the *Taliban* met in Bonn in December 2001. The meeting was sponsored by the United Nations. The Bonn Agreement[5] charted the roadmap for the political transformation of the county into a democratic state. The UN Security Council endorsed the agreement through its resolution 1383.[6] Under the leadership of Mr. Hamid Karzai, a Transitional Administration was established to guide the process of transformation. The interim administration obtained its authority through the *Loya Jirgha* (Grand Council) convened by former Afghan king Zahir Shah. In early 2002, international donors pledged about $4.5 billion in Tokyo for the reconstruction efforts in Afghanistan. In March 2002, the UN also established the UN Assistance Mission in Afghanistan (UNAMA). The constitutional *Loya Jirgha* adopted a new constitution in January 2004, with the presidential form of government. In April 2004 in Berlin, 23 donor nations pledged a total of $8.2 billion. aid to Afghanistan over three years.[7] Under the new constitution, presidential elections were held in October 2004 and parliamentary elections in September 2005. More than 75 percent voters participated in the presidential election and a significant number of women were elected to the National Assembly. The constitution also established legal protection for the private property and it was presumed that economic development in the country will be based mainly on the market economy. These were remarkable achievements for a country destroyed by decades of war. Once these landmarks were achieved, international community and the Afghanistan government agreed on the *Afghanistan Compact*[8] at the London Conference in 2005. The Compact set ambitious targets for security, governance, development, regional cooperation and counter narcotics. While reviewing the "*Afghanistan Compact*", at another international conference on Afghanistan in Paris in June 2008, international community made further commitments for the next five years.[9]

Achievements

According to the *Afghanistan National Development Strategy*[10] (ANDS), more than 5 million Afghan refugees have returned home since 2002. In 2006 alone 342,925 Afghan refugees returned from Pakistan and Iran and another thousand from other countries. The number of school going children has grown from under one million in 2001 to about 6 million in 2007 (one third of them are girls). In 2007, there were more than 9,000 schools (including 1,337 all girls and 4,325 co-educational). The number of teachers has increased seven fold to 142,500, which included 40,000 female teachers. In the health and nutrition sector, more than $1 billion has been invested in the last five years. As a result, percentage of people living in areas where basic health care facilities are made available has increased from 9 percent in 2002 to 85 percent in 2008. Infant mortality rate has been reduced by 26 percent in five years.[11] 76 percent of the children under the age of five have been immunized against childhood diseases.

It is remarkable that despite a difficult legacy, the macro-economic stability in Afghanistan has been maintained in the last few years (see table 1). This has been the result of disciplined fiscal and monetary policies. A new currency was successfully introduced. Till 2007, inflation remained reasonably low and exchange rate has been stable. More than a dozen private commercial banks, two private airlines and 13 micro-finance institutions are operating successfully. About 150 cities across Afghanistan now have access to mobile phone networks and internet provider services. Many multinationals are already operating or showing an interest in Afghanistan which includes Coca Cola, Siemens, Nestle and Etisalat. In 2001, only 15,000 people had access to telecom facilities. Today the number of telephone users (mainly mobile) has crossed 4 million, which is more than 15 percent of the population. Afghan Telecom has installed 86,000 fixed digital lines and 233,000 wireless lines in all 34 provinces. By mid-2009, the process of constructing a 3,200-kilometer optical-fiber network connecting major provincial capitals with one another and also with neighbouring countries will be complete. Broadly free and privately owned media sector has developed. Presently, Afghanistan has seven national TV stations (out of which six are private), numerous radio networks, plus a diverse and increasingly professional print media. According to government sources, about 12,000 kms of roads have been rehabilitated, improved, or built. This includes the 2,200 km long ring road which connects all major towns of Afghanistan, national highways, provincial roads and rural roads. More than $2 billion has been spent on roads. All these projects are implemented in difficult security situations, which are normally not mentioned while discussing broader security and strategic matters concerning Afghanistan.

Table 1: Some Macro-economic Indicators in Afghanistan

Year	*GDP Growth*	*Inflation*	*Exchange Rate to US$ (annual average)*
2004	8.0	NA	47.8
2005	16.1	12.3	49.7
2006	8.2	5.3	49.9
2007	12.1	12.9	49.8
2008	3.4	28.3	50.2
2009*	9.0	6.0	NA
2010*	7.5	6.8	NA

*projected

Source: Asian Development Outlook 2009 (ADB: 2009), pp. 296, 303, 314.

Security Situation and Narcotics

After initial successes till 2004-05, situation in Afghanistan has become more difficult, complex and challenging. One of the main reasons has been the deteriorating security situation, particularly in the south and east of the country. A major change that has happened in the last three years is the rise in suicide bombings which reached almost 150 in 2007 and further increased in 2008. As the following table shows the figures of coalition casualties in Afghanistan are growing with every passing year making 2009 the bloodiest year since 2001.

Table 2: Coalition Military Fatalities in Afghanistan, 2001-Sep 2009 (by year and month)

Year	*Jan*	*Feb*	*Mar*	*Apr*	*May*	*Jun*	*Jul*	*Aug*	*Sep*	*Oct*	*Nov*	*Dec*	*Total*
2001	0	0	0	0	0	0	0	0	0	3	5	4	12
2002	10	12	14	10	1	3	0	3	1	6	1	8	69
2003	4	7	12	2	2	7	2	4	2	6	8	1	57
2004	11	2	3	3	9	5	2	4	4	8	7	1	59
2005	2	3	6	19	4	29	2	33	12	10	7	4	131
2006	1	17	13	5	17	22	19	29	38	17	9	4	191
2007	2	18	10	20	25	24	29	34	24	15	22	9	232
2008	14	7	19	14	23	46	30	46	37	19	12	27	294
2009	25	24	28	14	27	38	76	77	56	NA	NA	NA	365

Source: http://icasualties.org/oef/

In addition, opium production continue to be a serious problem in Afghanistan although 2008 and 2009 opium surveys by the United Nations

Office of Drugs and Crime (UNODC) have shown that there has been some moderate decline in opium production. In 2008 it was shown that 98 percent of the total cultivation was confined to seven provinces with serious security problems. Five out of these provinces were in the south and two in the west of Afghanistan. The seven provinces that contributed to 98 percent of Afghan opium cultivation and production in 2008 were Hilmand, Kandahar, Uruzgan, Daykundi, Zabul, Farah and Nimroz, clearly showing strong linkages between opium production and the security situation. Opium cultivation in Afghanistan has decreased by 22 per cent, from 157,000 hectares (ha) in 2008 to 123,000 in 2009. In 2008, Hilmand remained the single largest opium cultivating province where 66 percent of total Afghan cultivation was done. In 2009, cultivation declined by a third, to less than 70,000 ha. in Hilmand. The 2009 survey also shows that compared to 13 in 2007 and 18 in 2008, 20 provinces (out of 34) were poppy free. All the seven provinces in the Northern region are poppy free in almost a decade. The survey righly asserts that "controlling drugs in Afghanistan will not solve all of the country's problems, but the country's problems can not be solved without controlling drugs".[12]

Various official and unofficial reports and studies have broadly pointed out that Afghanistan today is at crossroads. The *Afghanistan Study Group* report which was released in early 2008 sums up the mood by asserting that "the progress achieved after six years of international engagement is under serious threat from resurgent violence, weakening international resolve, mounting regional challenges and a growing lack of confidence on the part of the Afghan people about the future direction of their country."[13]

Similarly, the *Centre for Strategic and International Studies* (CSIS) report[14] sums up its findings as: (1) Afghans are losing trust in their government because of an escalation in violence; (2) public expectations are neither being met nor managed; and (3) Conditions in Afghanistan have deteriorated in all key areas targeted for development, except for the economy and women's rights.

In September 2008, the UN Secretary General in its report observed that "the overall situation in Afghanistan has become more challenging". Despite enhanced capacities, he notes that the "security situation has deteriorated markedly." Further, "the influence of the insurgency has expanded beyond traditionally volatile areas" and "incidents stemming from cross-border activities from Pakistan have increased significantly in terms of numbers and sophistication." In addition, he mentions that the humanitarian situation has also deteriorated. The report also draws particular attention to the increase in the number of civilian casualties, "which are caused mainly by anti-government activities but are also the unintended consequence of operations by pro-government forces".[15]

General Staley A. McChrystal, then commander of International Security Assistance Force (ISAF) and US forces in Afghanistan has warned that the situation is serious and "neither success nor failure can be taken for granted" and "many indicators suggest that the situation is deteriorating." He further writes that "we face not only a resilient and growing insurgency, there is also a crisis of confidence among Afghans—in both their government and in the international community—that undermines our credibility and emboldens the insurgents".[16]

Regional Economic Cooperation

Despite difficult security situation and limited capacities, Afghanistan is emerging as an important player in regional economic cooperation. All international and regional players have appreciated its approach towards regional cooperation. High economic growth in both Central and South Asian regions is also pushing policy makers to work for integration strategies. In this paper an attempt has been made to argue that developments in the area of regional cooperation involving Afghanistan have major implications for regional peace and stability as well as India's linkages with the Eurasian region.

Policy makers in Afghanistan believe that after decades of war now the country has a unique opportunity to realise its potential as a "land bridge" between Central Asia, South Asia and the West Asian regions. They also advocate that peace and stability in this strategically important country is also going to provide huge economic opportunities not only to Afghanistan but also to its neighbours. Increasingly it is pointed out that with enhanced cooperation, land locked energy rich Central Asia could be connected to energy deficient South Asia. Similarly, Afghanistan could also realise significant revenue as transit fee and improve its economic activities in the process.

Most official declarations indicate that Afghanistan is seriously committed to regional cooperation. It intends to share the benefits of its centrality through regional cooperation with its neighbours and countries beyond the immediate neighborhood. Two major documents *The Afghanistan Compact* and the *Afghanistan National Development Strategy* clearly show that regional economic cooperation is one of the main priorities of the government. Despite difficult conditions and limited capacities, Afghanistan government has been able to market itself as an important player in regional cooperation. This is evident through various international declarations like the Good Neighbourly Relations Declaration of 2002, the Dubai Declaration of 2003, the Berlin Agreements of 2003, the Bishkek Conference of 2004, the Kabul Conference Declaration of 2005, the Delhi Conference Declaration of 2006 and Islamabad Conference Declaration of 2009. Through these announcements, countries in the region have accepted the centrality of Afghanistan for economic cooperation.

Afghan Engagement with Regional Organisations

Afghanistan has requested for accession to the World Trade Organization (WTO). In December 2004, the General Council of the WTO established a working party to examine its membership. At the WTO General Council, its Ambassador Mr. Assad Omer reiterated that Afghanistan "hoped to re-establish itself as the land bridge for trans-continental trade". Apart from WTO, the country is also simultaneously engaged with many of its neighbours through bilateral and multilateral trade, economic and investment agreements. Afghanistan is an active member of the Economic Cooperation Organization (ECO). At the fourteenth South Asian Association for Regional Cooperation (SAARC) summit held in Delhi in April 2007, Afghanistan became the eighth member of the grouping. Afghanistan's membership in the SAARC has the potential to bring new dynamism in economic relations between the South Asian and Central Asian regions. Afghanistan also serves in the Contact Group of the Shanghai Cooperation Organisation (SCO). Through its membership in Central Asian Regional Economic Cooperation (CAREC), Central and South Asia Transport and Trade Forum (CSATTF) and UN Special Programme for the Economies of Central Asia (SPECA) Afghanistan is also trying to involve itself with various regional projects and activities associated with enhanced regional cooperation. Officially, it is claimed that "through regional cooperation, Afghanistan wishes to (a) improve trading opportunities; (b) integrate itself with the regional rail and road networks; (c) be an important partner in regional energy markets; (d) eliminate narcotics trade; and (e) achieve Millennium Development Goals".[17] The following table highlights the trade and transit agreements signed by Afghanistan in the last few years:

Table 3: Trade and Transit Agreements by Afghanistan Since 2003

Partner Country	*Type of Agreement*	*Signed on*	*Remarks/Signatory from Afghanistan*
ECO Trade Agreement (Regional)	Trade	17-07-2003	
SAFTA (Regional)	FTA	AFG entered SAARC on 1 April 2007	The government in the process of completing formalities to be part of SAFTA (negative list etc has been submitted)
Tajikistan	Commercial	13-09-2004	Minister of Commerce
India	Trade (PTA)	06-03-2003	Minister of Commerce
Turkey	Investment	10-06-2004	Minister of Commerce
Turkey	Commercial	10-06-2004	Minister of Commerce
Iran, Chabahar	Trade, Transit	18-12-1382*	DG, ACCI
Iran, Chabahar	Trade, Transit	17-06-1382*	Minister of Commerce
Multilateral (Iran, Tajikistan)	International Transportation	23-03-1382*	President
Iran	Trade and Economic Coop MOU	17-06-1382*	Minister of Commerce
Iran	Int'l transportation	15-10-1381*	Minister of Commerce
Multilateral (Iran, India)	Chabahar Transit, Delaram Zarang issues	15-10-1381*	Minister of Commerce
Multilateral (Iran, India)	MOU Multilateral Commission	15-10-1381*	Minister of Commerce
Iran	Commercial	15-10-1381*	Minister of Commerce
Multilateral (Iran, Uzbekistan)	Int'l transportation	28-03-1383*	
Kazakhstan	Trade and Eco coop	Hamal 1383*	Minister of Commerce
Uzbekistan	Trade and Eco coop	08-12-2003	Minister of Commerce
Uzbekistan	Transport	02-12-2003	Minister of Foreign Affairs
Uzbekistan	Transit and Trade	29-08-2004	Minister of Foreign Affairs
Turkey	Customs, transport	27-02-2005	Minister of Commerce
Turkmenistan	Trade and Economic Cooperation, Transit	05-07-2007	Minister of Foreign Affairs

* Afghanistan Calendar dates.

Source: *Ministry of Commerce and Industry of Afghanistan and Press Reports.*

Regional Economic Cooperation Conference (RECC) on Afghanistan

To publicise the concept of Afghanistan's centrality and to identify some regional projects, Afghanistan initiated an institutional mechanism called Regional Economic Cooperation Conference (RECC) on Afghanistan in 2005. The first RECC was held in Kabul during December 4-5, 2005 which was organised at the initiative of UK, the G-8 Chair at that time.

The Kabul Conference attempted to bring together 11 regional countries, namely China, India, Iran, Kazakhstan, Kyrgyzstan, Pakistan, Tajikistan, Turkey, Turkmenistan, UAE and Uzbekistan and G-8 representatives along with officials from the World Bank, Asian Development Bank, IMF, ECO, SCO, etc. The focus of the initiative was to promote specific forms of economic cooperation in areas of critical concern to the regional countries. These included specific sectors like trade, investment and transport facilitation, electricity trade and energy development, etc. At the end, an ambitious Kabul Declaration was adopted which incorporated decisions on areas that were identified as potential areas of co-operation. These areas included: (a) electricity trade and power development (b) sharing the benefits of water (c) counter-narcotics (d) transport (e) energy transport (f) trade facilitation and (e) business climate.

The second RECC was hosted by India in Delhi in November 2006. This meeting tried to build on the work done at the Kabul in 2005 and followed on the themes identified at Kabul. The countries which participated at Delhi meeting were Canada, China, Finland (EU Presidency), France, Germany, Iran, Italy, Japan, Kazakhstan, Kyrgyzstan, Pakistan, Russia, Tajikistan, Turkey, Turkmenistan, UAE, UK, US and Uzbekistan. In addition, ADB, Aga Khan Development Network, European Commission, European Council, IMF, ECO, SAARC, UNDP, UN and World Bank also participated. Major themes discussed in Delhi included trade and transport facilitation, investment, regional energy trading, and Turkmenistan-Afghanistan-Pakistan-India (TAPI) gas pipeline, etc. Special focus was also given to renewal energy and agriculture. In association with Afghanistan Investment Support Agency (AISA), concurrent business meetings were also held. Some of the recommendations of these meetings included:

- The creation of a Centre for Regional Cooperation in Kabul.
- Public-Private partnership as key aspect of regional development.
- Existing regional groupings should consider integrating their efforts into a larger single entity.
- Afghanistan would benefit more from a region specific approach to capacity development.
- New themes for the next conference were identified as mining, water, health, labour movement human resource development, and trade and transit.

Similarly, among other things, Delhi Declaration also decided that:

- Regional countries will undertake stronger credibility and confidence building measures and will intensify efforts to remove obstacles to overland trade and transit between countries and regions.
- The short-term focus of regional economic co-operation will be on practical win-win projects, notably in the fields of energy, transport and trade, agriculture and mining.
- There will be better information sharing, via prioritisation of key issues, among the countries and regional organisations in order to avoid duplication of efforts.
- ADB will undertake a study on regional integration strategies and will share key findings at the next Conference.
- Regional countries will work towards aviation liberalisation for greater regional connectivity.
- Work will be accelerated on TAPI gas pipeline to develop a technically and commercially viable project.
- The regional countries will encourage forging of institutional linkages with training institutes in the respective countries with a view towards capacity building of their work force, with the long-term objective of establishing regional training institutes in specialised areas.

At the Delhi conference it was decide that the next RECC will take place in Islamabad in 2007. However, due to political changes and other reasons, it was postponed many times. Finally, the third RECC took place in Islamabad in May 2009 where many issues concerning trade, energy, capacity building, agriculture and counter-narcotics were discussed. Among many other things it was agreed that priority will be given to the following items.

- Conclusion of Trade and Transit agreement between Afghanistan and Pakistan before the end of 2009.
- A pre-feasibility study of railways across Afghanistan linking major destinations within Afghanistan and its neigbours by the European Commission.
- Establishment of a Customs Academy in Kabul.
- Feasibility studies for the development of border economic zones around Afghanistan.

- An Afghan centre within the Ministry of Foreign Affairs to follow up on regional economic cooperation issues by the European Commission.

At the conference it was also agreed that next RECC will take place in Turkey.

Developments Targeting Regional Integration

It is not only that Afghanistan and its neighbours have signed some agreements; there is also significant development in actual realisation of some these of these initiatives.

Infrastructure

Afghanistan has practically no rail or water transport connections. Besides little air transport, the country relies mainly on road transport. Till 1980, Afghanistan had 18,000 kms of road network, out of which only 3000 km was asphalted. As a result of decades of conflict, the road network was completely destroyed. In the last few years, the country has started a major Programme of improving its road network. As per the Road Master Plan, Afghanistan has four kinds of roads: national highways (3,363 km), regional highway (4,884 km), provincial roads (9,656 km), and rural roads (17,000 km). For regional cooperation, improvement in regional roads is very important as they connect Afghanistan with its neighbouring countries, viz. Iran, Pakistan, Tajikistan, Turkmenistan and Uzbekistan. They also connect neighbouring countries with each other. With the help of multilateral agencies and donor countries (mainly USAID, The World Bank, Asian Development Bank (ADB), European Commission, Japan, Iran, India, Pakistan, etc) most of these regional road have been rehabilitated and/or constructed. Under this programme Rehabilitation of ring road has been given priority. This road connects the country as it starts from Kabul and after going through Doshi-Puekhumry, Mazar-e-eharif, Faryab, Badghees, Herat, Kandhahar, finally ends in Kabul. Total length of the road is 2210 km, out of which 1504 km (about 75 percent) has already been rehabilitated. Total cost of the project is USD 1142 million. It is expected that by 2009 the ring road will be complete. Secondly, the roads that connect Afghanistan with its neighbours and consequently connect countries in the region are Kabul-Torkham, Heart-Torghundi, Herat-Islamqala, Kandhahar-Spinboldok, Aquina-Andhkhoy, Delaram-Zeranj and Pule Khumri-Sherkhan Bandar Naibabad. Total length of these roads is 1,153 km. Out of this, 597 km have been rehabilitated so far.

As a significant portion of the national ring road has already been completed, it has helped lowering transit time through Afghanistan. The opening of Sher Khan Bandar "Friendship Bridge" connecting Afghanistan and Tajikistan was also another major milestone. This $37 million, 672 meters long and 11 meters wide bridge will not only connect two neighbouring countries but also help greater trade and investment flows in the entire region. The plans for connecting Afghanistan with Iran (Herat-Sangan project) and Pakistan (Chaman-Spinboldok railway) are at different stages of planning and implementation. With the completion of ring road and further connections with neighbours, Afghanistan can also plan to become a partner in North-South transport corridors. Improvement in transit facilities through Turkmenistan, Tajikistan and Pakistan and development of Regional Opportunity Zones (ROZ) on the Afghanistan-Pakistan border has the potential to further integrate the region.

Power

In the area of power, Afghanistan is already involved with serious cross border energy trade. Already imported power represents about 22 percent of Afghanistan's total power supply. Currently, it imports about 100 MW of power from four neighbouring countries viz. Iran, Turkmenistan, Uzbekistan and Tajikistan. Under North Eastern Power System (NEPS), Afghanistan expects to import another 300 MW of power from Uzbekistan by 2008-09. Similarly, through Central Asia-South Asia project (CASA-1000), it is expected that it will import another 1300 MW of additional power from Tajikistan and Kyrgyzstan by 2012. Out of this, about 300 MW of power will remain in Afghanistan and the rest 1000 MW will be exported to Pakistan. Various bilateral electricity trade deals like North-East power System (NEPS)[18] of Afghanistan together with evolving new multilateral projects like CASA-1000 could eventually lead to the creation of an integrated Central Asia-South Asia Regional Electricity Market (CASAREM). In January 2009, a project of transfer of electricity from Uzbekistan to Kabul covering a distance of 462 km over the Hindu Kush through the Salang Pass was inaugurated. The 202 km long 220 KV DC transmission line from Pul-e-Khumri to Chimtala and the substation project is one of the major Indian infrastructure projects in Afghanistan.

Reconstruction

Regional countries are also actively involved in the reconstruction efforts in Afghanistan in a big way. The present level of Indian assistance to the country stands at $1.2 billion, making it the 5th largest bilateral donor in

Afghanistan after the US, UK, Japan and Germany. This is a substantial amount for a non-traditional donor like India. India has already completed 30 projects and is involved in other 50 reconstruction projects. These projects are being implemented in the areas of hydro-electricity, power transmission lines, road construction, agriculture, industry, telecommunications, information and broadcasting, education, health and capacity building. Similarly, Iran has spent about $300 million in Afghan reconstruction mainly in infrastructure and capacity building. Pakistan has also committed about $300 million to reconstruction efforts in Afghanistan. Russia has also made settlement of Afghanistan's debt to former USSR which according to some Russian experts estimates totals to $10 billion. Chinese company has won a $3.5 billion contract to develop Afghanistan's Aynak copper field, the largest foreign direct investment project in the country.

Time for a Regional Approach in Security

Compared to regional approach to economic development which has been well appreciated by all concerned players, situation in security matters is more complex. As of July 23, 2009, almost all forty-two nations which contribute about 64,000 troops to the International Security Assistance Force (ISAF) are from outside the region. There are no troops from Iran, China, Pakistan, India, Russia or Central Asian republics. These are the countries which are actually going to be directly affected by developments within Afghanistan. Pakistan's involvement in security matters in Afghanistan is complicated. On one hand it helps the coalition forces in Afghanistan through logistics, intelligence, joint operations, etc as a non-NATO major ally. On the other hand, most of the Afghan insurgent groups have bases in Pakistan. In addition, they are given tactical support by many elements within the administration. Regional countries are not involved even in training of security personnel. This despite the fact that trainers from Iran, India, Pakistan and Central Asian region could communicate in local languages and will have more cultural understanding of the place.

Today what Afghanistan is facing is a typical insurgency. It has broadly two distinct insurgencies. One is Kandahar based insurgency which is mainly dominated by the *Taliban* in the south. The eastern insurgency is more complex. It is a loose confederation of affiliates such as the Haqqani Network and like-minded groups *(Al-Qaeda, Hizb-e Islami Gulbuddin,* and Pakistani militant groups *Jaish-e Mohammed, Lashkar-e-Tayyiba, Tehrik Nefaz-i-Shariat Muhammad).* Both the *Taliban* and eastern groups have support structures in Pakistan. Their shared goals include the expulsion of all foreign military forces from Afghanistan, the elimination of external government influence in their respective areas, and the imposition of a religiously conservative, Pashtun-led government.[19]

On the basis of 90 insurgencies world over since 1945, a recent RAND study[20] shows that it takes an average of 14 years to defeat insurgencies once an insurgency develops. Due to history and topography, it might take even longer in Afghanistan. Experience in the region also shows that a large number of boots on the ground are needed to mange any insurgency. The ratio in South Asia is somewhere between 1 to 30 or 35. Current estimates of *Taliban* and other insurgents in Afghanistan are between ten to seventeen thousands. It means to mange and defeat this insurgency a minimum 300,000 to 350,000 troops are needed in Afghanistan for at least ten to fifteen years. With current levels of about 1,90,000 (64,000 ISAF, another independently operating 35,000 US troops plus 90,000 Afghan National Army) it is going to be very difficult task to manage Afghan insurgency. In the absence of required numbers, the coalition forces have relied more on airpower in counter-insurgency operations. According to the a human rights report, 116 civilians were killed in 2006 in 13 bombings. Similarly, 321 civilians were killed in 2007 in 22 bombings while hundreds more injured. In the first seven months of 2008 at least 119 civilians were killed in 12 air strikes.[21] According to UNAMA, in the first six months of 2009, 1013 civilians died in Afghanistan due to conflict. Out of this, 59 per cent (595 deaths) were caused by anti government forces and 310 deaths by pro government forces.[22] The large number of civilian casualties further undermine the legitimacy of the Afghan administration.

Moreover, it is highly unlikely that many of ISAF contributing European nations will be able to commit their forces for the next ten to fifteen years. Many European nations including Germany and Italy are seriously debating their involvement in Afghanistan. So strategy in Afghanistan should be to raise Afghan National Army numbers to around 200,000 and involve some of the regional countries in security management of the nation. To give a concrete shape to this plan, two major things need to happen in the region. First, a rapprochement between the US and Iran must happen. Secondly, a dramatic improvement in relations between India and Pakistan is also a pre-requisite for this strategy. Therefore, the war in Afghanistan is not only about troop numbers alone but also a serious diplomatic engagement by the US to create a regional platform from where this war will be fought both militarily and diplomatically. Writing agenda for the new US president, the current US Special envoy to the Afghanistan-Pakistan region Ambassador Richard Holbrooke wrote in 2008 that "Afghanistan's future cannot be secured by a counterinsurgency effort alone; it will also require regional agreements that give Afghanistan's neighbours a stake in the settlement. That includes Iran—as well as China, India, and Russia. But the most important neighbour is, of course, Pakistan, which can destabilize Afghanistan at will- and has. Getting policy toward Islamabad right will be absolutely critical for the next administration- and very difficult"[23] So far there is no regional institutional mechanism to address this issue. What is needed is a sustained institutional forum within the region to continue with this engagement on a long term basis. Half day meetings in some European capitals will not serve any purpose except for some photo opportunities. The new Af-Pak policy of the new US administration also talked about exploring the possibilities of "creating new diplomatic mechanisms, including establishing a "Contact Group" and a regional security and economic cooperation forum"[24]. Despite declarations, nothing concrete has emerged yet.

Conclusion

Despite difficult security situation, the process of nation-building in Afghanistan is continuing. In economic matters, the country has the potential to play an important role in facilitating regional integration in different economies of South, Central and West Asia. If proposals concerning regional economic cooperation originating from Afghanistan are implemented by other countries in the region, this could ultimately improve chances of peace and stability not only between India and Pakistan but also in the entire Eurasian region. However, much will depend on the political and security situations in Afghanistan-Pakistan region. The security situation in Afghanistan as it has developed over the last few years will take at least ten to fifteen years to be controlled significantly. Ultimately it will need more involvement of regional countries in the security affairs of Afghanistan as many present contributing nations to the ISAF may move out the project in due course of time. A regional institutional mechanism in security matters should be the most important item on Afghanistan agenda. In addition, serious diplomatic efforts are needed to improve relations between the US and Iran as well as between India and Pakistan. Unless efforts are made in this direction, it will be difficult to make a major breakthrough in Afghanistan.

Notes and References

1. Grey Bruno, *Rethinking Afghanistan*, Daily Analysis, September 1, 2009, Council on Foreign Relations, available at http://www.cfr.org/publication/20114/rethinking_afghanistan.html
2. Remarks by the President (of the United States) on a New Strategy for Afghanistan and Pakistan, March 27, 2009, available at http://www.whitehouse.gov/the_press_office/Remarks-by-the-President-on-a-New-Strategy-for-Afghanistan-and-Pakistan/
3. "Obama Considers Strategic Shift in Afghanistan" The New York Times, September 23, 2009, available at http://www.nytimes.com/2009/09/23/world/asia/23policy.html
4. For details see *Operation Enduring Freedom and the Conflict in Afghanistan: An Update*, UK House of Commons Research paper 01/81, 31 October 2001, available at www.parliament.uk/commons/lib/research/rp2001/rp01-081.pdf
5. For text of Bonn Agreement see *Agreement on Provisional Arrangements in Afghanistan Pending the Re-establishment of Permanent Government Institutions*, available at http://unama.unmissions.org/Portals/UNAMA/Documents/Bonn-agreement.pdf
6. See UN Security Council resolution number 1383, December 6, 2001, available at http://daccess-ods.un.org/TMP/5722597.html
7. See *Berlin Declaration,* available at http://reliefweb.int/rw/rwb.nsf/db900SID/SNAO-634SXS?OpenDocument
8. See *Afghanistan Compact*, available at http://unama.unmissions.org/Portals/UNAMA/Documents/AfghanistanCompact-English.pdf
9. See *Paris Declaration*, June 12, 2008, available at http://unama.unmissions.org/Portals/UNAMA/Documents/Paris-con-Declaration-English.pdf
10. *Afghanistan National Development Strategy: A Strategy for Security, Governance, Economic Growth, and Poverty Reduction,* Kabul: Government of Islamic Republic of Afghanistan, 2008.
11. *Afghan Update* (Special Health Issue) UNAMA, No. 20, Summer 2009, p. 7.
12. For details see *Afghanistan Opium Survey 2008* (UN Office of Drugs and Crime, 2008); *Afghanistan Opium Survey 2009 Summary Findings* (UN Office of Drugs and Crime, 2009).
13. *The Afghanistan Study Group: Revitalising Our efforts, Rethinking our Strategies* (Washington DC: Centre for the Study of the Presidency, 2008), p. 5.
14. *Breaking Point: Measuring Progress in Afghanistan* (Centre for Strategic and International Studies, 2007).
15. *The Situation in Afghanistan and its Implications for International Peace and Security,* Report of the UN Secretary General to the General Assembly Security Council, September 23, 2008.
16. *Commander's Initial Assessment*, Unclassified Report prepared by Stanley A McChrystal, US Commander in Afghanistan, August 30, 2009, p. 1-1, available at http://media.washingtonpost.com/wp-srv/politics/documents/Assessment_Redacted_092109.pdf

17. For details see regional cooperation section of the Afghanistan Ministry of Foreign Affairs website http://www.mfa.gov.af/regional-cooperation.asp
18. NEPS consists of transmission lines of Hairatan (Uzbekistan border)—Pul-e-Khumri to Kabul - Jalalabad and Kabul - Gardeyz (original plan) plus Sherkhanbander (Tajikistan border) to Pul-e-Khumri and Turkmenistan border to Sheberghan—Mazae-e-Sherif—Pul-e-Khumri.
19. For details see *Report on Progress toward Security and Stability in Afghanistan* (Report to the US Congress in accordance with the 2008 National Defense Authorization Act, June 2008)
20. Seth G. Jones, *Counterinsurgency in Afghanistan*, (USA: Rand Corporation, 2008.
21. *Troops in Contact: Air strikes and Civilian Deaths in Afghanistan*, USA: Human Rights Watch, 2008.
22. "Afghanistan; Civilian Causalities Keep on Rising, Says UN Report", available at http://www.unog.ch/unog/website/news_media.nsf/(httpNewsByYear_en)/0A22BB5BFE041B76C125760400343AE3?OpenDocument
23. Richard Holbrooke, "The Next President" *Foreign Affairs*, September-October 2008.
24. See *White Paper of the Interagency Policy Group's Report on US Policy toward Afghanistan and Pakistan*, available at http://www.whitehouse.gov/assets/documents/Afghanistan-Pakistan_White_Paper.pdf

9

Role and Relevance of the Region in Afghanistan

Aunohita Mojumdar

The mantra of regional cooperation has received a fresh impetus from recent developments. The thaw in the US policy towards Iran following the election of Barack Obama, the spiraling insecurity in Afghanistan and the growing concern over the loss of control of state institutions in Pakistan have added some urgency to talk of the role of the region in Afghanistan. But will this talk lead to any substantive difference on the role of the regional countries? In fact, most of the talks about the role of the region has emanated from the West. Where is the region itself in all these talks about the region?

Afghanistan has indeed become a member of SAARC, but what has been the significance of this step? Has it become just another alphabet in the lexicon, a poorer and more underdeveloped member than any other, with little political clout? Or does the regional grouping really see a role for itself in the growing crisis in Afghanistan? Is there indeed a special role for the region or is that just the self-serving self importance of the regional countries given to themselves? Finally, is there a regional view on Afghanistan at all? This paper will attempt to look at the role and relevance of the region as it stands currently, using India as an example.

In a polarized world where the 'clash of civilisations' has become the template, providing the determinant value in evaluating differences in language, culture, religion and geography, plural societies such as India and Afghanistan do not fit the mould. To borrow from the American poet, Walt Whitman, we contain "multitudes", whether it is of religions, ethnicities, cultures or languages. Sometimes, we celebrate this diversity, sometimes we struggle with it. We in India are still trying to come to terms with this identity. What we do recognise however is that for survival, we need to acknowledge our plural identities, and attempts at reducing these to simplistic notions of 'us' and 'them' are invariably disastrous. While multiculturalism and pluralism brings its own share of problems, it is not inherently problematic as it is sometimes viewed in more linear political cultures. In fact, pluralism is the only bulwark against growing intolerance and Afghanistan's new nation state in the making must reflect this in order to survive.

Unfortunately, over the past seven years, the regional perspective has been completely missing from the efforts to rebuild Afghanistan. While many of the regional countries including India have made laudable bilateral efforts, there has been no coherent regional perspective emerging from these efforts, either collectively or even individually and responsibility for this troubled country in our neighbourhood has been virtually ceded to countries and power blocs much farther with very different political and strategic imperatives.

The initial trajectory for the western domination of the 'Afghanistan project' is not difficult to trace. The US intervention in 2001 was followed quickly by the deployment of NATO led troops largely from the western countries[1]. The bulk of aid which came into the country was also from the same nations. Between 2002 and 2007 the US alone accounted for one third of all aid coming into the country.[2]

Money and muscle power alone determined who would dominate the efforts to rebuild and reconstruct Afghanistan. However, the dominance of the west has also resulted in a paralysis of the regional countries. Perhaps overwhelmed by the extent of power exhibited by the western donor nations, the regional countries have retreated, preferring to engage with Afghanistan on a bilateral platform rather than become participants in the multilateral fora. While it is certainly true that most of the regional countries would have limited influence especially individually, they have chosen to stay away rather than exercise their limited leverage. India for example, is now providing aid of more than $1 billion to Afghanistan through a series of well executed project initiatives. However, its inputs into the international decision making process is very limited and it chooses to be a bystander on issues related to policy, security and governance rather than using its political influence. While an emphasis on bilateral relations is certainly desirable, in the context of Afghanistan, both a nation and state in the making, ignoring the multilateral geopolitics and interests is a willful disregard of the existing reality. The government of Afghanistan still does not have complete control either over the bulk of resources spent in its own country nor the forces providing security. Decisions on strategic, economic and political imperatives are being made on the basis of discussions and interests presented by different members of the international community, whether or not India, which calls itself a world player, chooses to be a participant.

Security

The most significant and visible area where the international community's decision making will have a direct impact on the region in the short, medium and long term, is that of security. Here there is a very real danger that decision-making may be overly influenced by short-term goals rather than long term objectives of stability of the region. The military intervention, which led to the removal of the *Taliban* came about in response to a very specific event—9/11—and had very specific objectives, i.e. the elimination of any threat from the *Al Qaeda* and the supportive *Taliban*. The *Taliban*'s denial of rights to large sections of its population proved useful in securing international support, but was never the cause for the intervention. The goals were so short term that at this point the then US administration famously asserted that it was 'not into nation building'. Indeed, while the US went after its security objective, the UN mandated NATO-led International Security Assistance Force was kept restricted to Kabul, a move that in retrospect is seen as being counter productive. The US forces, after carrying out operations, would move out of the area of operation, thus leaving behind a vaccum. The space was left unsecured and allowed the insurgents to regroup. Insufficient boots on the ground, inadequate resources and the complete neglect of the police force compounded the problem.

The short-term perspective with its limited goals also led to the use of the same warlords whose predatory behaviour had first allowed the *Taliban* to come to power and the same commanders whose brutality had alienated the local population. Many of them were rehabilitated as the face of the new Afghan leadership as were several 'leaders' whose conservatism was only a few degrees away from that of the *Taliban*. All these vested interests were absorbed as acceptable fellow travelers as long as they swore allegiance to the limited goal of mopping up the *Al Qaeda* remnants. The strategic imperative was to eliminate any possible threat to the western regimes emanating from these remnants and the tactical method that was used to achieve this, laid emphasis on body counts. As we can see today that strategy has had its limitations.

While the past few years saw a recognition that more resources were required, the single most important resource that has usually been missing from most strategic assessments is the resource of time and patience. With its eye on specific short-term goals, the western approach is predicated on an 'exit strategy' and 'end game', whereas the regional approach must necessarily be based on continuity. Unfortunately, the eagerness of regional countries to pay obeisance to the goal of fighting terrorism has become a goal in itself. Rather than evaluate the specific steps being taken in the name of the 'war on terror' for the implications they have on the security and strategic interests of our region, our countries seem to have suspended their critical faculties in their eagerness to become paid up members of the club executing the 'war against terror'.

Forthcoming Steps with Relevance to Regional Security

There is indeed a lot of focus on Afghanistan and its security situations within India, whether in the media or within the government. However, 99.9 percent of this centres on Pakistan and its role in fuelling this insecurity. While certainly the role of Pakistan bears scrutiny, monitoring and advocacy, the Pakistani dimension is not the only aspect of security in Afghanistan. Reducing the larger strategic issues into this narrow bilateral political agenda has cost India its relevance and leverage on the issue, and even more dangerously stymied any understanding or grasp of the changing strategic contours in the region.

There are several steps that will unfold in the near future having a direct bearing on the region. The first is the ongoing influx of more international troops. While the official Indian position is that it is supportive of the UN mandated troop deployment, there seems to be no attempt to take a rigorous look at the specificities of this deployment. Is the presence of this large scale deployment in the neighbourhood beneficial to the interests of the region? Are there caveats to this approval? Troop supply routes are being recast through the Central Asian countries. What will be the impact of this? What about the troops deployed under the direct command and control of the US? When the US increases its troops in Afghanistan, would it be under NATO command and control or under the US command and control?

The second aspect of the deployment will be the operating procedures of these troops. Has the military strategy been able to meet the threat or has it actually increased instability in the region? What will be the implications of the growing public alienation and anger over the continuing civilian casualties caused by the operations of the international military forces?

Another new security related policy that is likely to cause a major change on the situation on the ground is the proposal to arm the tribes as a means of meeting the shortfall in resources. Several sections of the international community have voiced their misgivings over this, pointing out that the rearming of the tribes would escalate the level of violence within communities. It would also run counter to the programmes of disarmament and demobilisation of the armed groups, bringing more guns to the civilian population centres rather than taking them out. Stable areas of the country, deprived of this muscle power, could react violently. Given the vitiated rivalries of the years of conflict such rearming could result in tribal rivalries being settled with arms in an increasing cycle of violence and retribution. However, despite this the proposal seems to have some powerful backing especially from military commanders who are getting tired of the hard going in the military battle, and the proposal may soon turn into policy with a pilot project already underway. Is there any debate on this issue in the region? If there is, it is so quiet as to have no influence on policy making.

There has been similar silence on the issue of drug trafficking. The international community has vigorously debated the pros and cons of the policy to combat opium production and trafficking. According to some analysts, the emphasis on targeting poppy farmers rather than the drug traffickers has been counter productive. Though the country saw a marginal drop in the cultivation of opium the drop was attributable to a number of factors including the drought and the high food prices this year and even the UN's Office of Drugs and Crime expressed fears that this slender gain might be reversed. Countries in the region stand to lose a great deal from the continuing trafficking of opium and heroin from Afghanistan, becoming natural conduits for the route taken by the drug traffickers, with its concomitant increase in crime, corruption and instability. Yet most of the concern on the drug trafficking seems to have emanated from the west with no regional input on the counter narcotics policy. Cooperation with regional countries has been initiated at the behest of the western donors.

International Interests

An uneasy Russia, which has been watching the presence of the international troops expand in its backyard, has now started flexing its muscles, evident in the pressure it has brought to bear on Kyrgyzstan to close down the Manas air base used by the US troops. Russia would like to have more say on the access of the international troops to bases and routes in the Central Asian region, and to use this leverage to enhance its own position and strategic importance. With NATO needing new supply routes through

Central Asian countries in lieu of the problems on the supply routes running through Pakistan, the importance of the Central Asian region will grow in the next few years. The economy and the political configuration of the Central Asian states as well as their relationship to each other is likely to be rewritten during this period. Does our region have a strategy or viewpoint to deal with these changes including the considerable changes in the oil and gas energy interests that are likely to increase as a result?

The region's relationship with Iran has also been driven by US interests on this issue. India has all but abandoned its ties with Iran, in an attempt to keep time with its new friendship with the US. While the thaw in the US-Iran relationship is certainly a welcome sign, the initiative is still of the US' own making rather than any step taken by any of the countries in the region.

AID delivery

Between 2002 and 2007 Afghanistan received $15 billion in aid. While the money, per capita, fell far short of the money spent on other post-conflict areas like Kosovo or East Timor, the main shortcoming was the manner of delivery and distribution of the aid. Donor funding cycles are usually annual. By the time the money is actually released to the beneficiary; there are only a few months left for the actual execution of the project. An estimated two thirds of the aid money is through the external budget or outside government spending. The Afghan government has continuously argued and with good reason that this erodes both its credibility as well as its legitimacy since it lacks control over the lion's share of resources spent in the country. This approach also prevents the Afghan government from being able to make long-term plans and strategic sectoral policies. Scattered and direct spending by donors makes it difficult for the government to get a clear picture of the spending on any particular sector. In education for example a donor might invest in building school buildings. While these are much needed, they cannot work unless there is a commensurate commitment for teachers. Unfortunately the donor funding is driven by the donor reporting approach where the donor and the implementer are accountable to the domestic governments of the donor agencies rather than to the Afghan beneficiaries or the Afghan government. The emphasis, therefore, is on numbers and the speed with which projects are executed, rather than community involvement, sustainability and an emphasis on the end users.

The aid is disbursed through a process of contracting and sub-contracting where commissioning agencies absorb a significant share of the money of the project while the beneficiaries receive only a trickle of the project amount. With a small amount of the money coming to those actually executing the project, the tendency is to cut corners and use sub-standard material and resources. The short-term approach of the donor cycle makes it unlikely that there will be any accountability or repercussions beyond a few months even if the building collapses or the road disintegrates. A conservative estimate puts the money going back to donor countries at 40 percent of the allocation.[3]

In addition, the major donors are putting the bulk of their money in areas where their troops are based. In 2007 for example DFID, the UK government's aid agency was putting a fifth of its budget for the next three years in the southern province of Helmand where British troops are based. At the same time the US Agency for International Development had concentrated more than half its budget on Helmand and three other southern provinces[4]. The reasoning behind this was to have a combined military-reconstruction approach. The troops, it was felt, would clear out areas and the reconstruction would begin, thus showing people the beneficial impact of peace and building a stake in allegiance to the government. It would also help mitigate the adverse fallout of the military operations and the collateral damage arising out of it. Unfortunately, though the situation changed on the ground, the policy did not. Money is being poured into areas in continuing conflict which often do not have the capacity to absorb the aid, resulting in high costs, wastage and unsustainable projects. Projects can be executed under heavy armed presence but using them subsequently becomes problematic for the local population.

A community based approach which could use the inherent technical know-how of similar geographical conditions, cultural preferences, usage and materials could be extremely beneficial for the better utilisation of scarce resources. But countries like India, whose aid programme has been successful, have had no influence on the aid delivery of the international community, being content to point out that they are in a different category.

Economic Model

Most surprising perhaps is the unquestioning adoption of the free market economic model for Afghanistan. It is not clear where and why a decision was made to place the burden of economic recovery on a non-existent market.[5] Certainly the model was pushed forward at the behest of the votaries of free market and without much discussion. After thirty years of war, however, Afghanistan has none of the conditions required for a free market economy. Infrastructure was completely decimated including roads, power and water supply. According to recent government statistics, currently only "20 percent of the population have access to public power (grid-supplied) on certain days for a limited number of hours. On a per capita basis, the electricity generating capacity is "well below what it was in 1978"[6]. The present goal of electricity availability set for 2010 is below 40 kw per capita. While roads have been built, spiraling insecurity has increased the costs of road transport and made road travel impossible in some areas.

Currently Afghanistan lacks the capacity to utilise its rich resources, including its mineral wealth. An example is the agreement on the Aynak copper mines. While the agreement with the Chinese government on the exploitation of the mineral wealth of this mine is being touted as a success story since it would net the government an enormous revenue, what is not being emphasised is the fact that the copper will leave this country as raw material without any form of processing or value addition. Value addition would have generated employment and also increased the revenue generation. However, the current condition of infrastructure in Afghanistan makes it more lucrative for any mining company to take the ore out of Afghanistan and have it processed elsewhere the technology is available and can be used at a lower cost.

Let alone copper refining technology, Afghanistan is not producing the basic necessities of everyday life since there are few industries that can compete in the market on an economically viable basis without a regular power supply. Afghanistan's markets are awash with cheap Chinese household goods and second hand Pakistani clothes. Even a slight escalation in quality puts most of the goods above the reach of the ordinary Afghan consumer.

While Afghanistan and especially urban centres like Kabul are awash with plenty of money—either from aid or through the drugs and criminal economy, the wealth is not spread evenly. In the seven years of post-*Taliban* development there are almost as many people who feel they were more prosperous under the *Taliban* regime (36 percent) as feel they are more prosperous now (39 percent)[7] While this could be dismissed as a matter of perception, there is no way of dismissing the stark figures relating to poverty. Despite repeated calls for greater attention to food security, the numbers of those who cannot meet their minimum dietary needs in Afghanistan is on the rise, growing from 30 percent to 35 percent between 2005 and 2008.[8] The crisis is expected to worsen over the next few months as the impact of local drought and high global food prices push more Afghans into food insecurity. Today, on average, an Afghan family spends 77 percent of its income on food, compared to 56 percent it used to spend in 2005.

Despite the urgency, and awareness among international monitors, concern has not translated into relief. A Joint Emergency Food Appeal launched in July 2008 by the Afghan government and the UN, calling for $404 million to "feed Afghanistan's most vulnerable people who are in desperate need of food aid," was dismally under-funded. The $604 million Humanitarian Action Plan appeal launched by the UN in 2009, partly in order to meet this shortfall, also remains underfunded till date while billions is allocated for security.

According to Oxfam, the health of over a million young children and half a million women is at serious risk due to malnutrition. One out of every two Afghan children under five is stunted and 39 percent are underweight, the humanitarian agency says. In a memo to US President Barack Obama, Oxfam has warned of the possibility of significant food shortages in 2009 that could "adversely affect public health and even spark displacement and unrest."

Though 80 percent of Afghanistan's population is dependent on agriculture, the sector has been one of the most under-funded, receiving only $500 million out of the $15 billion spent on non-security related reconstruction in this country. The country's leading donor, the United States, is estimated to have spent less than 5 percent of USAID's budget for Afghanistan since 2002 on agriculture. In 2007, US spending on agriculture amounted to less than 1 percent of what it spent on security.[9]

Democratic Institutions

Nowhere has the absence of vision made itself felt more starkly than in the sphere of building of institutions of state. Afghanistan has always been a country where the centre has exercised varying degrees of control over the provinces and outlying areas. The fragmentation of the state power in the decades of war has been too well documented to bear repetition. Yet, when the western compact sat down to arrive at a consensus on the form of government that would be most beneficial in the post-conflict period, it chose a centrist form of governance with most powers concentrated in the hands of the president. It agreed upon a parliamentary democracy but subsequently chose to ban political parties from participation. In any other country this would have been described as autocratic undemocratic governance. In Afghanistan, the western countries celebrated it as a major achievement in democracy.

The parliament which was elected was kept out of decision making. Without political parties, it was much easier for a handful of powerful commanders and warlords turned parliamentarians to dominate the proceedings. Currently, parliament functions as an opposition to the government, blocking the functioning of the government as a means of leverage. Disputes are settled through deal making. Provincial councils were set up and not empowered either with political or economic powers.

The centrist model was quite in keeping with the American preference of supporting strongmen to solve intractable problems in countries in the region, seen so disastrously in the support to successive military dictators in Pakistan. Nowhere has this been exemplified better than in the person of the incumbent president Hamid Karzai. First anointing him as a messiah, the international community put all its eggs in the basket, expecting that concentrating all powers in his hands would help since he was seen as a politician willing to listen to the international community. Now that this approach has not delivered, Karzai has become the whipping boy, and all problems are being attributed to him.

The approach was not limited to the man at the top. Through the chain of governance, individuals were supported and empowered in preference to institutions. The hope that amenable individuals would help smooth the way for certain western countries, whether in the pursuit of the beneficial task of aid delivery or the more self serving interests of domestic agendas of these countries has left Afghanistan weakened, its political institutions and instruments of governance undermined, and its justice sector in complete disarray.

Rather than acknowledging that it was inadequate attention to institutions of democracy and governance that has caused this problem, the international compact has now started questioning the model of democratic governance asking whether Afghanistan is really ready for democracy or really requires it. The new mantra in support of "traditional forms of governance" is getting growing influence. However, the truth is that thirty years of war have completely changed the complexion of traditional mechanisms whether they relate to governance or delivery of justice.

Within our region however there has been no discussion on the form of governance and political system in Afghanistan. While Indian diplomats claim that this reticence is a result of their unwillingness to interfere in another country's sovereign decisions, the reality on the ground is that these issues are being debated and decisions being made under the influence of an international compact and presence. A regional input can only help by broadening the debate even if it is only to point out the problems and benefits of systems of governance including the different models of democracy in the region. Long-term sustainable relationships can only be built with Afghanistan if its institutions of governance and state are robust and provide continuity. Individuals, however pleasing, cannot replace this, and even in the short term, this approach may prove counter productive as evident from the souring of the relationship between President Karzai and the US government.

Democratic Practices

The last but perhaps most significant failure of the region including its civil society is to make linkages with democratic trends within Afghanistan. A brief window of opportunity for encouraging groups and ideas that foster democratic practices in relation to political and civil rights, human rights, women rights, media freedom and public participation is rapidly closing. Conservatism has seen a sharp increase over the past two years as has intolerance. Freedoms and spaces that had opened up in the immediate aftermath of the removal of the *Taliban* are now closing and closing fast. More conservative elements have been inducted into the government. Both the parliament and the government are seeking curbs on media freedom. Human rights are being described as a western phenomenon and women's rights as an alien concept.

While Afghanistan certainly needs to arrive at its own balance with the concept of different rights and how it implements them, there are certain fundamental freedoms and inalienable rights that cannot be negotiable in this day and age, amongst them the right to life, liberty, protection from violence and fair trial. Yet, all talk of women's rights, for example, now frequently invokes the mantra that it is all an imported concept, an argument that even some within western governments are buying into.

While Afghanistan certainly needs to arrive at its own understanding of the role of women and socially appropriate behaviour, what cannot and should not be negotiable in the name of tradition is the women's right to life and liberty. Honour killings, captivity of women and marrying girls who are underage cannot be condoned in the name of tradition. Yet, many westerners who began with simplistic notions, such as viewing the burkha or the absence of it to liberation of women, have now swung to the other extreme, some even advocating the return to customary laws, parts of which are abhorrent and a denial of the basic human rights.

This is exactly where the regions can play a very positive role. We in this region know that human rights does not mean abdication of the rights of the state, women's rights does not mean a rebuttal of Indian culture, freedom of media is not an antithesis of tradition. A Benazir Bhutto or Indira Gandhi can rule in their traditional attire. Village sarpanches in rural India sometimes wear the full ghunghat or face veil. We have and fiercely defend media freedoms but we also have the censor board. While it is true that there are social tensions in our countries that are often posited as a conflict between tradition and modernity, the noblest vision of this country is one that accepts that the best of traditional values and modern principles can coexist side by side.

In Conclusion

Recently, there has been an outcry on discussions linking India, Pakistan and Afghanistan and on how the Kashmir issue is linked to this. While a US intervention on Kashmir may certainly not be beneficial, what cannot be disregarded is that instability in the region is linked. Whether it is the relationship between India and Pakistan and its fallout on Afghanistan or the general rise in intolerance in the region—whether it is in the name of Hinduism or Islam, ethnicity or language, the social trends are linked to each other. India will not be able to isolate itself if the growing intolerance in the regional countries continues. The spillover effect will be devastating. Rather than wait for the western compact to bestow relevance on the role of the region and to decide the contours of this role, it is time the region itself began taking an initiative.

Notes and References

1. The United States currently accounts for 24,900 of the 56,420 troops, the UK 8,300, and Germany with 3,460. The other largest troop contributing nations are, in order of numbers: Canada, France, Italy, Netherlands, Poland and Australia. All other nations provide less than 1000 troops each. (Source ISAF placemat February 13, 2009)
2. Acbar Advocacy Series: Falling Short: Aid Effectiveness in Afghanistan, March 2008.
3. Former NATO Senior Civilian Representative Daan Everts in an interview with the author published in *Al Jazeera.*
4. The author. Interviews with DFID and USAID official cited in an article in *Financial Times.*
5. More recently, the approach was enshrined as one of the defining tenets of the vision for Afghanistan as "a society of hope and prosperity based on a strong private sector-led market economy" in what is known as Afghanistan's National Development Strategy (ANDS), finalised and adopted at the Paris Conference in June 2008.
6. ANDS.
7. The Asia Foundation, Afghanistan in 2008, A Survey of the Afghan People.
8. UN Humanitarian Action Plan for Afghanistan, February 2009.
9. Oxfam, Memo to US President, 2009.

10

Idea and Politics of 'Reconciliation' with the *Taliban* in Afghanistan

Vishal Chandra

> *"We have a common task—Afghanistan, the US and the civilized world—to launch a joint struggle against fundamentalism. If fundamentalism comes to Afghanistan, war will continue for many years. Afghanistan will turn into a centre of world smuggling for narcotic drugs. Afghanistan will be turned into a centre for terrorism."*[1]
>
> — Former Afghan President Najibullah in his interview to *The New York Times*, March 1992

The idea of engaging, co-opting, incorporating or integrating elements of the former *Taliban* regime in the ongoing political process is as old as the 'war on terror.' In fact, Pakistan had first proposed the thesis of 'moderate *Taliban*' immediately after the overthrow of the *Taliban* regime in Kabul in November 2001.[2] Since then the idea of talking to the *Taliban* and the politics around it has come a long way. *Taliban* are often regarded as indispensable to any effort aimed at national reconciliation and peace in Afghanistan. From a mainly Western perspective, it is one viable way of stabilising the country and thereby ensuring an early withdrawal of the Western forces from the region. However, the *Taliban* leadership, supposed to be based in Pakistan, has so far rebutted all offers of negotiations. They have, instead, successfully exploited the weaknesses in the Western approach and strategy and have transformed the war to their advantage.

The nine-year-old US-led war is a striking account of a war gone awfully wrong, of losing while winning, of undoing the done. The narrative on the idea and politics of national reconciliation evolved as the *Taliban* returned from the periphery to the centre of Afghan politics and conflict. In the larger Western perspective, the Afghan war is an unavoidable war with an unavoidable defeat. The confusion over ways and means of dealing with the widened Afghan conflict is more than palpable. What were considered as unacceptable or not-so-acceptable propositions in early years of the war on terror are now put forth as the way forward. Since 2006-07, the idea of reconciliation with a particular variety and category of *Taliban* has been integral to the mainstream non-US Western discourses on Afghanistan. This is not to suggest that the US, despite differences of opinion within the Obama Administration, remains opposed to Kabul's idea of reaching out to the *Taliban*. The January 28, 2010 international conference on Afghanistan in London, the June 2010 National Consultative Peace *Jirga* in Kabul, and the July 2010 Kabul Conference, have only reinforced Karzai Government's growing quest for an international as well as national consensus on its reconciliation plans.

This paper is a modest attempt to examine the evolution as well as prospects of the idea and politics of 'reconciliation' with the *Taliban* in Afghanistan. The paper posits that the surge in reconciliation efforts aimed at the *Taliban* is an inevitable outcome of the shortcomings in the West-sponsored political process in the country and the ambivalence of the US' allies— both Pakistan and NATO. In prospective, the *Taliban* are likely to emerge stronger, and thereafter it may either mutate and metamorphose into a more virulent movement or get splintered and subsumed in the intra-Afghan power dynamics in the coming decade. However, as of now, much would depend on the West's staying power and extent to which the US is able to pressurise and transform Pakistan. At a much broader level, the Afghan war is a war of ideas, reflective of the politico-religious transformation brought about by the jehadisation, militarization and internationalisation of the Afghan civil war during the 1980s. It will continue to pose a serious challenge to the socio-political stability and the centuries-old synergetic Islam of the south-central Asian region and even beyond for decades to follow.

It needs to be emphasised here that the *Taliban* are also a manifestation of Pakistan's geo-politics of the 1990s. The paper recognises the rising limitations of the US in the region, yet argues that the idea of reconciliation with the *Taliban* in its present form is not workable. It would only strengthen the position of the *Taliban* and their allies, especially *Al Qaeda*. It would also reinforce the pro-*Taliban* elements within the Pakistani establishment in particular, which in turn would regionalise the conflict and further complicate matters for the US. It would be prudent to remember that unlike the *Taliban* (whether Afghan or Pakistani) and their sponsors east of the Durand Line, the West has much to loose by exiting and re-abandoning Afghanistan. However, as the West scouts for an exit strategy, and the Karzai Government rushes for reconciliation, it would be interesting to see how the reconciliation process towards the *Taliban* has been shaping up over the years, the challenges inherent, and its likely implications.

Evolution of the Discourse and Strategy

The key objective of the US-led war on terror, launched on the Afghan soil in October 2001, was not to fight the *Taliban* and their ideology in every nook and corner of the country. It was primarily focussed on destroying *Al Qaeda* and the *Taliban* regime which sheltered them. The US approach was thus short-term and narrowly defined. The US invasion of Iraq in March 2003, while the nascent transitional government under Hamid Karzai was still grappling with the issue of legitimacy, proved fatal. It not only led to diversion of much-needed resources and international attention critical to institution building in Afghanistan, but also provided the *Taliban* and its allies a window of opportunity to reconstitute and prepare for a long haul. The pro-*Taliban* elements within the Pakistani establishment and the polity too felt vindicated. It was aptly observed by Ahmed Rashid:

> Indeed, in March 2002, just three months after the defeat of the *Taliban*, the United States began to withdraw its Special Forces, surveillance satellites and drones from Afghanistan to prepare for war in Iraq. Distracted by Baghdad, it did not notice what was happening in the tribal agencies. By the time the Pakistan army entered South Waziristan in March 2004, the extremists were so well entrenched that 250 Pakistani soldiers were killed in the first encounters.[3]

Interestingly, both the US, and to a lesser degree, Kabul, in a way, adopted a policy of trivialising the potential threat from the *Taliban* regrouping along and across the Durand Line. While the US was engaged in a protracted struggle to 'liberate' Iraq, Karzai was busy in curbing the influence of the former United Front or the Northern Alliance within his government. It is noteworthy that in July 2004 Karzai had referred to private militias of various factional commanders as the greatest threat, greater than the *Taliban*, to the stability of the country.[4] However, at the same time, he was aware of the urgency to shore up support among the Pashtuns who remained sceptical of his leadership as well as the West-sponsored Bonn process.

In the run up to the October 2004 presidential election, Hamid Karzai had first offered amnesty to the *Taliban* and Hezb-e-Islami (Hekmatyar group) cadres, excluding the 100-150 top members from both the groups. In March 2005, he appointed Sebghatullah Mojadeddi, a veteran Afghan leader, as the head of the newly initiated *Programme Takhim-e Solh* (PTS) to wean away the middle and lower ranking *Taliban* and Hezb fighters. In May 2005, Mojadeddi reportedly extended the amnesty offer to even Mullah Omar and Gulbuddin Hekmatyar, including the *Taliban* detainees at Guantanamo Bay and Bagram detention centres.[5] In March 2007, while speaking to a German daily, *Der Spiegel,* Karzai expressed his willingness to 'embrace' Mullah Omar and Hekmatyar for peace and stability in Afghanistan. However, at the same time, Karzai stated, "it is the Afghan people who should decide on the atrocities committed against the Afghan people."[6]

Meanwhile, the British commanders in the Musa Qala District of the southern Helmand Province had entered into a pact with the *Taliban* in October 2006, a month after the Waziristan Pact was signed with the local *Taliban* in Pakistan. These pacts, which ensured nothing more than a brief ceasefire, only strengthened the *Taliban*. The Musa Qala Pact withered away within months and the *Taliban* held on to the district for nearly ten months, from February to December 2007, in the face of full presence of the British forces. The NATO operations in other parts of southern Afghanistan also brought to the fore the lack of preparedness and conviction on its part towards the Afghan mission.

On May 8, 2007, a bill calling on the government to open talks with the Afghan *Taliban* was reportedly passed by the upper house of the Afghan Parliament or the Meshrano *Jirga.*[7] Interestingly, two senior former *Taliban* officials based in Kabul— Mullah Wakil Ahmed Muttawakil, the former *Taliban* foreign minister, and Mullah Zaeef, the former *Taliban* ambassador to Pakistan—called upon Kabul to open talks with the *Taliban* at the same time.[8] The National Front (NF) of Afghanistan or the Jabha-ye-Milli, comprising of former United Front (or the Northern Alliance) leaders and some ex-communists, declared in early April 2008 that they had been negotiating with the *Taliban*. The NF spokesperson had reportedly asked for recognition of the *Taliban* as a political or a military party.[9] The very next month, in May 2008, Mostafa Zahir, the only member from the former Afghan royal family to have joined the National Front, had reportedly proposed the establishment of a transitional government comprising members from the present government and the *Taliban* and other anti-government groups.[10]

Interestingly, despite the failure of the Musa Qala Pact, British intelligence agents continued to negotiate with the *Taliban* in Helmand.

The Daily Telegraph, in a report published in December 2007, alleged that the British MI6 agents had had several meetings with the local *Taliban.*[11] The British tactic of negotiating with the *Taliban* at the local level was resented by both Karzai and the US commanders. Karzai in January 2008 categorically stated that Helmand "was one part of the country" which "suffered after the arrival of the British forces" for until then his government had been 'fully in charge' of the province.[12] He thereafter appointed former *Taliban* governor of Urozgan Province as the chief of the Musa Qala district. The very next month in February 2008, the newly appointed governor of Helmand Province, proposed to initiate negotiations with "second and third-tier *Taliban*" at the behest of the central government.[13] In the same month, Karzai expelled a European Union official and former advisor to the British High Commission in Islamabad, Michael Semple, for negotiating with the *Taliban* without the consent of the Afghan Government.[14]

Interestingly, though the NATO has officially been opposed to any dealing with the *Taliban*, the individual member-states, especially those involved in counter-*Taliban* operations, have had their own perception and strategies to deal with the *Taliban* at the local level. Their tactics have played a role in re-shaping the Western discourse on ways and means of stabilising Afghanistan which led to a surge in efforts to explore the prospects of reconciliation with the *Taliban* by 2006-07. A caveated NATO was more likely to call for reconciliation with the *Taliban* and an exit strategy. Apart from the British, the Canadian and Dutch commanders too had reportedly been trying to reach out to the local *Taliban.*[15] In fact, the Af-Pak strategy announced by the Obama Administration on March 27, 2009 was reflective of the growing consensus in the West that there were no military solutions to the Afghan conflict and that their involvement in Afghanistan was not open-ended. The Obama Administration's decision to deploy 21,000 additional troops in Afghanistan had evoked a mixed reaction among the European allies. The March 2009 Af-Pak strategy had also referred to the need to integrate "non-ideologically committed" and "reconcilable insurgents" while reinforcing the military and civilian component in the US-led effort. The impact of the European discourse and the growing impatience of the American public as well as the political class on the new US strategy were thus clearly evident.

As for Kabul, it has been trying reach out to the *Taliban* elements willing to renounce violence and accept the Afghan Constitution since 2004-05. The Karzai Government, in fact, had integrated some of the former *Taliban* elements in the government structures, especially at the provincial level. However, Kabul has always been suspicious of the reconciliation initiatives being made without its knowledge by various extra-governmental and foreign entities as it undermined its authority and instead reinforced the position of the *Taliban* and its allies. At the same time, Kabul has been forthcoming in soliciting support from foreign actors with influence either over the *Taliban* or Pakistan or both, especially Saudi Arabia and Turkey, in opening channels of communication with them.

But, what is significant here is the extent to which the *Taliban* are willing to yield space and work towards a negotiated settlement. It is difficult to be definitive about the *Taliban shura* to which Kabul could be talking to or the extent to which the Afghan Government has been able to reach out to the senior *Taliban* leadership and the Haqqanis based in Pakistan. In this context, it is worth quoting Siraj-ud Din Haqqani, son of senior *Taliban* commander Jalal-ud Din Haqqani, who had stated, "We cannot go outside Afghanistan to participate in any talks, as we face difficulties in our movement. In case of any talks, we send fifth or sixth-rank leadership to negotiate."[16] Though the *Taliban* publicly denounce the legitimacy and the authority of the Karzai Government, negotiations between the two cannot be completely ruled out.

At the same time, there also seems to be a perception among the *Taliban* leadership that there is no point in negotiating with Kabul, a losing side, especially when they have an upper-hand. With the Obama Administration in its revised strategy announced in December 2009 referring to a time frame for beginning the withdrawal of American forces by mid-2011, *Taliban* could be sensing 'victory.' In their view, a yet another superpower is about to be humbled on the Afghan soil. In fact, their policy and approach, and those of their Pakistani-sponsors, remain largely driven by their long-held conviction that the West will have to sooner or later withdraw from Afghanistan. Even from the conditions attached by both Kabul and the *Taliban* for initiating the negotiations, it is clear that they remain strongly sceptical of each other's exact objectives and machinations. For the *Taliban*, Kabul and their Western backers are out to divide and weaken the movement, and for Kabul and the US, the *Al Qaeda* aligned Afghan *Taliban* leadership is uncompromising and beyond the scope of reconciliation. However, even if the top *Taliban* leadership is in touch with Kabul through its intermediaries, the possibility of it being part of the *Taliban* tactic to wait out the West cannot be ruled out at all.

The Pakistan-based core Afghan *Taliban* leadership have all through been consistent in its opposition to the idea of 'moderate *Taliban*.' As early as November 2001, Mullah Omar had asserted that "there is no such thing in the *Taliban*" and that "all *Taliban* are moderate." He opined,

"There are two things: extremism ("ifraat", or doing something to excess) and conservatism ("tafreet", or doing something insufficiently). So in that sense, we are all moderates - taking the middle path."[17]

Eight years later in March 2009 when President Obama initially referred to the prospects of reaching out to reconcilable *Taliban* elements in an interview to *The New York Times,* the purported *Taliban* spokesperson had dismissed it as "illogical" and said that it "does not require any response or reaction". He had asserted that "the *Taliban* are united, have one leader, one aim, one policy" and wondered as to "why the US is talking about moderate *Taliban*" and "if it means those who are not fighting and are sitting in their homes, then talking to them is meaningless. This really is surprising the *Taliban*."[18]

In April 2009, Siraj-ud Din Haqqani, too had categorically denied the presence of 'moderates' in the *Taliban* rank and file. He rhetorically stated that the *Taliban* are the ones "living in the mountains, spending sleepless nights and eating dried bread, but struggling to liberate their homeland from occupation forces" and not the ones who have renounced jihad and are leading a luxurious life.[19]

Prospects: Key Questions and Issues of Concern

The Obama Administration in its revised Af-Pak strategy of December 2009 has announced another additional deployment of 30,000 US troops, over and above 21,000 US troops deployed as part of its March 2009 new Af-Pak strategy. The idea is to break and reverse the *Taliban* momentum so that greater security responsibility can be transferred on to the Afghan security forces and the Western troops can subsequently begin to withdraw by July 2011. With the deployment of Western troops crossing the 100,000 mark, the Afghan war is certainly peaking and entering into perhaps a new phase. On the idea of reconciliation with the *Taliban*, the revised strategy, similar to the March 2009 Af-Pak strategy, supported the Afghan Government's initiatives "to open the door to those *Taliban* who abandon violence and respect the human rights of their fellow citizens."[20]

With the revised US strategy giving out a time-frame for starting the troop pullout and endorsing Kabul's initiatives to woo the *Taliban*, numerous sets of queries assume critical importance. First of all, where is the incentive for the *Taliban* to reconcile with Kabul, or for their Pakistani-sponsors to act against the Afghan *Taliban*? Despite recent US pressure, Pakistan Army remains averse to taking action against the Haqqani network operating out of the North Waziristan region as well as the leadership council or the *rahbar shura* of the Afghan *Taliban* based in Quetta or Karachi. In the given circumstances, are Kabul and the West in a position to lay down terms and conditions for negotiating with the *Taliban*? Given the weak negotiating position of Kabul, what are the terms and conditions on which the *Taliban* are willing to talk to Kabul? What are the potential implications for Afghanistan's current constitution, evolving state structures, and its foreign policy? Will the *Taliban* guerrillas disarm or will they be integrated into the Afghan national army and police? To what extent is the *Taliban* leadership willing to work with the minority ethnic groups? Are the *Taliban* willing to sever their links with *Al Qaeda* and host of other Islamist entities active in the south-central Asia region? The answers to the above queries are too well-known to be elaborated here.

The above issues indubitably have far-reaching consequences, especially as the West is stuck and is looking for an 'honourable exit' out of Afghanistan. There are no two opinions that growing demand for reconciliation with the *Taliban* in its current form and position will only work to the advantage of the *Taliban*, sponsored and supported by elements across the Durand Line. It only reinforces their resolve to continue with their 'jihad' at the expense of the Afghan government and the nine-year-old state-building process in Afghanistan because of the shortcomings in the West's Afghan strategy.

It is doubtful if a weak Kabul and a divided Western coalition eager for an exit holds any incentive even for those willing to defect and be part of the reconciliation process. The Afghan national peace and reconciliation commission too has failed so far in realising its objectives. Both Kabul and the commission were never in a position to provide security and effectively rehabilitate the *Taliban* elements willing to join the new political process. There is no doubt that a well-resourced multi-level national reconciliation programme is required to wean away the more amenable *Taliban* elements from the hardcore, but it cannot be at the expense of the fundamental values on which a modern Afghan state is being built. Kabul's effort to reach out to the disgruntled elements and groupings should be within a well-defined policy framework. At the same time, it is worth emphasising that national reconciliation efforts are doomed to fail unless Afghan state structures and institutions are strengthened. As for the two key elements of the Kabul-led peace process – reintegration and reconciliation – the focus should be on integrating and rehabilitating low-level fighters or relatively independent mid-level *Taliban* commanders. Reconciliation, which is aimed at the senior elements of the *Taliban* leadership based in Pakistan, is too risky for Kabul.

It is equally important to bear in mind the security concerns of some of the regional countries, especially Russia, India, Iran and the bordering Central Asian Republics, with regard to the rising power of the *Taliban*, and its potential demonstrative and motivational effect on aspiring Islamists across south-central Asia. Interestingly, there was hardly any reference to the US partnering with regional countries on the Afghanistan issue, except for Pakistan, in the Obama Administration's December 2009 revised strategy in contrast to the Af-Pak strategy unveiled earlier in March 2009. Though establishing an "effective partnership" with Pakistan is one of the three key components of the revised strategy, the limitations of the US' perceived leverages over Pakistan is more than evident. It is difficult to comprehend at the moment whether the US' greater engagement with Pakistan would lead to any substantive transformation or bring about any notable structural change in the policies of the Pakistan military establishment.

With the Obama Administration explicitly stating that the Afghan mission is not an open-ended affair, where is the need for Pakistan to give up its existing or prospective leverages within Afghanistan. For the emboldened pro-*Taliban* elements within the Pakistani establishment, it is time to extract maximum concession and aid from the West, and to create conditions for the grand bargain with the US on the Afghan issue. As for Kabul, it has been under increasing pressure to reconcile with sections of *Taliban* in view of the West's growing quest for a quick, unambiguous, and a well-scripted exit strategy from Afghanistan. However, unless Pakistan gives up its Cold War era policy of sponsoring and using a wide range of radical religious outfits to further its perceived regional agenda, Kabul's reconciliation initiatives will continue to be rebuffed by the *Taliban*. To sound a note of caution, those attempting reconciliation must ensure that it should not lead to greater violence, religious extremism and instability in the region.

Moreover, the US has to acknowledge that its selective approach towards other militant Islamist groups operating out of Pakistan has only strengthened the *Taliban* and the pro-*Taliban* elements within the Pakistani state structure over a period of time. During the last eight years, Islamist radical groups of all hues have come together despite their ideological differences and coordinated their activities in an effective manner. Many of the India-focussed jihadi organizations have relocated to the tribal areas and have been working with the *Taliban* and *Al Qaeda* against the interests of the US. Ironically, their nexus with ISI is an acknowledged fact in the West. Be it the March 2009 new Af-Pak or the December 2009 revised strategy, the US remains fixated with its stated core goal of disrupting, dismantling, and defeating *Al Qaeda* and its safe havens in Pakistan, and to prevent their return to Pakistan or Afghanistan. What is to be understood here is that both *Taliban* and *Al Qaeda* are not acting independent of various Pakistan-based extremist Islamist groupings who have made a common cause with them.

It is therefore imperative to the success of the Western mission in the Af-Pak region to galvanize regional support and stay the course until Afghan state institutions are relatively strong. The only way forward, as well as the way out, is to help build institutions of governance in Afghanistan and to bring about an effective structural transformation within the Pakistani state. Meanwhile, a sustained military pressure on anti-government and extremist groups in the Af-Pak region is critical to developing the capacities and strengthening the authority of the Afghan state. President Obama rightly pointed out that it is a "war of necessity". It is also worth quoting from the concluding remarks made in the March 2009 White Paper of the US Interagency Policy Group's Report on US Policy toward Afghanistan and Pakistan that "there are no quick fixes to achieve US national security interests" in the region and "the danger of failure is real and the implications are grave."[21] Therefore, any stop-gap measure or a short-term approach to dealing with the Af-Pak challenge at this stage has the potential to destabilise the entire region. If re-abandoning Afghanistan-Pakistan region is the strategy in the making then the West may have to come back sooner than later to 'fix' the region again, and to fight the more virulent descendants of the *Taliban* and the likes. The West still has a choice.

Notes and References

1. Edward A. Gargan, "Afghan President Says US Should See Him as Ally against Militant Islam," *The New York Times*, March 10, 1992.
2. It was said that Pakistan had tried to convince the former anti-Soviet and later a *Taliban* commander, Jalal-ud din Haqqani, to carve out a faction of 'moderate *Taliban*' who could be included in the Bonn Process. However, Haqqani reportedly refused to yield to the Pakistani pressure. See Syed Saleem Shahzad, '*Taliban*'s New Commander Ready for a Fight', *Asia Times Online*, March 20, 2006, at http://www.atimes.com/atimes/South_Asia/HE20Df02.html. Also see, 'Jalal-ud Din Haqqani', at http://www.pbs.org/wgbh/pages/frontline/taliban/militants/haqqani.html.
3. Ahmed Rashid, "Looking for Osama", *Indian Express*, March 06, 2006, at http://www.indianexpress.com/oldStory/89037/.
4. Carlotta Gall and David Rohde, "Afghan President Describe Militias as the Top Threat", *The New York Times*, July 12, 2004, at http://www.nytimes.com/2004/07/12/world/afghan-president-describes-militias-as-the-top-threat.html?pagewanted=all.
5. 'Kabul Hints at Amnesty for Omar, Hekmatyar', *Dawn*, May 9, 2005, at http://www.dawn.com/2005/05/10/top7.htm.
6. 'Afghanistan Open to Dialogue with Militants', *Der Spiegel*, March 6, 2007, at http://www.spiegel.de/international/0,1518,469876,00.html
7. 'Afghan Bill Calls for Talks with *Taliban*', *The New York Times*, May 9,

2007, at http://www.nytimes.com/aponline/world/AP-Afghan-*Taliban*-Talks.html.

8. 'Afghan Papers See Taleban as Possible Talks Partner', *Sabawoon Online*, February 16, 2007, at http://www.sabawoon.com/news/miniheadlines.asp?dismode=article&artid=35569.
9. Zubair Babakarkhil, "AUNF for Recognition of *Taliban* as a Party", *Pajhwok Afghan News*, April 30, 2008, at http://www.pajhwok.com/viewstory.asp?lng=eng&id=54259.
10. 'Ex-Prince Wants *Taliban* Brought into Afghan Government', *The New York Times*, May 7, 2008, at http://www.nytimes.com/reuters/world/internationalafghan-crisis.html.
11. Thomas Harding and Tom Coghlan, "Britain in Secret Talks with the *Taliban*", *The Daily Telegraph,* December 26, 2007, at http://www.telegraph.co.uk/news/uknews/1573687/Britain-in-secret-talks-with-the-*Taliban*.html.
12. David Charter, Anthony Loyd and Richard Beeston, "The British have made matters worse, says Afghan President", *The Times*, January 25, 2008, at http://www.timesonline.co.uk/tol/news/world/asia/article3248318.ece.
13 "New Helmand Governor Confirms Desire for Talks with *Taliban*", *Radio Free* Europe/Radio Liberty, *March 21, 2008, at http://www.rferl.org/content/article/1079672.html.*
14. Henry McDonald, "We Can Persuade *Taliban* to be Peaceful – Expelled EU Man", *Guardian,* February 16, 2008, at http://www.guardian.co.uk/world/2008/feb/16/afghanistan.terrorism.
15. Graeme Smith, "Canada Reaches Out to *Taliban*", *The Globe and Mail,* May 1, 2008, at http://www.theglobeandmail.com/servlet/story/LAC.20080501.AFGHAN01/TPStory/TPInternational/Asia/.
16. "No moderates in *Taliban* ranks: Haqqani", *The News*, International Edition, April 17, 2009, at http://thenews.jang.com.pk/top_story_ detail.asp? Id=21576.
17. "Interview with Mullah Omar – transcript", *BBC Pashto*, November 15, 2001, at http://news.bbc.co.uk/2/hi/south_asia/1657368.stm.
18. "*Taliban* Say Obama's Call on Moderates "Illogical"", *The New York Times*, March 10, 2009, at http://www.nytimes.com/reuters/2009/03/10/world/international-us-afghan-taliban-obama.html.
19. "No moderates in *Taliban* ranks: Haqqani", *The News*, International Edition, April 17, 2009, at http://thenews.jang.com.pk/top_story_detail.asp?Id=21576
20. See "Remarks by the President in Address to the Nation on the Way Forward in Afghanistan and Pakistan", December 01, 2009, at http://www.whitehouse.gov/the-press-office/remarks-president-address-nation-way-forward-afghanistan-and-pakistan.
21. See "White Paper of the Interagency Policy Group's Report on US Policy toward Afghanistan and Pakistan", March 01, 2009, at http://www.whitehouse.gov/assets/documents/Afghanistan-Pakistan_White_Paper.pdf.

11

Empowering Grassroots through Capacity Building Measures: Indian Initiatives in Afghanistan

Mondira Dutta

Introduction

Afghanistan is seen as a bridge connecting India, Central Asia and Iran. From a security point of view, Afghanistan is critical to the rest of South Asia. The massive loss of lives, the continued food insecurity, the displacement of approximately six million people and the disabling of another three million, in addition to the severe reduction in social services, are some of the major problems that grip Afghanistan today. Even with trilateral discussions on in the West and Pakistan getting active in the Swat valley, ending of the tragic conflict in Afghanistan still seems to be shrouded in mystery. Promoting national reconciliation, ushering in lasting peace, stability and respect for human rights in the country seem to have become a distant dream.

The perception about Afghanistan in the present situation is far from being nostalgic. It is hardly a scene of the shared history of our common past. If one studies the rise in violence in Afghanistan's history and the deterioration of our own internal security environment, it is visibly clear that there exists a strong positive correlation between them. Issues of terrorism, security, extremism compel India to consider Afghanistan from a contemporary viewpoint rather than one from the point of view of our shared history.

The US led war in Afghanistan following the 9/11 attacks brought the world community together pledging support towards assisting the tattered and battered Afghanistan in its reconstruction process. Post *Taliban*, India came out in a big way providing aid and participating in the reconstruction efforts. India has been one of the fore runners in the reconstruction process and developing the capacity building measures of Afghanistan. Compared to the needs of the Afghan people and the Afghan government, India's contribution may be considered a miniscule but India has been able to restore full diplomatic relations, and has provided USD 1.2 billion in aid for Afghanistan's reconstruction and development so far. It has entered into partnership with the Afghan government in a wide range of sectors such as hydro-electricity, road construction, agriculture, industry, telecommunications, information and broadcasting, education and health. Today India is among the top four countries who are actively participating in the reconstruction process.

According to experts, by rebuilding Afghanistan, India not only hopes to achieve greater regional stability, but also aspires to counter Pakistan's influence in Kabul, while countering terrorism and extremism movements. India is also conscious that Afghanistan is a potential route for accessing the Central Asian energy. India is an observer of the Shanghai Cooperation Organisation. It has been pursuing better relations with Central Asian states for energy cooperation through its status as an observer of the Shanghai Cooperation Organisation and through TAPI.

Some of the sectors of Afghanistan identified by the Afghan government as priority areas for development, have been helped significantly by India. All the projects undertaken in partnership with the Government of Afghanistan are in alignment with the Afghanistan's National Development Strategy with a focus on local ownership of assets. As a result India's reconstruction effort becomes distinctive. It is not only guided entirely by the priorities of the government of Afghanistan[1] but the majority of the reconstruction programmes are implemented by India itself without involving the other countries and thus making it cost effective. Indian Prime Minister's visit to Kabul aimed at consolidating these efforts and sending out a message of solidarity and trust to the war-scarred nation, deeply divided along ethnic lines.

Besides assisting with the reconstruction process, India has also engaged in empowering and strengthening the local capacity of the Afghans at the grassroots level. This is an important factor in achieving sustainability of a project. The challenge to absorptive capacity in fact has been the most important concern of India's assistance. No assistance can be considered as complete without incorporating the absorptive capacity. A great deal of the international aid in Afghanistan is not carefully structured and hence acts as barriers and pose hurdles for programmes to get executed. There are not enough bases created in terms of manpower, maintenance and in terms of sustaining that particular project after it has been handed over by the concerned donor agency. This is a common problem faced by the developing countries who receive external assistance. The issue of absorptive capacity needs to be factored in and India has tried to do so by bringing in the element of consistency between the capacity building programmes and the projects undertaken. The challenge is to ensure that there is an adequate number of technical manpower available in Afghanistan to run all the projects after they are handed over. If not, the failure would be a reflection of the donor agency rather than that of the concerned Afghan ministry.

The purpose of this paper is to highlight India's assistance to the reconstruction process of Afghanistan particularly in terms of capacity building measures and empowering the capacity of the local Afghans.

Limitations of External Assistance

There are limitations to any recovery process especially in a conflict ridden zone like Afghanistan. While external assistance is necessary for the reconstruction process and developing the capacity building measures, the donor agency is at times unable to deliver the necessary visibility and transparency due to several limitations. There is no short-cut method of developing capacity building for the local Afghans. The empowerment of programmes for the locals, if undertaken in a quick fix manner, tends to get implemented in a biased ad hoc mode. It rather requires a long term multi dimensional commitment and needs to be implemented in a long drawn phased manner.[2]

Since most of the capacity building measures adopted in Afghanistan are externally driven, the recipients' priorities and local capacities are seldom considered. Sometimes the agenda of the external actors are served rather than that of the recipient's and western models are imposed on the host country in the name of capacity building. The sustainability of such projects have not come about due to a lack of ownership.[3]

There exists insufficient coordination among the donor agencies.[4] The measures may be supplementary and duplicate each others effort. Despite the existence of guidelines from the international agencies, the programmes are run uncoordinated with disparate interests and different mandates. Further a delayed assistance could lead to a lack of trust and hope. The delays between pledges, commitments and disbursement in Afghanistan have often led to discontinuation of a project.

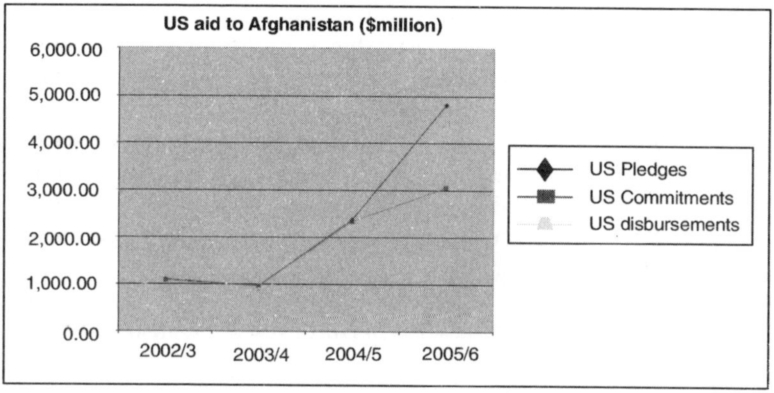

Figure 1

Figure I, shows the wide gaps between pledges, commitments and disbursements. Moreover, more than 75 percent of all aid to Afghanistan fund projects that are either directly implemented or contracted by donors. Such a gesture defeats the whole purpose and discourages the state from assuming legitimacy and responsibility. "A government that cannot report to its parliament about public expenditure can hardly be called democratic; no matter how many elections it holds".[5] A prompt translation of the promise goes a long way in touching the lives of the poor. Lengthy procedural formalities should be done away with.

The lack of priorities among the donor agencies often leads to the training capacities being imparted in a fragmented approach.[6] The donors' propensity for financing a plethora of small scale projects across a large number of sectors have very often been falsely justified as 'doing something is better than doing nothing'. The poor rate of return for any particular project has also led to the right priorities getting ignored.

Indian Efforts towards Reconstruction

India has played a significant role since 2002 in the reconstruction process of Afghanistan. This was mainly initiated to reinstate democracy and development back in the country so that Afghanistan becomes a source of regional stability and can avoid the path of extremism and terrorism.

India has undertaken projects virtually in all parts of Afghanistan, in a wide range of sectors. A few of the major projects are mentioned below:

- Construction of Transmission Lines
- Humanitarian Food Assistance Programme administered through World Food Programme
- Construction of roads such as (Zaranj to Delaram)
- Reconstruction and completion of Salma Dam Power Project in Herat province
- Construction of Afghan Parliament
- Reconstruction of Indira Gandhi Institute of Child Health (IGICH) in Kabul
- Reconstruction of Habibia School
- Digging of 26 tube wells in Northwest Afghanistan
- Gifting vehicles
- Setting up of 5 toilet-cum-public sanitation complexes
- Telephone exchanges in 11 provinces connecting to Kabul
- Expansion of National TV network

The completed projects in Afghanistan initiated by the government of India since (2002 to 2007) may be clubbed together under six heads. These are (Refer Table 1):

Table 1: Completed Projects in Afghanistan by Government of India (2002-2007)

S. No.	*Project Heads*
1	Social Development
2	Infra Structure Development
3	Training, Skill and Capacity Building
4	Economic Development
5	Contribution to Reconstruction Fund
6	Technology and Scientific Upgradation
	Total

Source: http://meakabul.nic.in

1. Social Development includes consignment for immediate humanitarian relief, medicines, educational kits, books, reconstruction of schools, donation of desks and benches for the school, and construction of toilets
2. Infrastructure development includes the supply of aircrafts, busses and vehicles. It also considers the construction of transmission lines and solar electrification
3. The third sector focuses on the development of capacity building measures through training of school teachers, ICT

professionals, doctors, diplomats, skill development, providing of sewing machines, banking, etc.

4. Economic development includes digging deep wells, agriculture, and construction of cold storage, etc.
5. The Contribution to reconstruction process includes Afghan Government budget and World Bank managed Afghan Reconstruction Trust Fund
6. Technology and Scientific Upgradation include the restoration/revamping of Information systems, TV satellite, telecommunication, setting up of common facilities service centre, TV studio, a TV transmitter, a mobile TV satellite uplink and a TV relay centre.

Figure No. 2 Depicts the Budget Expenditure on Each of the Sectors.

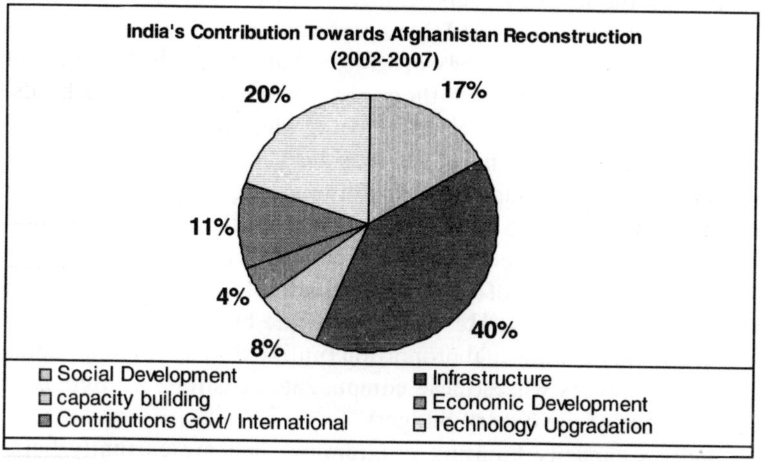

Figure 2

The figure shows infrastructure development has the highest priority followed by technology and scientific upgradation and social development.[7] A section of the pie (8 percent) goes towards training, skill and capacity building measures. Some of the programmes under other heads, such as infrastructure, technology and scientific upgradation, and social development also incorporate capacity building and skill upgradation programme.

Capacity-Building and Skill Upgradation

Building capacity and empowering the local institutions in conflict ridden Afghanistan is a challenge for the world community. A participatory approach with an aim at social empowerment seems to be a possibility despite the massive restriction of political environments. The degree of development intervention depends on the extent to which institutional capacity can be built. In a situation where the ingredients of institutional capacity building are not in the right places, 'participation and empowerment' emerging from the development initiatives may become short-lived but there will be an element of contribution (however small it may be) towards building a foundation for longer-term improvement in the quality of life in Afghanistan. Therefore, it is of immense importance that capacity building measures are implemented on a regular basis.

During the last few years Afghanistan has entered an important period of history where the Afghans are seeking to rebuild their society with external assistance. They are aware that ultimately this effort is primarily to be directed by them and carried forward. With skill development and capacity building being identified as the key areas of priority, the Indian initiatives may lead the way in tackling the massive challenge of institution building in Afghanistan. The Indian initiatives have tried to be in conformity with the local government priorities and have been in co-ordination with other donors. A maximum utilisation of the locally available sub-contactors and materials, as far as possible, has reduced the budget on security and salaries to only a miniscule proportion (unlike the case of other donor agencies/countries where these components constitute as high as 65 to 85 percent of the overall budget).

India's capacity building programmes that are currently being implemented are ambitious. Most visible ones of these are the scholarships awarded to persons who finish school and come to India for graduate and undergraduate studies. These scholarships are awarded to people who are already working either in government or elsewhere. They come to India for short courses to enhance their own technical skills and technological capabilities. These scholarships will help in training the next generation of persons who would act as the resource persons deeply committed to Afghanistan and be available to the Afghan government for addressing its future needs. Inclusive in the capacity building are a range of other programmes. There are some civil servants who are attached to different ministries who act as trainers.

There are currently about five thousand Indian workers and security personnel working on different relief and reconstruction projects in Afghanistan. Since 2006, following the increased incidents of kidnappings and attacks, India has also sent the country's paramilitary force to guard its border with China and to guard its workers. In addition there are about five hundred police currently deployed in Afghanistan.

Some of the Indian initiatives for capacity building are summarised as:

- 500 Indian Council for Cultural Relations (ICCR) long-term university scholarships
- 500 short-term Indian Technical and Economic Cooperation (ITEC) training programmes for Afghan nationals annually from 2006-07 onwards
- 30 Indian civil servants are deputed for Afghan Public Administration programme envisaged to build capacity in various Afghan Ministries
- CII project for training 3,000 Afghans in the trades of carpentry, plumbing, welding, masonry and tailoring
- SEWA project for technical assistance to Women's Vocational Training Centre in Bagh-e-Zanana
- Since 2002, several thousand Afghans have trained/studied in India under the various Government of India sponsored training programme.
- 15 Indian doctors and 15 paramedicals have been deployed for Medical Missions (IMMs) in Kabul, Kandahar, Jalalabad, Mazar-e-Sharif and Herat. Each IMM is treating several hundred patients daily
- Patients are also provided free medicines supplied by India
- India is also implementing community-based, small development projects ($20 million) in the fields of agriculture, rural development, education, health, vocational training, etc. with short gestation periods having direct and visible impact on community life, with focus on local ownership and management.

The various completed projects related to capacity building of the local afghan nationals are displayed in Table no. II. Some of the projects cater to both the creation of infrastructure and upgradation of training skills. It is evident from the table that education has a major role in the capacity building measures. Capacity building initiated with a holistic approach begins from the school and extends up to the universities, people working in fields and the technical capacities which are available with the Afghan government. Inclusive in the capacity building are a range of other programmes including Afghan judges and lawyers who were trained at the Indian Law Institute in New Delhi. There are some civil servants who are attached to different ministries to act as trainers.

Table 2: Completed Projects by Government of India Since 2002

S. No.	*Project Description*	*Approx Exp (in million USD)*
1.	Computer Training Centre at Kabul, Herat, Kandahar, Pul-e-Khumri, Jalalabad	0.5
2.	8646 educational kits gifted to students of Habibia School in Kabul, Laboratory equipments and sports goods for schools in Nimroz Province, Books to Kandahar and Khost universities and teachers training	7.4
3.	Restoration/revamping of Information set up, including setting up of printing press, 100 KW-SW Transmitters, TV Satellite uplinking/down linking facility for 10 TV Stations	3.5
4.	Emergency restoration of telecommunication network infrastructure in 11 provinces	11.1
5.	Setting up of Common Facilities Service Centre and Tool Room at Pul-e-Charkhi industrial Park	3.1
6.	Teachers (English language) in Kabul, Jalalabad, Kandahar, Mazar-e-Sharif and Pule-Khumri	1.5
7.	Supply of 110/20 KV and 20/0.4 kV substation equipment/110kV and 20 kV Transmission line material in Faryab province and extension of warranty period for eqpt and continued presence of experts	8.2
8.	Skill development programme	0.02
9.	Training of 1126 Afghan personnel in India	2.05
10.	Supply of 1000 Sewing machines	0.4
11.	F&B training at Presidential palace	0.01
12.	Training of 20 doctors of IGICH at AIIMS	
13.	School training programme for 15 teachers of Habibia School trained at Sanskriti School in N. Delhi for 2 months in Jan-Mar, 2006	0.02
14.	Training of 20 Afghan diplomats at FSI	0.15
15.	Training of 1326 Afghan personnel in India Since 2002, more than 1300 Afghan trainees have been trained in various training institutes in India	2.05
16.	Banking team in Da Afghan Bank and Millie Bank	2.13
17.	Eqpt & trg of digitizing of negatives at BNA	0.01
18.	Digging of 26 tube wells in 6 North West provinces (9 in Herat; 6 in Balkh; 6 in Baghlan; 2 in Badghis; 2 in Faryab; 1 in Jawzjan)—WAPCOS	1.22
	Total	40.26

Source: http://meakabul.nic.in

Most of the completed capacity building projects relate to software skill upgradation, training of teachers, training in setting up of transmitters, banking, photography and skill development. India has also imparted training to Afghan police, Afghan national army, parliamentary training to Afghan officials, judicial training, helping to develop media, information and broadcasting, support and training in the fields of telecommunication, information technology, etc.

Table 3: Ongoing Projects by Government of India Since 2002

S. No.	*Ongoing Project/Pledge*	*Amt in ($ m)*
1.	500 Scholarships for Afghan students for university education in India	$ 1.75
2.	500 short-term training programme for Afghan trainees	$ 2.55
3.	Setting up of a Skill Building Initiative by CII in Kabul	$ 1.4
4.	Women's Vocational Training Centre in Bagh-e-Zanana, Kabul	$ 0.6
5.	Setting up of 11 multipurpose Community Tele-centre	$ 0.33
6.	Setting up of a Hindi department in Nangarhar	$ 0.02
7.	Deputation of 30 civil servants as advisors with key Afghan ministries under UNDP's proposal for creating Capacity Development Facility for Afghanistan	$ 1.08
8.	Small Development Projects: to be implemented in collaboration with Afghan Ministry of Economy	$ 20
9.	Training of BNA officials at PTI	$ 0.02
10.	Setting up of a training facility for M/EW in Kabul	$ 0.99
11.	Setting up of a Afghanistan Academy of Agricultural Sciences (AAAS) (yet to take off)	
12.	Supply of medical equipment to Afghan National Army (yet to take off)	$ 0.5 m
13.	Conservation of Afghan historical sites and manuscripts (under review)	$ 0.17
14.	Deputation of 5 experts to Kabul Municipality (under review)	$ 0.18
15.	Assistance in setting up of a Rural Enterprise Development Programme Unit at Afghan MRRD (deputation of 2 experts)	

Source: http://meakabul.nic.in/intpage/assistancetoafghanistan.pdf

The projects that are ongoing and those which are nearing completion have been displayed in Table no. III. The regular scholarships for the young afghan students have helped them in obtaining university education. Some of the other programmes have been initiated by private organization, such as the CII, the NGO—SEWA, and others in collaboration with international organizations like the UN, World Food Programme, etc. In addition in 2002, officials from Reserve Bank of India were deputed to the Central Bank of Afghanistan besides the team of 30 Indian doctors who treat thousands of afghan patients every week.

All this is despite the fact that trade is rather restricted as Pakistan allows only the Afghan exports to India via Wagah, but not vice versa. Thus, every day, a large numbers of trucks cross Wagah carrying dry fruits and carpets but return back empty.

Implications for India

Indian initiatives in Afghanistan's reconstruction process and capacity building measures have widely covered all sectors of the economy. India has been involved in a wide array of development projects in Afghanistan. It includes building of several key roads such as the Zaranj-Delaram highway in southwest Afghanistan near the Iran border, helping Kabul build its new parliament building, training Afghan police officers, diplomats and civil servants and providing support in the areas of health, education, transportation, power, and telecommunications.

The opening up of Zeranj-Delaram highway with the help of the Indian Army's Border Road Organization (BRO) who were involved in the construction of the road has made Pakistan perceive this to be at the cost of Gawadar port in Balochistan. These developments no doubt challenge Pakistan's hegemony as the single point of access to the landlocked Afghanistan and Central Asia as well. The greater the Indian involvement in reconstruction and in training of the Afghan nationals, the greater would be the Indian gains in Afghanistan in terms of closeness and bonding. But at the same time India would continue to be a target.

Today, India is increasingly being looked upon as a friend by the young Afghans. Close cultural ties between the two nations will no doubt work towards re-establishing the old historical linkages. This would be at the cost of India being perceived as a threat for the separatists in the tribal regions and Balochistan. It is thus obvious that such developments will be under constant attack in order to curtail the increasing Indian influence. The Indian influences could also be perceived as a threat to sever ties between Afghanistan and Pakistan, resulting in serious implications for Pakistan. There is significant anti-Pakistani sentiment in Afghanistan because of the perception of Pakistani interference in their country. In contrast, Afghan attitudes in general are far more positive towards India because of India's increased assistance.

The US President's new approach to the conflict is particularly laudable. It promises to usher in a speeding up of the Afghan reconstruction and a greater involvement of other regional players like India, Pakistan and Iran. On account of the mounting pressure from the US, Pakistan has launched a massive operation on its western borders. For bringing peace and stability in the South Asian region it is important that India and Pakistan develop their dialogue and enhance bilateral cooperation. Think tanks have suggested that the geopolitical nexus of Pakistan-FATA-Afghanistan-India must be seen as a regional crisis that requires a holistic politico-military approach. So any reconstruction programme in the region cannot ignore the region as a whole. A failure to bring peace and restore the minimum level of stability in FATA will automatically trigger off widespread repercussions for the whole region and the world at large.

By offering economic and developmental assistance to Hamid Karzai's government, India has been able to establish a sphere of influence, which has alarmed the Pakistanis. However Islamabad has now realised that the insurgent *Taliban*, which they used to block Indian moves in Afghanistan, was no longer an asset.

Despite the hurdles, India is much closer to Afghanistan today. India's interests are quite loud and clear. Under no circumstances is it prepared to allow the *Taliban* to resurface and it wants the new Afghan security structure to be free of anti-India elements. With the current trilateral talks between US, Afghanistan and Pakistan, it is a moment of crucial significance and opportunity for India. It will prove beneficial if India forges ahead to extend military and other support to Pakistan at this crucial juncture in its war against Al-Qaeda and the *Taliban*.

Notes and References

1. The Afghanistan Compact and the I-ANDS: www.ands.gov.af.
2. Cockell, John G (2000): "Conceptualizing Peace-building: Human Security and Sustainable Peace" in Pugh Michael (ed.), *Regeneration of War Torn Societies*, London: Macmillan, 2000.
3. Zeewu, Jeroen De: *Building Peace in War Torn Societies, From Concept to Strategy,* Conflict Research Unit, Clingendael, The Hague: 2001. Netherlands Institute of International Relations,
4. Dutta, Mondira : *Emerging Afghanistan in the Third Millennium*, New Delhi: Pentagon Publishers, 2009.
5. Rubin, Barnett R.: *Making Aid to Afghanistan Effective*, Testimony before the House Committee on International Relations, New York, 2006.

6. Gall Carlotta and Somini Sengupta, "Afghan Electorate's Message: The Provinces Need Public Works and Restoration of Order", in *New York Times*, September 20, 2005.
7. Dutta, Mondira, "India-Afghanistan Relations: Opportunities and Challenges" in World Focus, *India's Foreign Policy: Issues and Challenges*, 347-348, Nov-Dec 2008, Annual Number, New Delhi, 2008.

12

The Afghan Cauldron Beyond Kabul

P.L. Dash

Seldom one comes across a country in the annals of history that remains in international limelight for so long. It is nearly three decades since the Soviet troops moved into Afghanistan on the Christmas eve of 1979 that Afghanistan has become the nerve centre of international relations. The Soviets had come and gone, the *Taliban* have appeared and disappeared and are once again reappearing. Many governments of various hues have shuffled power. The US led coalition forces have been running the country since October 2001 through President, Hamid Karzai. But the country's tumultuous journey to democracy remains unfinished and highly uncertain. Ravaged by nagging and internecine wars, the Afghan economy remains shaky. Millions of people are maimed and crippled. On an average men die at the age of 40 and women at 43 years of age. 85 percent of the country's 25.8 million people live in rural areas, whereas half of the rest who live in urban areas stay in Kabul. The social fabric of the country has been shattered. Infant mortality is high at 38 percent. Poverty is abject and people are ready to flee to neighbouring countries as soon as they get an opportunity, resulting in 2.5 million refugees in Pakistan, 1.5 million in Iran and over 150,000 migrating to western countries. This is the grave picture of Afghanistan around March 2009 that the official website depicts of the country of Karzai.

Sustained international endeavour to better the prospects of Afghanistan has met with resistance of religious zealots. Organised crime that kills employees engaged in humanitarian aid and infrastructure building across the country, growing poppy cultivation that ferments a booming narcotic trade, rising extremism and Islamic fundamentalism that breeds intolerance are the present hallmarks of Afghanistan—a country deep in the mire of misery from where there seems no escape route. It is a country where Muslims are killing Muslims, defying all logics of Islam. Rising Islamic fervour coupled with democracy deficit in the periphery has continued to polarise the international efforts to bring Afghanistan to the mainstream of life. The US led coalition forces have stayed in the country for nine years now to fight the *Taliban* and *Al Qaeda* and combat terrorism and narcotic trafficking and build democracy, but their success has been dubious. Although Hamid Karzai's fate is unknown, he does one thing dear to his heart very clearly: pursues the grand regional strategy of the US on the chessboard of international politics. This article deals with issues, both internal and peripheral, that beset Afghanistan bizarrely on this chessboard. It analyses the depth of their implications for the plethora of stakeholders, who all are at interplay with cross-purposes.

Factoring Pakistan

In the aftermath of 26/11 Mumbai attack, former US Secretary of State, Madeleine Albright had called Pakistan an 'international migraine.' A couple of moths later, at the end of January, 2009, participating in a panel discussion on US relations with the Muslim world organised by the Council on Foreign Relations, Albright reiterated her stance and identified Pakistan as the 'most dangerous place in the world' by saying "it has nuclear weapons, extremism, poverty, corruption and a very fragile system and is in a very difficult location."[1] Her statement, coming at a time, when the US has been considering a policy recast on the region, is laden with nuances of analysis, particularly by a person who had dealt with Pakistan under the Clinton administration and this is surely likely to carry weight in fathoming the gravity of terrorism and extremism in the periphery of Pakistan. Afghanistan and Indian state of Jammu and Kashmir are two likely candidates for the repercussions of this analysis in the months and years to come. Further, with a view to accentuating this danger, Pakistani *Taliban*'s readiness to extend Jihadi help to the country's army revealed a new page in the conspiracy theory of a closer alliance between the Islamists and the Armed Forces within Pakistan. When Bill Roggio, an American counter-terrorist expert wrote in similar vein that "Baitullah Mehsud's commitment to back the government confirms the policy of the Pakistani military and government of creating strategic depth by supporting the *Taliban* in Afghanistan and a host of other Islamist groups inside Pakistan and Kashmir, he was perhaps speaking about the extant reality. The Pakistani army believes that the terror groups will provide manpower and logistics in case of a war not only with India, but also with any of Pakistan's neighbours. The army/ISI in Pakistan have a definite agenda, carved out in close connivance of the *Al Qaeda/Taliban* leadership to spread global jihad and anything coming as an impediment to realise this agenda ought to be ruthlessly crushed, including by using the methods of war, in exigent situation. That Afghanistan and NWFP will serve as an impenetrable fortress in the rear in case of an invasion" is a foregone conclusion.[2] It is in this complex context, a Pakistani think tank considered 26/11 Mumbai attack and the subsequent Indian dossier on it "as a Hindu-Jewish-American plot to dismember Pakistan and divest it of its nuclear crown jewels by provoking a dual Indian-US invasion from opposite flanks.[3] This is precisely the strategic mindset that embraces Talibanisation, terror and *Al Qaeda* as something native and everything else as meddling by alien powers. Baitullah's comments are no exception. Baitullah Mehsud was the chief of an Islamic group called *Tehrik-e-Taliban*. With anti-India rhetoric becoming a daily refrain in Pakistani press, growing Talibanisation of the country is being increasingly felt. Roggio's statement only candidly reveals and justifies part of the extant four pronged Pakistani conspiracy to divert attention from the real issue of spreading terrorism.

First, Baitullah has expressed not only his personal commitment to *Jihad* but also the devotion of thousands of his followers, who are suicide bombers, who could spread across the uncontrolled terrain from Pakistan Occupied Kashmir (POK) through Durand line to Herat and elsewhere deeper inside Afghanistan. In this Space, there are four possibilities the first of which has been aired by Roggio that Indo-Pak borders will be the war zone, the territories of entire Pakistan will be the core, PoK will be the frontier and NWFP and adjoining Wajiristan will be the rear of continued Jihadi support in the event of an Indian attack on Pakistan. That will bleed India to the end through its proposed thousand cuts.

Secondly and precisely, continued Islamists support will flow in the event of a war Pakistan has to fight with Afghanistan, where over 60,000 allied forces led by NATO are concentrated to fight the *Taliban* and terror. 17,000 more troops are likely joined after President Obama's decision to replenish force strength in Afghanistan. For Pakistan, it will be a jigsaw puzzle because it has signed a ceasefire deal with the very *Taliban* the Americans are targeting to fight in the Swat valley. In that case of a prolonged conflict, the Durand line will be a war zone, Waziristan will be the frontier, Pakistan will remain the core and PoK will be the rear of Islamists support to perpetuate the war and that would bleed Karzai, the allied forces and the US through another thousand cuts on Pakistan's north western flank.

Thirdly, strategists in Pakistan plan that in the event of an Afghan war with northern alliance/Central Asian countries or even with Russia, Pakistan could open up a northern front. In the event of such an exigency, Wakkhan corridor will be the frontier, the treacherous terrain along the Tajik-Afghan and Uzbek-Afghan borders will be a perennial war zone, Pakistan will be the core, PoK and NWFP on both flanks of Pakistan will serve as the rear to continue a protracted war. And that would possibly cut the Central Asian adjoining states to size, besides making thousand cuts on the Russians should they venture to challenge the *Taliban/Al Qaeda/* ISI/Pak army nexus. Fourthly, in the event of an Iran-US rapprochement and the possibility of an attack on Pakistan from its western neighbour, Iran, the Iran-Pakistan borders will be the active war zone. The long stretch of Afghan-Iran borders will be the war zone too, where Islamists will rule the day. Resource rich Baluchistan will be the frontier, the warlord dominated territory will be backyard and *Taliban* controlled territories across both countries will be the rear. Pakistan will remain the core as usual.

This is an army/ISI plan and not the plan of the Pakistani government, nor that of the Pakistani people. All illicit and illegal activities such as narcotic trafficking, arms and money laundering will help perpetuate the protracted Pak-Afghan and Pak-India conflicts. Pakistan will be able thus to engage the US in the region forever and milk the American cow as it wishes, and whenever it desires. Once entangled in this messy situation, the US cannot so easily disentangle itself to a safe exit. Pakistan will behave truant to deal with the *Taliban* because it is Pakistan that has provided the *Taliban* with a safe haven all through the Musharraf years. However grandiose this plan may sound, there is always a possibility of the Pakistani core altogether collapsing, thereby pushing the country and the region to turmoil and chaos under a possible *Taliban-Al Qaeda* control of Pakistan as well as its nuclear arsenal. The US must consider such a situation emerging in near future.

Further, the rear-to-front coordination will be managed entirely by a coordination team comprising top Generals of the Pakistani army, ISI, *Taliban* clergy and *Al Qaeda* leadership. Their nexus and objectives are clear: strategic planning for an unending war in the region is more than obvious and behind rhetoric or flip-flop diplomacy lay a labyrinth of truth that strategists must ponder over while dealing with *Taliban* as a localised phenomenon of Islamic insurgency, which it no longer is. *Taliban* has been acquiring a global character. Or else how could one prove the post-Mumbai mayhem of 26/11, terror taking a U-turn toward Indo-

Pakistan war on borders? The global war on terror is an international issue, Pakistan's territory is being used to run a terror factory that must stop, if not by Pakistan, then by the international community and a bilateral war is nowhere near the picture here. As British Prime Minister, Gordon Brown had pointed out to Pakistani leaders, even in Britain, two third of all terrorist strikes are nailed down to Pakistan.

It is more than clear that far too long, Pakistan has been running with the hare and hunting with the hound. It is a part of global anti-terror mechanism, a partner of the US in the global war on terror. Yet it is a breeding ground of terror itself. The irony cannot forever benefit Pakistan. Flexing military muscle with India will not yield the desired result. Islamic terrorism is likely to consume Pakistan from within in a few years. A poor Pakistan with its nuclear capability and with up to 120 potentially dangerous nuclear warheads that has been going with a begging bowl to the international agencies to bail out the country from economic doldrums would find it excruciatingly painful to come out of the mess, a war with India would create for that country. If past lessons of three Indo-Pak wars are any indicator, the Pakistani leadership, both military and civil, ought not provoke India but restrain itself from going to a war. An Indo-Pakistan war will be no solution to the problems of terrorism; nor is likely to curb growing Islamism within Pakistan.

In the pretext of seeking strategic depth, the US has remained Pakistan's stoic supporter through the Cold War and post-Cold war years. Incremental increase in Islamism, growing threat of terror in the region, the menace of narcotic and drugs coming from this volatile area are all sinister signs to the US for a policy recast vis-à-vis Pakistan. It is a country that does not deserve financial and military aid. It is a country that has become really a permanent migraine. And it is a country likely to cause pain to all in the region and beyond. Therefore, it is imperative that all flow of US aid to Pakistan must stop forthwith to choke that country's line of supply to terror and find ways and means of how to help its suffering millions. This is the responsibility of a responsive world community; and not exclusively that of India or the US. Pakistan's strategic depth for the US will outlive its utility as India would grow economically prosperous and militarily more powerful and as Indo-US strategic partnership will flourish in the years to come.

At a time of intensely explosive situation brewing the stew of war in West Asia, with continuing Israel bombardment on Gaza strip, Pakistan's double standard in the fight against terror and its encouragement to the *Taliban* and its *jihadi* cronies are serious matters to ponder over. What the

US has been trying to preserve, Pakistan has been feigning to protect, while in reality it has been decimating the very values the US stands for. The US, and alone the US, could help assuage the situation with help from the international community. The US has already doled out $ 10 billion post 9/11 to Pakistan without any conditionality attached and now it is the US who could ask for the accountability from Pakistan, admonish it to stop the double speak. Far too long Pakistan has played the India card beyond the Cold War years. Those equations have changed. It cannot expect the Americans forever to feed it with milk and butter. The Musharraf years are gone too. As a Britain based Pakistan observer wrote, "In 2009, the situation for the Pakistan army and ISI is going to be a great deal more uncomfortable."[4]

Nebulous Nexus

Much as we talk about combating terrorism, the war on terror cannot be won, if it is alone pursued by the intelligence agencies or the military or the police of one or many countries. Both Afghanistan and Pakistan have been passing through trying times. While both countries have miserably failed to combat terror, even after being part of the global anti-terror campaign headed by the US, the anti-terror mechanism has not acted against terror operating in Afghanistan or Pakistan primarily because terror intertwines with Islam in an intricate antique manner. To extricate terror from Islam is tough because people believe in Islam. The political leaders, who ought to act against terrorists, tend to be believers of Islam too. Jihadists and terrorists are inseparable and both are believers of Islam. The terrorists believe in Islam and the religious bigots misinterpret every line of the Quran. The people are largely alienated from the state. The state considers the *Taliban* and terrorists as non-state actors and sometimes as freedom fighters. The state patronises terror acts as and when it suits it. Instead of motivating people to take arms against terror, the perpetrators of terror are encouraged to take up arms against the state as in Afghanistan, oppose all developmental projects that the Afghan state has undertaken in building the Ring Road around the cities where population is concentrated and take up arms against all those who extend help in building infrastructure. Terrorist activities such as the Indian Embassy bombing in Kabul by the ISI agents or killing of Indian engineers working on the road projects are evidences of terrorism. In this sort of situation, all elements in Pakistan agree on one common enemy: India. And all elements in Afghanistan can agree on one common enemy, the West led by the US. Fanned by nationalism in their respective countries and using Islam that connotes Peace to whip up terror, the Pak-Afghan nexus is too intricate to be so easily broken.

In Pakistan the army is as much convinced as the ISI that India is supporting the *Taliban*, while reality is the reverse. In Afghanistan the people believe that Pakistan is supporting the *Taliban* return to power. The *Taliban* in fact has been extending their power base in all far flung areas and successfully launching terror acts wherever and whenever they wish to launch one. Thus, the *Taliban* in Afghanistan and Pakistan are a closely knitted group, who regroup in their endeavours to capture power be it in Pakistan or Afghanistan. Taking advantage of the divide prevailing in Pakistan after Pervez Musharaff quit power, the *Taliban* supported by Al-Qaeda elements and encouraged by the clerics in Pakistan assumed strength that could prove detrimental to regional stability in the years to come. The recent events in the Swat valley and across the Durand line is demonstrative of the growing *Taliban* influence in the tribal belt of Waziristan and the result is: 1200 killed in the Swat valley in the past one year, 2-5 lakh people displaced, 3000 *Taliban* insurgents have taken shelterin the valley, 15,000 government troops deployed to handle the situation, 170 schools including 100 schools for girls are shut down by the *Taliban*.[5] This shows the dichotomy between what the Karzai-Zardari governments wish to protect and what the *Taliban-Al Qaeda* nexus wishes to preserve. Thus a clear divide is discernible in Pakistan and Afghanistan. In the case of Pakistan, the divide exists between the civilian government and the army-ISI combine joined by a third pole of power held by the *Taliban* Islamists. In Afghanistan it is the warlord-Islamist combine including *Al Qaeda* elements on the one hand and the Karzai government on the other. Karzai rules the centre while the opposition rules the periphery. Precise conclusion from this divide is that the people are largely on the side of the Islamists while the government grapples with the problems of how to bridge the divide and ensure harmony among various social groups. The outcome is: what is wild west for Pakistan in NWFP is logically Afghan anarchy along the Durand line.

When people are not with the government, when people are swayed by the preaching of the Mullahs, when political illiteracy prevents them from real participatory democracy, when terrorist groups operate within the Islamic umbrella against the state and the United States, the state becomes virtually numb or it acts with duplicity. Aligning with the *Taliban* and siding with the terrorists have not prevented Pakistan from simultaneously siding with the US that leads the international war on terror. This piquant situation was deftly handled by Musharaff's duplicity by bargaining with the US pecuniary gains for Pakistan—a country he salvaged from the economic slump and piloted for nearly eight years. Concurrently holding two top jobs, politically as President and militarily as Army Chief, it depended on Musharaff and his followers in the army to have assuaged the situation, who called the final shots throughout post 9/11. Whether Pervez Musharaff or Pervez Kayani, the rule of the game has not changed although Cold War architecture of international relations and regional equations in South Asia have vastly changed. Much as the US may wish to nurture democracy on the debris of military dictatorship, the agenda is doomed to fail. Otherwise how could one explain the self contradiction of Pakistani leadership right from the Musharaff to Zardari years? The fight against terror at the global level and the encouragement to running terror factory within the country against neighbours is an irony facing Pakistan. Musharaff spent his eight years in this self-contradiction, Zardari has been experiencing this self-contradiction ever since he assumed office. The horrific incident of 26/11 exposed Pakistan's conceit more than ever earlier, when its leaders tried to pull wool over the eyes of the world by their contradictory statements. Leaders, who failed for months after Pakistani elections to hammer out a power sharing arrangement, need not necessarily be trusted as faithful followers of democracy. They need to be admonished, and if necessary coerced to follow what the international community considers legitimate and licit.

This inherent internal contradiction within the Pakistani political elite was self evident first, when Musharaff effectively effaced the influence of the judiciary by removing its Chief Justice, who he was forced to reinstate under growing protest by the lawyer community. Secondly, far too long Musharaff stuck to his military uniform and did not abdicate his position as Army Chief until he was forced by the US to pave way for democracy. Post-Musharaff, Pakistan passed through trying times when for the first few months after elections, the elected political elite could not form a government by consensus. The final bickering within the Pakistani ruling elite was exposed in the aftermath of the 26/11 Mumbai attack, when a Pakistani terrorist was caught alive and Pakistan downplayed his nationality. Bit by bit, the endeavour to wash hands off the Mumbai terror attack, embroiled Pakistan in a vicious pool of blatant lies from where it has not come out so far. Denying knowledge of the terror strike in Mumbai was too naive a proposition for a responsible country, that too a nuclear power, that has committed to fight terror internationally. Pakistan government first offered to send the ISI chief to India to help in investigation, but subsequently backtracked under pressure from the army. When goaded to reveal the truth, the Pakistani Prime Minister refrained over and over again that the Mumbai attack was staged by non-state actors and the Pakistani state was not involved. From A.Q. Khan to Shuja Pasha all were state actors. Thus the state had encouraged terrorist all along to take arms and perpetrate terror as per the direction of the ISI-army nexus.

Then the Prime Minister of Pakistan openly said that Kasab was not a Pakistani, when its own former Prime Minister Nawaz Shariff was on record attesting his nationality and the denial mode continued until American FBI visited Kasab's village and came out with evidence of his Pakistani origin. Meanwhile, a melodramatic situation had prevailed over the village from where Kasab hailed: the village was cordoned off, his family not allowed to speak and right up to the moment of accepting that he was a Pakistani citizen. But why to dismiss Durani, Pakistan's National Security Advisor, from the job for revealing the truth? The double-speak was obvious in all these actions. From the moot question of how to fight terror and deflate tension, attention of the Pakistani leadership riveted on Indo-Pakistani relations, the so called danger posed by India and the finger pointing at an impending war as if India was the culprit, and not Pakistan whose territory has been systematically used to launch terror strikes that has maimed hundreds of innocent citizens, including Americans and Israelis. For days together a sort of war hysteria swept the Pakistani leadership, and thanks to American shuttle diplomacy, the situation was brought under control. When evidence pointed at Pakistan's involvement in terrorist activities, it was a naivety to deny complicity. Whether it was Kandahar hijack, or Kabul bombing of the Indian embassy or the killing of the American journalist, Daniel Pearl, or Mumbai attack, on all occasions it was terrorists from Pakistani soil, who had a nebulous nexus with Pakistani establishment. The British Prime Minister had rightly told President Zardari that the matter of terror was a grave international concern.

The denial mode continued. First it was revealed by the Pakistani authorities that Maulana Masood Azhar was under house arrest. Then suddenly he was not in Pakistani custody and vanished from the intelligence radar. Such contradictions happen only when the state treats international fugitives like Dawood Ibrahim and Masood Azhar as state guests and intentionally harbours them by downplaying their pernicious role. Ultimately they will consume Pakistan from within and the state will have to crumble under their weight. Musharraf was attacked on several occasions, Benazir Bhutto was killed, many more will be killed and state guests would outlast everyone. A state with such duplicity and with virtual access to Afghanistan via the tribal belt in Waziristan, is a danger for the whole region and the stake holders are many. It is Pakistan in the Afghan periphery that would prove to be fatal than Afghanistan or India. A failed state with a hard currency reserve of just $ 4 billion in November, 2008 that would cover 4-5 weeks of its import,[6] with a nuclear bomb in hand and with hundreds of terror camps operating from its territory, ventured to launch a daring attack on India and dared too to deny that it was involved. It seems a state within the state, the Pakistani army and ISI have a larger than life role that has been funded by the US in the exclusive period of Soviet involvement in Afghanistan. That reason in particular, and the Cold War equations in general have outlived their longevity by a decade and half ago. Yet, Pakistan is determined to live on the Cold War paradigm is a strange desire that has generated enough heat worldwide, particularly in the US that the generals in Pakistan must feel.

Flowers that Kill

What compounds the complicated political fabric of both Pakistan and Afghanistan with greater regional ramifications is the poppy culture. The poppy field on bloom across Afghanistan looks beautiful. The colour of the flower on poppy plant mutates from light to salmon pink to red and violet before it bears a fruit that yields poppy. The raw poppy is then processed to yield opium and opium is further processed with addition of chemicals to make heroin and other drugs. It is these drugs that kill people across the globe. The anti drug front, a Russian NGO, has recently reported that 70 people die every day of heroin consumption in Russia.[7] The countries in the proximity of Afghanistan have been the immediate victims of the drug abuse. Year after year the UN drug reports convey the gruesome details of narcotic production, trafficking and transport, precursor procurement, laboratory refinement and final march of the product to profit. From Afghanistan to Europe, from the source of production to the target of consumption, the cost manifolds as it shuffles hands of the profiteers. All efforts, singular and joint as well as all interdiction measures taken by Afghan authorities have yielded little positive results to either curb poppy cultivation or combat the menace of its consequences. Acreage of poppy cultivation has been steadily growing and the perimeter of the drug trafficking has been widening as if the narcotic traders have made mockery of the combat efforts of authorities.

It is simply because illiterate and innocent Afghans have taken recourse to poppy cultivation as a source of livelihood. In the absence of irrigation facilities on the mountainous terrains or arid deserts, alternative crop cultivation is a remote possibility. Poppy comes as the saviour of livelihood, handy in the most unfavourable climatic conditions; and most importantly it yields profit to the farmers. This profit could be gauzed from the cost escalations as heroin travels from one place to another. In Gorno-Badakshan of Tajikistan a kilogram of heroin costs $408 thousand, in Dushanbe the cost escalates to $12-17 thousand, in Tashkent its worth is $30-40 thousand, the same amount of heroin in Moscow costs $150-200 thousand, while in Europe it is sold at $250-300 thousand.[8] As capitalism permeates to the private lives of innocent Afghan villagers, the demand for money grows correspondingly and poppy sale provides the much needed succour. The dearth of money and prevalence of abject poverty drive farmers to the doorsteps of money lenders, who are warlords too, to act as middlemen; often procuring the entire poppy crop in exchange of the money lent to farmers on usurious interests. Money is not recovered; instead poppy is recovered and in connivance with the warlords, processed, refined and marketed in a chain of well connected network that Karzai or no Karzai, none will be able to stop. The roots are in the villages, in the abject poverty of farmers and in the highly loyal patriarchal societal system, where village headmen are extremely loyal to warlords. It is there the poppy grows, it is from there the poppy spreads, and it to that place interdiction measures are to be directed.

The failure of the authorities to curb poppy cultivation and resultantly the narcotic trade stemming from Afghanistan is the evidence of a futile saga of exercises by the government machinery. Russian sources have reported that compared to the 1990s, when 70 percent of world poppy cultivation was concentrated in Afghanistan, in 2002 a huge increase of 1400 percent was found to be in acreage increase in cultivation. As a result, opium based narcotic production witnessed a huge surge in Afghanistan, entailing in trade spurt and consequential affliction in the periphery and beyond. In 2001, under the *Taliban* clampdown, Afghanistan produced only 185 tons of opium a year. The *Taliban* imposed a 10 percent direct tax on opium production and sale that deterred poor farmers from poppy cultivation, yet this money was used by the *Taliban* to run 80 training bases of their supporters across the territory they controlled.[9] However, in subsequent years, following the installation of Karzai government in Kabul, there was a significant increase in both acreage coverage of poppy cultivation as well as in opium production: in 2002 around 2700 tons and in 2003 more than 7000 tons that constituted 87 percent of the world consumption and almost 100 percent of consumption in Europe. This figure in subsequent years increased to

12,000 tons in 2004 and 15,000 tons in 2006 and further escalated in subsequent years. There is very little difference between Russian and UN data in this regard then and since.[10]

Since Karzai seems to have no control over the periphery of his country, where the poppy cultivation flourishes, the area coverage as well as production and sale goes uninterrupted and largely unreported. In 2003 only 1.7 million Afghans earned their livelihood from poppy cultivation, their number in 2006 stood at 3 million. The nexus between the licit money earned from narcotics and illicit activities such as terrorism is so intricate that there is clear interconnection right from the grassroots levels to the level of international drug barons. It is simply hard for the government to break this intricate nexus at each level; and without breaking that, it is not possible to combat both narcotics and terrorism. Thus, by producing 90 percent of the world's opium based narcotics, the Afghan narcotic business is evidently at the forefront. Fifty percent of Afghan GDP comes from the sale of narcotics and the yearly transactions stand at $ 30 billion. Obviously Afghanistan is a narcotic state, deeply connected with narco-terrorism.[11] When illiterate Afghans grow poppy for livelihood and look to their religious leaders for spiritual succour, no extraneous power can influence them to course correction; let alone foreign powers.

Foreign involvement may temporarily help to ameliorate the situation, but can never eradicate the root cause of the ills plaguing Afghanistan. And the root causes are a highly hierarchical society, deeply embedded patriarchal laws still prevailing, literacy and liberty being denied to women and excessive reliance on Islam and the way it is misinterpreted by the clergy. All these aspects put together make a combustible combination of an explosive that has destroyed the traditional societal fabric of Afghanistan rather than building western style democracy by the Karzai government. Karzai does not command grassroots support, the *Talibanised* clergy does, and in tandem with the warlords, it is they who rule Afghanistan and not Karzai whose writ does not stretch beyond the periphery of Kabul.

Political Equations

For the past three decades, Afghanistan has been passing through a fluid political situation. The major reason for failure of the Soviet venture to build socialism was lack of grassroots support. The people, believers of Islam, normally thought that their religious guru, the Mullah was the representative of Allah on earth and socialism was an alien intervention.

Similar mindset has not changed even today. Post 9/11, when the fight to the finish against the *Taliban* began in Afghanistan and the US bombarded that country, Russia supported the Northern Alliance as did many other countries to oust the *Taliban*. On the thick of this fight, Pakistan supported the Pushtun community—the traditional rulers of Afghanistan—until it changed course to side with the US led coalition under American pressure. This had polarised the internal political situation in a bizarre manner. On the one hand stood the US led coalition supported by president Musharraf of Pakistan. With them stood President Hamid Karzai. On the other hand there were innumerable political factions, opposing this virtual American takeover. These likeminded groups were politically alert to think that American involvement was no solution, rather it is an impediment. The possibility of an Afghan-Russian rapprochement has already fizzled out by the time Karzai was saddled in power. Grassroots participation in the democratic process of Afghanistan remains by far a daydream.

Taliban ouster was just the beginning of the long process of another Afghan reconciliation process based entirely on different parameters than did the Soviet experiment for ten years. The Peoples Democratic Party of Afghanistan under its various dispensations could hardly reach out to the Afghan grassroots because socialism was religiously opposed. That precisely served the breeding ground for the radical zealots of Islam that begot the *Taliban*. The American-Pakistani support to these zealots was obvious throughout Soviet involvement in Afghanistan. The Al-Qaeda symptom is entirely a different connotation of Osama's connections to 9/11 and the consequential overthrow of the *Taliban* that led to Karzai appearing on the political firmament of Afghanistan. The rest is history, but the shadow of that history continues to linger on Afghanistan, polarizing its society as never earlier. There is, however, a discernible divide among the Islamists with regard to their political loyalty. As *Wahabism,* the radical strand of Islam, made inroads from Saudi Arabia to Pakistan and Afghanistan with billions of dollars of aid and literature pouring in for spiritual renaissance, it became evident that the society has been bifurcated into Nakshabandis, who practised Sufi spirituality in their efforts to reform Islam and Deobandhis, who saw nothing but jihad as their ultimate goal to save Islam from the infidels. Over the years, the Deobandhi trend has been growing in Afghanistan and Pakistan. "Today 10,000 Deobandhi *madrassas* are active around the world and many of them unfortunately preach jihad."[12] Historian Charles Allen, who called *Wahabism* as the 'nursery of global terror' feels that there are two versions of the Quran: one that talks of *Allah* the merciful and his compassion; and the other that spreads intolerance and violence. And there seems to be more intolerance in the later *Quran* followed by the Deobandhis.[13]

As religious zealots align with the grassroots to misinterpret Islam, the society gets further polarised on the ethnic basis. In the absence of credible data on ethnicity in a country that has not conducted any census since 1979, Afghanistan throws figures sporadically from time to time. As per data available for 2000 on the official Afghan website, there are 25.8 million people of whom 54 percent are *Pushtuns.* This is the dominant nationality in Afghanistan. In order of their numbers, second comes the *Tajiks,* third the *Hazaras*, fourth the *Uzbeks* and fifth the *Kyrgyz*. All of them are, however, considered minorities in all 34 provinces of Afghanistan. This is precisely the ethnic polarity of a nation in shambles. *Pushtuns* are not *Talibans*; they are victimised by the *Taliban-Al Qaeda* combine, who cleverly juxtaposes religion against ethnicity and wishes to establish the rule of religion.

In addition to the religious and ethno-national dichotomies, there is political polarisation within the country. Hamid Karzai and his team of ministers are largely non-resident Afghans supplanted by the US led coalition forces in Kabul and subsequently formalised in the post of President by the 2004 presidential elections. Before the elections, in 2003, when political leaders and military commanders proposed a coalition with the Northern Alliance, Karzai refused to toe the line. As a result Karzai and his cronies enjoy power in Kabul and in the precinct of it, but the local powers rest with the powerful warlords, who control the provinces and virtually control everything under their provincial jurisdiction. The political vacuum of the centre's writ is evident in the periphery, where nothing could be decided without the consent of local headmen or provincial chieftain. The hierarchical nexus is too well knitted to be broken. Karzai's top-to-bottom democracy has no effect on the Afghans in the periphery. In this situation the country requires a bottom-to-top participatory democracy, which is largely absent.

There are over 80 political parties in Afghanistan[14] and their ambition to win a political space in the ongoing process of transformation is a legitimate aspiration Hamid Karzai ought to address. Leaders of various political persuasions led by the National Democratic Party of Afghanistan vied to win popular mandate by uniting themselves into a National Front, a virtual predecessor of which was the Northern Alliance that united likeminded forces to oust *Taliban*. The composition of the national front is a strange amalgam of many powerful political parties and leaders. They included B. Rabbani, a former Afghan President and presently a member of parliament and head of Islamic Society of Afghanistan, National Movement headed by a former Vice President Z. Masud, party of New Afghanistan headed by Parliament speaker, U. Kanuni, National Islamic Movement of Afghanistan with A. Dostum as Chairman, energy and water resources minister, M. Ismail Khan and so on. All these leaders except Dostum, who is an Uzbek, are Tajik. The family members of former Afghan king, Zahir Shah and many prominent members of the National Democratic Party of Afghanistan, currently having a majority in the parliament that ruled Afghanistan under the Soviets also participated in the alliance. All these groups stand opposed to the government of Karzai. The crux of the political dispute between Karzai and the National Front centres on the future shape of political system slowly evolving in Afghanistan. While the National Front favours a parliamentary form of federal government, both at the centre and in provinces, Karzai stands for presidential form of government with domination of the central government in provincial affairs. He is also unwilling to curtail his absolute, executive powers in any way. The tussle continues and the victim is democracy in Afghanistan.

Thus we have a bizarre political picture where the ruling President is isolated from the mainstream politics in provinces, nay grassroots. Religious leaders are alienated from the president. The people are alienated from the power centres, their leaders are sidestepped from central politics. The way Karzai treated his former defence minister, M. Fahirn, was evident enough of the rift apparent in ruling circles in Afghanistan. Everyone expected Fahim to be offered the post of first Vice President, but that was not to happen. Instead the post went to Zia Masud, younger brother of A. Masud.[15] As a result, nine years after American involvement, no cohesive political force is visible to steer clear the Afghan political mess created successively by the Soviets, the *Taliban* and the American machinations over the past three decades.

The Stakeholders

The volatility of the Afghan political situation has brought a field many stakeholders. The first and foremost victim is the idea of liberal democracy. In a country, where extremism, *Taliban*isation and intolerance to anything modern have held sway over the years, talk of democracy is a misnomer. Fundamentalist Islam holds sway over moderate Islam and Sufi thoughts are a far cry. Super-charged with religious extremism juxtaposed to the determination of Karzai to pursue western style presidential form of government supported by the presence of NATO and alliance forces, the chances of democracy seem bleak as much in the short run as in the long run amid growing resistance to the process of modernisation. Democracy has to evolve from within, from the grassroots participation of Afghans in the process of political formations and from bottom to top. But this is unlikely to happen in the present Afghan situation that plants democracy from top to bottom. Further the American experience of top to bottom democracy building in Somalia, Haiti, Kosovo and Iraq are stark reminders of perennial warfare and bloodshed rather than anything akin to democracy. Afghanistan is possibly taking no different course.

The second biggest stakeholder is US and NATO forces trying for stabilising the Afghan situation, but in vain. More American troops to Afghanistan will not yield any better democracy or stability. It cannot contain the growing menace of the *Taliban* and the *Al Qaeda* and their spreading popularity. It can only help them unite against foreign occupation forces to fight them to the finish. Afghanistan will be a litmus test for the ultramodern NATO forces verses archaic mode of rustic fight rendered by the *Taliban*. This is possibly why engineers building roads and hospitals are kidnapped and killed to teach foreigners a lesson and telling them not to meddle. But Afghanistan is in such a mess that invites international intervention to salvage that country from the sunken predicament of decay without which it can never be modernised. Apart from the very significance of asymmetric force used in the Afghan imbroglio, there is a serious component of infeasibility and that is "the sheer unaffordablility of an open ended war in Afghanistan for the US economy."[16] And this will weigh heavily in Obama's Af-Pak policy in the months to come so as to minimise what is at stake.

The third stakeholder is Pakistan. An unstable Afghanistan at the doorstep of Pakistan is a permanent danger to building democracy in Pakistan. Religiosity is consuming both Pakistan and Afghanistan from within; and it is never too late to wake up to the challenge of Islamic extremism to the very existence of their statehood. Stability and democracy in either country will supplement the situation in another because of their close proximity coupled with similar adherence to Islam. Pakistan's president has openly admitted the widespread presence of the *Taliban* inside Pakistan and the more it grows, the more it would pose a menace to modernisation and democracy. The unfolding events of the *Taliban* dominance in the Swat valley in the wee months of 2009 are a stark reminder of the shape of things to come.

The fourth stakeholder is Central Asia. The spill-over effects of growing fundamentalism has been widely felt across Central Asia. The narcotic impact is well known too. The illegal arms smuggling, money laundering, human trafficking and all that is rejected by a modern state are home to Afghanistan. Since three countries of Central Asia—Turkmenistan, Tajikistan and Uzbekistan—share borders with Afghanistan, they have been feeling the brunt of the Afghan syndrome on their territories itself for the last fifteen years. Much as these countries wish to refrain from what has been happening in Afghanistan, regrettably, they have failed in their endeavour. The Afghan shadow is overwhelming their socio-cultural lives, where Islam comes as the driving force of motivation. However, so far, what has minimised the risk of spreading Islamism to Central Asia is the high literacy level and the consequent level of fathoming the benefits of Islam and differentiating it from the fundamentalist strand.

Another stakeholder is Russia. Endangered by growing influence of Islam, Russia is concerned about the Afghan situation. Ten years of building socialism in that country between 1979-1989 did Russia no good until its leader, Mikhail Gorbachev, admitted openly that Afghanistan was the 'bleeding wound of the USSR' and gracefully evolved an exit strategy that finally disentangled the Soviet Union from Afghanistan. Russia's Afghan concerns are further accentuated by growing Islamic influence along its southern underbelly straddling from Agediye via Chechnya and Dagestan in the northern Caucasus to Kazakhstan and beyond to Tatarstan and Bashkorotostan in its heartland, where the population is largely Muslim. The feeling of socio-cultural affinity to rising Islam in Afghanistan vis-à-vis rising Russian influence within their republics may pose a danger for the Russian leadership to handle. The more this Islamic affinity grows between Afghanistan and the countries of the Russian southern fringe, the more troublesome it would prove for Russia in the years to come.

There is a lot for India at stake too. In fact, as all neighbouring countries have been feeling the Afghan heat, India must not be singled out as an exception. India's External affairs Minister, Pranab Mukherjee has called the *Taliban* a "terrorist organisation and threat to humanity" The Indo-Afghan territorial proximity dates back to the days immemorial. For millennia, both countries have been neighbours. With intentions of ensuring a peaceful Afghanistan, India's efforts to help that country in the field of education and healthcare is commendable. The current situation puts everything at stake by carving out a *Taliban* niche on a swathe of land that has witnessed ancient civilisations, including the Buddhist heritage at the Bamyan and the Harappa civilisation in Larkana. Indian heritage is at stake. At stake is also global peace. If for Carl von Clausewitz, "war is the continuation of politics by other means" for the *Taliban* terrorism is the continuation of war by other means. Therefore, the war on international terror must focus on all other means of diplomacy inclusive of the use of asymmetric force, if required, because international security is at stake.

Conclusions

While it is tough to delineate a political future course for Afghanistan in the current scenario, it is equally difficult to demarcate the path of democracy for Pakistan. So far the native agenda for the future of Afghanistan and Pakistan has been deeply rooted in Islam that has been lopsidedly interpreted by the clergies as it suits them against all infidels such as the Soviets, the US, and India. In true sense, building of democracy is off this agenda. While various options are being explored to stabilise the current situation and ensure peace in the region, a tangible possibility is not to exclude the *Taliban* from the process of governance. Use of force by foreign powers has never succeeded in Afghanistan. None of its rulers in the past two hundred years has died a natural death in that country. The specifics of history matters while determining a future government. It is the ninth year the Karzai government has not succeeded in putting the country under its control. The country has turned to be a terror factory to absorb all activities of the *Taliban* and *Al Qaeda* operating from the safe sanctuaries in neighbouring Pakistan. It would be prudent to approach the Afghan situation in a wider regional context by including Pakistan and Iran and neighbouring Central Asia that would also address the interests of other powers including the US, India, Russia and China.

Notes and References

1. *Sunday Mumbai Mirror*, February 1, 2009, p. 13.
2. Indrani Bagchi, "Pak Military, *Taliban* Unite against India", *The Times of India*, December 25, 2008, p. 1.
3. Brahma Chellaney, "Foil The Terror War", *The Times of India*, February 18, 2009, p. 18.
4. Shaun Gregory, "It's Time for Army and ISI to Feel the Heat", *Sunday Times of India*, January 4, 2009, p. 12.
5. "*Taliban* Gets Pak to enforce Sharia in Swat", *The Times of India*, February 17, 2009, p. 1.
6. *The Economist*, November 1, 2008, p. 36.
7. www.antidrugfront.ru 17 February,2009 newsletter.

8. P.L. Dash, "Central Asia: The Heroin Highway to Hell in Eurasian Vision", Mahavir Singh and Victor Krassilchtchikov (eds.), New Delhi: Anamika Publishers, 2003, p. 307. For the source, please refer to Irina Komissina and Adzhar Kurtov, Narkotiki Tsentral'noi Ajii: Novaya Ugroza tsivilizatsii, Rossiya I Musulmanskyi Mir, No. 1, 2001, 59.
9. Maxim Starchak, protivodeistvie Afghanskomy Narkotrafiku, Rossiya I Musulmanskii Mir, No. 10, 2008, p. 105.
10. Shoislam Akmalov, Afghanistan: Etapi uregulirovanniye I posledstviya postkonfliktnoi Situatsii, Rossiya I Musulmanskii Mir, No. 2, 2007, pp. 107-108.
11. Maxmim Starchak, *op. cit.*, p. 107.
12. Charles Allen, "All their Fatwas are on Computer", An interview published in the DNA, *Sunday*, Mumbai, November 19, 2006.
13. *Ibid.*
14. Yu. Laletin, Perviye Shagi Novogo Politicheskogo Obedeneniya v Afghanistane, Russiya I Musulmanskii Mir, No. 9, 2008, p. 100.
15. *Ibid*, p. 104.
16. M.K. Bhadrakumar, "How to Wind Down the Afghan War", *The Hindu*, October 20, 2008, p. 12. Please refer to the ten commandments in the same article as guidelines to resolving the problem.

13
Afghanistan: A Security Challenge for Eurasia

Sreemati Ganguli

The Soviet withdrawal from Afghanistan in 1989 was followed by a reign of terror, chaos and anarchy that went on for over two decades in Afghanistan. A near-simultaneous event of Soviet disintegration in 1991 and the collapse of the Soviet security architecture led to a pervasive security vacuum in the region covering the post-Soviet space. The insecurity scenario within Afghanistan poses a negative spill-over effect on the five Central Asian countries to an extent that we may talk of their forming a regional 'security complex' in Barry Buzan's terms. Such a security complex is defined by Buzan as "a group of states whose primary security concerns link together sufficiently closely that their national securities cannot realistically be considered apart from one another".[1] Buzan talked of five factors, namely, social factors of ethnic linguistic and historic importance; economic factors, military factor, political factors and environmental factors that constitute a security complex involving states of a region.[2]

This article, however, identifies two areas where the insecurities of Afghanistan and of these countries of Eurasia are interlinked—religious extremism and narcotics trafficking. There are two other areas where there is scope to develop linkages between security among them—energy and economy. The paper also takes into consideration the involvement of Russia in the security situation in Afghanistan in the post-Soviet withdrawal era, as well as the process of democratisation that is underway in the region.

Religious Extremism

The unenviable experience of remaining the theatre of superpower rivalry for 10 long years (1979-1989), the eventual Soviet pull-out (1989), the disintegration of the USSR (1991) and the emergence of the new states of Central Asia along its borders have redefined the nature and scope of Afghanistan's battleground. The political vacuum created after the Soviet pull-out, the inter-ethnic wars, the failure of *Mujahedeens* in building some form of political stability, the alarming growth of drug-trafficking, the proliferation of small arms leading to the 'kalashnikov culture' and a devastated economy—all these factors helped create an ideal atmosphere for militant religious extremism to flourish in Afghanistan.

On the other hand, the Central Asian states got an exposure to radical religious movements in Afghanistan since the days of the Soviet involvement there. In 1990, the anti-Armenian riots in Dushanbe were labeled as 'freedom movement' or 'internal revolt' against the 'Soviet subjugation' by Burhanuddin Rabbani and Ahmed Shah Masoud[3]. During the Tajik crisis of 1992, Shadmon Yusufov, Chairman of Democratic Party, made a public appeal to Afghanistan for assistance against the 'interference' of CIS forces in Tajikistan's 'internal crisis'[4]. Even a Tajik government-in-exile was set up in Taloqan in Afghanistan by a combination of Islamic Renaissance Party, Democratic Party, National Front and Lal-e-Badakhshan[5].

The increasing clout of militant Wahabi radical groups like the Birlik, the formation of armed bands in Ferghana Valley and influx of Uzbek and Tajik refugees and Afghan radicals from Afghanistan, led towards the consolidation and politicization of Islam in Uzbekistan. Alarmed by the possibility of the Tajik-Afghan border being turned to "an open gate" for arms smuggling and drug-trade to all the CARs, Uzbek President Islam Karimov appealed to the UN Secretary General on March 14, 1993 to ensure "the security and inviolability of border between Tajikistan and Afghanistan." He also apprised the UN of training-camps "for terrorist groups in Afghanistan for sabotage and subversion" in Central Asia.[6] The predominant terrorist group in Central Asia is the Islamic Movement of Uzbekistan (IMU) under Tahir Yuldashev and Jumabai Namangani. Some grave incidents of its terrorist attacks in the region may be cited: a series of bomb attacks in Tashkent in 1997, an unsuccessful attempt on President Karimov's life in 1999 and the Batken incidents of 1999 and of 2001. Its main base is in Afghanistan, and it has secured the support of the *Taliban* in setting up training camps there. The American 'War on Terror' acted as a blow for the IMU as they lost their training camps and their leader J. Namangani during the operations. Later they tried to re-organise the group in the Pashtun Tribal belt of Pakistan. In 2002, a splinter group of the IMU formed the Islamic *Jihad* Union and is known to be based in North

Waziristan of Pakistan and has close relations with an important neo-*Taliban* group of the region, the Haqqani network. They also have connections with the *Al Qaeda* network as they share "the same enemies: the United States, the Coalition in Afghanistan, the Karzai government as well as all the regimes in Greater Central Asia".[7] The spill-over effects of all these developments became manifest in growing illegal traffic of arms and narcotics from Tajikistan into Osh through the Afghan-Pamir route as well as in increasing presence of radicals in Kyrgyzstan. There is no denying the fact that there continues to be an obvious Afghan angle in the scenario of terrorism in Central Asia, as Robin Raphael, the US Assistant Secretary of State for South Asia, told the US Senate in May 1996 that "Afghanistan has become a conduit for drugs, crime and terrorism that can undermine Pakistan, the neighbouring Central Asian states and have an impact beyond Europe and Russia".[8]

Narcotics Trafficking

According to the UN Regional Representative Office for Drug Control and Crime Prevention, approximately 65 percent of the narcotics from Afghanistan follow the route Afghanistan-Tajikistan-Kyrgyzstan-Kazakhstan-Russia-Europe. A 2002 Report by the US State Department mentioned another permanent route: Afghanistan-Turkmenistan-Uzbekistan-Kazakhstan-Russia-Europe.[9] Also, according to Russian sources, of the main six routes for shipment of narcotics to Europe, four are through Central Asia—Kandahar-Herat-Turkmenistan-CIS-Europe; Kandahar-Balkh-Janjan-Uzbekistan-CIS-Europe; Kunduz-Tajikistan-Russia-Europe; Peshawar-Chitral-Afghan Badakhshan-Gorno-Badakhshan-Kyrgyzstan-CIS-Europe.[10] According to UN, ODCCP, though 65 per cent of narcotics-export from Afghanistan goes through Central Asia, only 5 percent of this can be intercepted by the law-enforcement agencies there.[11] And these figures corroborate what Asa Hutchinson, Director of the US Drug Enforcement Administration, commented—that the link between narcotics trafficking is primarily geographical: terrorists and drug-traffickers seek for a base in countries where law is weakly enforced. Another link is financial: terrorists need stable financing for their operations that narcotics provide overwhelmingly.[12]

The ten-year long war against the Soviet occupation and the following civil war nearly destroyed Afghanistan's crop-irrigation system and now opium is not only Afghanistan's only significant cash crop, it is the dominant currency, traded for arms, food and shelter. On the other hand, economic stagnation, weak law-enforcement system, growth of armed political movements, lack of adequate border protection, and limited institutional capabilities to make use of local resources, have made the Central Asian states increasingly vulnerable to the proliferation of narcotics trade and related crimes. The UN Office on Drugs and Crime in a Report put stress on some other reasons of Central Asia becoming an easy transit route for Afghan narcotics: the geographical location of the Central Asian region between Afghanistan and the major markets of Russia and Europe; widespread corruption facilitating illegal activities including narcotics-trafficking; illegal labour migration providing ready-made channels for the clandestine transport of narcotics; and ill-capacity of law enforcement agencies of Central Asian states for interdiction of narcotics due to lack of resources, training and equipments. And major deficiencies in intelligence-collection and sharing between the Central Asian states and Afghanistan affect effective policing of common borders in a number of ways—"a lack of understanding of the value of information in assisting effective law enforcement; a lack of planned, structured, systematic information gathering procedures within national law enforcement agencies, a lack of analytical capacity and skills; and a lack of inter-agency cooperation and consequent sharing of law enforcement related information." So, there arise difficulties in "designing strategies to counter drug trafficking" in a joint way.[13]

Energy

The locational advantage of Afghanistan to the South Asian market has made it an important transit state for energy routes from Central to South Asia. The viability of the TAGP (Turkmenistan-Afghanistan Gas Pipeline) project has been totally dependent on the stability and security situation in Afghanistan. Turkmenistan's recognition of the *Taliban* regime and the initial US negligence of the menacing effect of the *Taliban* factor on the security of the Central Asian region were linked to the possibility of implementation of this project. Shireen Hunter noted that there was a connection between the Afghan civil war and the issue of getting an outlet for Central Asian energy and commented that "It is clear that the desire to find a southern outlet for Central Asia's oil and gas that would bypass Iran has complicated the Afghan civil war, first and foremost as a factor in the rise of the *Taliban*".[14] Ahmed Rashid also discussed the involvement of international oil companies like Bridas, Delta and Unocal as well as of the US and Pakistan in 'romancing' with the *Taliban* to build the pipeline and referred to the comments made by Yasushi Akashi, the UN Under

Secretary General for Humanitarian Affairs that 'The outside interference in Afghanistan is now all related to the battle for oil and gas pipelines. The fear is that these companies and regional powers are just renting the *Taliban* for their own purposes".[15] Here the geopolitics of providing alternative energy routes, bypassing both Russia and Iran, to the CARs was given priority over the economic logic or wider security considerations.

But in future, Afghanistan may become more directly and more positively involved in the energy security scenario of the Central Asian region, as the Report by the US Geological Survey and the Afghan Ministry of Mines and Industry has suggested, in March 2006, that undiscovered energy resources in Northern Afghanistan range from 3.6 to 36.5 trillion cubic feet of natural gas and 0.4 to 3.6 billion barrels of oil—an 18-fold increase in Afghanistan's potential oil resources and more than triple the gas resources.[16]

Economic Cooperation

The need for long-term and sustainable development of the region has become a facilitator for a number of projects that would develop the infrastructural as well as institutional capacities to focus on energy, trade and transport within the region and beyond. The October 2007 Meet of the Council of Ministers of Economic Cooperation Organisation (involving Turkey, Iran, Kazakhstan, Kyrgyzstan, Tajikistan, Turkmenistan, Pakistan and Afghanistan) in Herat discussed plans for the regional transport and energy infrastructure and deliberated on taking up the grandiose plan for establishing a free trade area in the region by 2015.

The Central Asia Regional Economic Cooperation Programme or CAREC (that includes China, Mongolia, Azerbaijan, Kazakhstan, Kyrgyzstan, Tajikistan, Uzbekistan and Afghanistan and six other multilateral financial institutions like ADB, EBRD, IMF, UNDP, World Bank and Islamic Development Bank) focuses particularly on intra-regional cooperation in the areas of trade, transport and energy. The 2007 Ministerial Conference in Dushanbe approved a trade and transport strategy to develop six priority transport corridors and discussed the need for an integrated CAREC Energy strategy.

The Special Programme for the Economies of Central Asia (SPECA), consisting of Azerbaijan, Kazakhstan, Tajikistan. Uzbekistan and Afghanistan, is another initiative to support regional cooperation in trade, transport, water, environment and social development. The Central Asia

South Asia Regional Electricity Market or CASAREM promotes the development of the CASA1000 transmission project to build electricity transmission infrastructure among the four member-states—Kyrgyzstan, Tajikistan, Afghanistan and Pakistan.

The need to involve Afghanistan in all these regional economic cooperation initiatives is to engage Afghanistan economically. The move to use Afghanistan as a bridgehead between Central and South Asia, as is evident in the Greater Central Asia-South Asia project is another indicator of the role Afghanistan might play in the region. The success of these initiatives might lead to the solution of another menacing problem—the cultivation of opium as the main cash crop of Afghan farmers as they might then get an opportunity to think of other alternatives as livelihood. Afghanistan presents the prime example of both "the transnational and regional character of contemporary armed conflict and the difficulties in achieving regional post-conflict reconstruction" and so, it is suggested that "Just as regional cooperation may be essential for Afghanistan's sustainable recovery, Afghanistan's sustainable recovery may be essential for regional cooperation".[17]

Russia's Involvement in Afghan Security Scenario

Whereas the Central Asian states are involved mostly in the economic cooperative ventures with Afghanistan, Russia's involvement is centred in the security scenario of Afghanistan. The rise of the *Taliban* was the prime mover for this change in Russia's stance as Russia showed a disinterest in Afghan domestic affairs since the Soviet troop withdrawal from Kabul in 1989.

Taliban's seizure of Kabul and Jalalabad in September 1996 prompted Russia to organise a meet of the Heads of the Central Asian states in Almaty in October 1996 to give a shape to the formation of a unified anti-*Taliban* coalition. This move later became institutionalised to make a viable resistance movement of the United Front with external support from Russia, Iran and all the Central Asian states, except Turkmenistan.

During the War on Terror in 2001, Moscow offered close cooperation with Washington on several levels—intelligence sharing, use of Russian air corridors for humanitarian deliveries, increased support for the United Front, endorsement of decisions by the Central Asian Republics to grant the US forces access to their military bases and airfields in Manas, Karshi-Khanabad, Kulyab, Kokaidy and Termez, and participation in search and rescue operations. Russia stopped short of direct participation in military campaigns as Russian policy-makers were guided by Russia's own problems in Chechnya and the possible repercussions of getting further embroiled in a war, evidently laden with anti-Russian overtures. They were also motivated by the post-Soviet experience in Afghanistan.

Russia was later an active participant in the 6+2 dialogue (involving the six neighbouring states of Afghanistan—Iran, Pakistan, China, Tajikistan, Uzbekistan and Turkmenistan as well as Russia and the US) for the reconstruction of post-War Afghanistan and also in the UN-sponsored Bonn Conference. However, noted Russian analyst Dmitri Trenin commented that "Russia did have an urge to play a lead role in the Afghan reconstruction effort but that its history in Afghanistan and its limited financial resources prevented it from doing so."[18]

However, in the post-*Taliban* period, Russia donated approximately $100 million to Afghanistan and donated hundreds of military trucks, jeeps, radios, wireless and communications units and heavy artillery spare parts to the Afghan National Army.[19] Interestingly, Yuri Krupnov, Russian political analyst and the head of the Development Movement and the Institute for Demography, suggested a more active Russian involvement in Afghan security and development scenario, in the Report titled "The Path to Peace and Concord in Afghanistan will be Determined by the Position Russia Takes".[20]

Both SCO and CSTO—the two regional security initiatives where Russia plays a significant role—project focus on Afghanistan through Working Groups. The SCO Contact Group on Afghanistan considers the security matters of Afghanistan and their impact on the region covering China and held a Conference, under the SCO Regional Security Group in March in Moscow, on the situation in Afghanistan and its influence on neighbouring states as well as to boost joint efforts to counteract terrorism, illegal drug trade and trans-border organised crime from Afghan territory. The CSTO established a Working Group on Afghanistan in 2005 to develop recommendations on strengthening Afghan security institutions and on anti-drug trafficking measures. CSTO also has plans to develop its own security relations with Afghanistan, involving training of Afghan army personnel, supply of arms and providing support to counter-narcotics operations. The offer made by CSTO to create a joint CSTO-NATO cooperation mechanism on Afghanistan, the Uzbek suggestion to revive and transform the 6+2 Contact group on Afghanistan, into a 6+3 formation by involving NATO as well as Uzbek President Karimov's offer to sign a NATO-Uzbek agreement to provide a transit corridor to deliver non-military cargo to Afghanistan through Termez-Kheyraton, during the April 2008 NATO and Euro-Atlantic Partnership Council Summit[21] are marked signs of the need for coordination among all involved powers in Afghanistan.

The recent event of the Russian consent to provide a transit corridor to supply food, non-military cargo and some types of non-lethal military equipments to Afghanistan for the ISAF at the request of the US and NATO may be an important development for the future of Afghanistan. This Corridor through the Russian territory will help avoid the extremely hazardous route through Pakistan, through which at least 70 percent of the supplies go at present and it will also cut the air-shipping costs as airlifts to Afghanistan costs $14,000 for a tonne, whereas it will cost only about $500 a tonne by railroutes from Europe to Afghanistan through Russia.[22]

The so-called return of Russia to Afghanistan seems to be an irony for some commentators, as the US seeks Russian help to combat in Afghanistan, an area where the US-Soviet rivalry was at its worst during the Cold War period. But this move reveals the realization of the ground situation in Afghanistan, as the US faces a daunting task of combating an ever-strengthening *Taliban* coupled with the closure of its military bases in Uzbekistan and Kyrgyzstan.

Democratisation

There is another significant trend that is intrinsically linked with the wider and deeper security considerations of the whole region, and that is the process towards democratisation. This process started in the early 1990s for the Central Asian States, whereas Afghanistan joined the process a decade later. Samuel P. Huntington termed the process of democratisation engulfing Europe and Latin American countries in the 1970s and the Communist regimes of Eastern Europe in the late 1980's as the third Wave of democratisation, after the first wave of 1828-1926 in Europe and the second wave of 1943-62 in the developing world.[23] Taking a cue from him, authors like Archie Brown termed the process of transition from the Communist rule as a fourth wave.[24] But none of them included the Eurasian countries or Afghanistan in their analyses. But the region as a whole is undergoing this process, under whatever wave one may call it.

For the Central Asian states, the promises of building a democratic state, with a truly independent media, non-governmental groups and opposition parties are not yet fulfilled after nearly two decades of their independence. In these states, "political power remains concentrated in the hands of the President, tolerance levels for opponent views are low and successive elections are used as tools for perpetuating the rules of the reigning authorities. Different socio-political patterns characterise the processes of establishing government set-ups: In Uzbekistan and Turkmenistan, strong tribal identities form centres of power in the highly centralised governmental structures; whereas regional identities are a potent force in Kazakhstan, Kyrgyzstan and Tajikistan. Family connections also control decision-making in a significant way. So there is the trend that hinders the democratisation processes in these Republics and there is the suggestion that the variation in the region is different shades of authoritarianism, "from the totalitarian dictatorship in Turkmenistan to the hard authoritarian regime in Uzbekistan and up to the more or less 'soft' authoritarian regimes of Tajikistan, Kazakhstan and Kyrgyzstan".[25]

For Afghanistan the process is much more complex as Afghanistan, termed as "one of the most savagely traumatized countries"[26] in the world, faces a myriad of challenges. After nearly three decades of (1979-2001) of war and the resultant chaos, it is in the process of building up a democratic, stable and tolerant state and each poses a most difficult challenge for the state as it faces simultaneous crises of institutional decomposition, elite fragmentation, the most intolerant kind of religious authority and so on. The 2004 Presidential elections and the 2005 Parliamentary elections may be called the first few steps towards democratization, though Afghanistan has the prior experiences of relatively free Parliamentary elections in 1965 and 1969 during the era of 'New Democracy' from 1964-1973.

There is a long-drawn debate in the arena of international relations, as whether democratisation actually leads to peace and stability, as the followers of Democratic Peace theory suggest or whether democratising states face increased probability of internal conflicts or civil war in the transition phase and secondly, whether democratisation is used as a foreign policy tool for expansionist and interventionist moves by external powers. Whereas Boutros-Ghali stated that as democratic states are more legitimate, they are less likely to get involved in regional wars, or Huntington argued that "the spread of democracy in the world means the expansion of the zone of peace in the world",[27] Layne argued that that illusions of achieving peace through democracy probably would lead to "disastrous military interventions abroad" and "strategic overextension"[28] and Mansfield-Snyder criticised the theory and suggested that democratising states are much more war-prone, as during the transition phase, the power vacuum in the ruling circles and absence of democratic institutions result into a chaos as "threatened elites from the collapsing autocratic regime...use nationalist appeals to compete mass allies with each other and new elites".[29] A study by Hegre and others also suggested that "...regime change clearly and strongly increases the probability of civil war in the short run".[30] The 2001 War on Terror and the 2003 Iraq War highlighted this debate even more. Pursuing wars to promote democracy may be termed, as Chan called it, 'democratic crusades'.[31] N. Panagiotu commented pertinently that "pursuing a policy of democratisation may create wars in precisely those situations where the intention is to avoid them."[32]

For Afghanistan the process of transition to democracy is tumultuous. A noted analyst enumerated a number of challenges to transition process in Afghanistan, like state-building, regaining trust of the people and establishing society.[33] But the kind of democratization that is not forced upon would be the best. As Joseph Nye Jr. suggested that the main lesson to be learned from the Iraq War 'is that while the development of democracy can be aided from outside, it cannot easily be imposed by force'[34] and a sort of democratization that includes all the ethno-religio-linguistic complexities of Afghan society is the only way for a stable polity. Because the promotion of genuine democracy is the determining factor in building sustainable human development and lasting peace, through enforcement of rule of law and protection of human rights. And also because in that sort of a polity, people get more chances to voice their grievances against authorities in a peaceful manner as otherwise, the lack of truly representative political institutions, along with the socio-economic crises Afghanistan faces now, would result in more people turning to religious extremism as the last resort to register protests, as that is the case with the Central Asian states to a certain extent. The development of such political institutions will also have better opportunities to provide the political space needed for genuine public participation, to limit selective political exclusion (like in cases of ethnic communities or gender) and thus to initiate the process to build political pluralism (which allows each part of society to get involved in the political process) to thwart the sense of alienation on the part of any section of society—either ethnic, or regional or religious or gender. And that polity will then be able to confront the challenges of conducting viable economic reforms and establishing security within itself. An Afghanistan, secure with itself, may become one of the guarantors of peace, security and stability in the Eurasian region as well. It is a long-term task with dangers all around. But, we may quote what Andrei Shleifer-Daniel Treisman commented for Russia's experiences with economic reforms, in the context of the transition process in Afghanistan: It is like "embarking on a journey through mountains without a map.... To understand their (the mountaineers') chances of success, it is not enough to consider their will power, their integrity, and the climbing kits or cash international friends have supplied. One also has to consider the shape of the mountain".[35]

Notes and References

1. Barry Buzan, *People, States and Fear: An Agenda for International Security Studies in the Post-Cold War Era*, London, New York: Harvester Wheatscheaf, 1991, p. 190.
2. Hooman Peiman, *Regional Security and the Future of Central Asia*, London: Praeger, 1998, p. 18.
3. Agence France Presse Report, February 15, 1990.
4. Short Wave Broadcasts, *SU 1379*, May 13, 1992.
5. K. Warikoo, "Cockpit of Central Asia: Afghanistan Factor in Tajikistan's Crisis" in K. Warikoo (ed.), *Afghanistan Factor in Central and South Asian Politics*, Occasional Pape r 1, Himalayan Research and Cultural Foundation, New Delhi, 1994.
6. SWB, *SU/1642,* March 20, 1993.
7. See D. Chaudet, Islamist Terrorism in Greater Central Asia, *www.ifri.org*
8. Robin Raphael, Testimony to the Senate Foreign Relations Sub-Committee on the Near East and South Asia, May 11, 1996. Cited in Ahmed Rashid, *Taliban: Islam, Oil and the New Great Game* in *Central Asia,* New Haven: Yale University Press, 2000.
9. See International Narcotics Control Strategy Report, 2002, March 2003, *www.state.gov/g/int/rls/nrcrp*
10. Nezavisimaya Gazeta, March 17, 2001, cited in Sultan Akimbekov, "The Conflict in Afghanistan: Conditions, Problems and Prospects", in Boris Rumer (ed.), *Central Asia: A Gathering Storm?,* New Delhi: M.E. Sharpe, Aakar Books, 2003.
11. Erika Dailey, 'Government and International Responses to Human Rights Abuses at Tajikistan', *www.eurasianet.org*
12. See A. Sirotin, "Narkotiki Is Afghanistana", *Chika*, Vol. 1, No. 17, 2002, *www.chayka,org/article*
13. See United Nations Office on Drugs and Crime, Securing Central Asia's Borders with Afghanistan Outline Action Plan, September 2007
14. Shireen T. Hunter, 'The Afghan Civil War: Implications for Central Asian Stability' in Robert Ebel-Rajan Menon (ed.), *Energy and Conflict in Central Asia and the Caucasus*, New York and Oxford: Rowman and Littlefield, 2000.
15. See Ahmed Rashid, *Taliban, op. cit.*
16. See Stephen Blank, "Afghanistan's Energy Future and Its Potential Implications", *www.eurasianet.org*

17. Barnett R. Rubin and Andrea Armstrong, "Regional Issues in the Reconstruction of Afghanistan", *World Policy Journal*, Spring 2003
18. In a Seminar organised by the Carnegie Endowment for International Peace, March 7, 2003, http://www.carnegieendowment.org/events.
19. "Russian Envoy Questions Presence of US Military Bases in Afghanistan", http://www.redorbit.com,/modules/news
20. "Russia must come back to Afghanistan", *http://www.globaliamagazine.com*
21. Roy Allison, *"Security Cooperation between Western States and Russia over Central Asia/Afghanistan: The Changing Role of Uzbekistan"*, Programme Paper, Chatham House, November 24, 2000
22. Vladimir Radyuhin, Russia Returns to Afghanistan, on request, http://www.hinduonnet.com
23. Samuel P. Huntington, *The Third Wave: Democratization in the Late Twentieth Century*, London and Norman: University of Oklahoma Press, 1991.
24. Archie Brown, 'Transnational Influences in the Transition from Communism', *Post-Soviet Affairs*, Vol. 16 No. 2, 2000.
25. Eugheniy Zhovtis, *Democratisation and Human Rights in Central Asia,* CEPS Policy Brief, No. 134, July 2007.
26. Quoted in William Maley, "The Dynamics of Regime Transition in Afghanistan", *Central Asian Survey*, Vol. 16 No. 2, 1997.
27. S.P. Huntington, *The Third Wave*, *op. cit.*
28. Cited in Nikolaos Panagiotu, "Is the Process of Democratization The Mean For A Peaceful World?", *www.ceeol.com*
29. E. D. Mansfield, and J. Snyder, "Democratization and the Danger of War", *International Security,* Volume 20, Number 1, Summer 1995.
30. Hegre Harvard, T. Ellingsen, S. Gates, N.P. Cleditsch, "Toward a Democratic Civil Peace?", *American Political Science Review,* March 2001.
31. Steve Chan, "In Search of Democratic Peace: Problems and Promise", *Mershon International Studies Review*, cited in N. Panagiotu, *op. cit.*
32. *Ibid*
33. See William Maley's comments in "Political Transition in Afghanistan: The State, Islam and Civil Society", *http://wilsoncenter.org*
34. Joseph S. Nye Jr, "Does increasing democracy undercut terrorists?", *The Christian Science Monitor*, September 22, 2005
35. Andrei Shleifer-Daniel Treisman, *Without A Map: Political Tactics and Economic Reform in Russia,* Cambridge: MIT Press, 2000.

Section III

Mitigating War Effects Through Development Interventions

14

Development Interventions in Afghanistan

Abdul Rahman Ulfat Mahmoodi

Introduction

Three decade long war has left deep imprints on Afghan society and has thoroughly destroyed the social and physical infrastructure. Not only that, but during the mentioned period, the Afghans did not have the opportunity to update their capacities with the needs of modern day resulting in a significant vacuum of human resources while a number of intellectual personalities were lost to the civil war. However, the involvement of international community in the country, especially NGO sector during early 1990s, provided an opportunity for a number of Afghans to learn state of the art development practices.

Considering the fact that Afghanistan has been through a long period of war, there has been significant effects of the war in the country. The effects of the destruction are visible not only in the overall status of the country but in the minds of individuals as well. A recent survey of Oxfam International shows that almost 80 percent Afghans are faced with psychological problems. The above mentioned status of Afghan society requires significant but coordinated efforts in order to mitigate the effects of war and transform the Afghan society into a normal socio-political and socio-economic society. The coordination means that all official and unofficial development assistance is utilized as per a consistent development strategy while involving local capacities.

Refugees

Although Afghanistan is not yet to transfer from conflict to post-conflict country, the neighboring countries have already started deporting the refugees from their territories. On the other hand, the Government of Afghanistan is not in a position to fully integrate the returnees in to a beneficial day to day labour.

Afghanistan is currently in greater need of dealing with the problem of unemployment due to the unavailability of industries and other job opportunities, while the returning refugees are adding to the problem. In order to meet with the problem as well as approach the resolution of other problems being faced by the society, comprehensive development interventions are required to be initiated and long-term and short-term job opportunities must be considered.

Agriculture

One of the development interventions that can play a vital role in mitigating the effects of war is employment generation activities in Agriculture sector. Agriculture is proposed because the overall economy of Afghans rests upon this sector. The major activities in the sector could be reconstruction of agricultural infrastructure through utilising Afghan labour which in turn will provide access to the people to employment. On the other hand, the reconstruction of agriculture infrastructure would help the increase of agricultural products resulting in food self-sufficiency as currently the country is importing wheat and other food items from other countries, while during early in 1970s Afghanistan was exporting wheat to international market.

The above proposed interventions would also enable the 4.2 million returnees to settle back in their own backyard in rural areas (as about 70 percent Afghan population lives in rural areas). This would help not only deal with settlement of returnees but also would avoid increasing urbanisation while ensuring that agriculture, the backbone of Afghan economy, is back on track.

Education

Education is the most important sector which requires special consideration in a development strategy capable of reducing negative effects of war, because on the one hand a long lasting devastating war destroyed educational infrastructure of the country, while on the other hand, current insecurity is preventing around 300,000 school students from going to schools in the south and south west of the country. This is while the bombing or closure of more than 700 schools by either the *Taliban* or terrorists makes the sector on of the most vulnerable sectors requiring urgent attention and rehabilitation efforts.

Therefore, a development intervention supported by both long-term and short-term strategies must provide educational opportunities, which could be created through construction of school buildings, provision of books and other related materials and awareness among masses about the importance of education. Moreover, community based education structure could also play an important role in the areas where robust education infrastructure development is not possible. Additionally, the activities could be designed around building the capacities of teachers in modern teaching skills. Besides, the teachers' community should be further supported through provisions of other subsistence facilities.

Women Empowerment

A comprehensive development process would not be possible without empowerment of women, since they form 55 percent of the overall Afghan population. However, in a culturally restricted society like Afghanistan, proposal of drastic changes can result in opposition of masses. Nevertheless, the strategic importance of the issue could not be ignored. Therefore, in order to deal with the issue, religion could be used. Considering the fact that Afghan society is very much religious, explanation of women rights in Islam can help people respect women rights. This will not only help women access their rights but also would provide them with very strong allays in the shape of male members of their families.

It is important to underline the fact that ensuring full participation of women in socio economic mainstream requires time and patience of a developing society because educational disparity between males and females starts early in life. Primary school enrolments reflect the inequality that starts at the beginning, and the disparity increases in secondary and higher education. Afghanistan has the lowest female literacy rate in the world, between 9 percent and 18 percent. Violence against women is pervasive, a silent epidemic due to the low status of women, and compounded by long exposure to hostilities and conflict. It is a major obstacle to achieving gender equality and needs to be overcome through multiple efforts, including the rule of law, awareness creation, utilisation of religion as mentioned above, and gradually changing cultural practices and mindsets. Above all, it requires political commitment and leadership at the highest levels to take actions that will concretely improve the rights of women.

By allocating 25 percent of the seats in the lower house of the National Assembly to women, Afghanistan has taken steps to bring about gender parity in the formal representation of women in decision-making. This needs to be followed by similar steps toward the effective participation of women in decision-making at all levels. But substantive participation by women will, above all, depend on the progress of education and economic empowerment.

Environmental Security

Although environmental security is an important facet of development of a society, probably, no intervention could succeed in this sector without economic development of Afghan citizens. Therefore, extreme efforts should be made towards economic development before initiatives on environmental preservation could be made. Currently, very few environment preservation laws exist in the country while awareness of people is also very low. Therefore, there is a need for legislation in this regard while it would require rigorous efforts from the Government to implement the laws, to explain more about the environmental security. The forest cover appears to have been cut in half since 1978 as a result of lack of energy alternatives to firewood and demand for timber in both Afghanistan and Pakistan. Only percent of the population have access to a regular supply of electricity. Due to drought and the destruction of water management systems, the water table has sunk in many areas. The growing population is mining the country's deep aquifer water reserves, and water quality is declining. Eighty percent of the rural population drinks contaminated water. With the return of millions of refugees, cities, overwhelmed by air pollution, sewage, and waste, has become swollen with transient populations living in slums, where an estimated 75 percent of the urban population lives.

Afghanistan must increase the proportion of land area under protected forests and restore the forest cover, while developing a system capable of implementing forest protection in the face of resistance from powerful timber mafias. The Afghan population needs access to cheap non-solid fuels. The experience of other poor countries shows that it is possible to change from the exclusive use of coal and wood toward a mix of energy including gas and solar energy over a period of 20 years. Rural electrification should be actively developed. Increased access to improved water sources and improved sanitation will not only contribute to sustaining the environment but also improve the overall health of the population, especially by reducing child morbidity and mortality.

Having proposed all above interventions, measurement of results would play crucial role. Currently, a huge amount of development assistance is invested without a real measurement of affect. Consequently, no lessons are learned and as such a number of mistakes are repeated again and again. Hence, systematic monitoring and evaluation of the interventions must be based on broader development indicators. Moreover, all these efforts should be fully coordinated and aligned with the national development strategy in order to result in broader and lasting change.

Poverty

Poverty measurement in Afghanistan is severely constrained by lack of data. Available data suggests that about 20 per cent of rural Afghans are chronically unsure of obtaining enough food, and another 18 per cent are vulnerable. The Afghan diet, consisting mostly of grains, has little variety, creating a serious problem of malnutrition. Nearly 40 per cent of the children under 3 years old are underweight, and more than half of the children in that age group are stunted. Both calorie intake and dietary diversity are greater for families that are closer to the market: households farther from the market consume fewer calories and have a less diverse diet.

Afghanistan needs a secure environment and sustained growth over at least over the next 10 years to reduce poverty significantly by 2020. This growth would have to actively favour the poor by building their productive assets. Much of this growth will have to come from (non-poppy) agriculture, which contributes more than 50 percent of the licit gross domestic products and provides employment to two-thirds of the workforce. Investment in rural roads, power, and water will increase access to markets and provide impetus to the rural economy, reducing hunger and malnutrition. A massive rural public works programme to build a reliable rural road system and irrigation will help generate rural employment and wages, connect the rural population to the market and create necessary conditions for poverty reduction.

Infrastructure

Among landlocked developing countries, Afghanistan has one of the longest distances to a seaport (over 2,000 kilometers) over exceedingly harsh land. The country has no railroads and one of the world's lowest degrees of road penetration, about 0.032 km of roads per square km of area and only 16 percent of roads paved, with the definition of "paved road" appearing to be "a road that was paved at one time."

As a poor landlocked country seeking to emerge from violent conflict, Afghanistan needs international partnership to connect to the market, provide employment, particularly to youth (a major factor in preventing violence), and invest in basic institutions and services. Afghanistan and its neighbours need to transform their relationship from one based on fears of destabilisation to one based on a common interest in cooperation. Key to this change is the transformation of Afghanistan to a "land bridge" for the region through investment in regional transport infrastructure, simplification and harmonisation of border procedures, management of water resources, and encouragement of labour migration. Hence, Afghanistan needs cooperation and increasing economic integration with its neighbours, in addition to global aid.

Mortality Rate

Life expectancy at birth is under 45 years, 20 years less than any other Asian country. Over a fifth of all Afghan children die before the age of five. Of these, a third die soon after birth, and more than half within the first year. High mortality rates are due to lack of food, poor sanitation, and low literacy, especially of women. About 70 per cent of the rural population and 40 per cent of the urban population have no access to clean water. About 41 per cent of the rural population and 13 per cent of the urban population have no access to proper sanitation. The measles immunization programme has been a success in Afghanistan, with 75 percent of children aged less than 12 months having being immunized. Owing to much higher immunisation coverage of children in urban as opposed to rural areas, infant and child mortality rates in the rural areas are around 25 percent higher.

Due to the existing poverty, Afghanistan has the highest rate of maternal mortality in the world except Sierra Leone and Angola. Overall maternal mortality is estimated at 1600 to 2200 deaths per 100,000 live births. As a result of the low level of female education and gender segregation, fewer than 15 percent of births are attended by medically trained personnel (who must be female), and only 10 percent by a traditional midwife; 75 percent of births are attended only by family members. Nearly 16 percent of Afghan girls are married before the age of 15 and 52 per cent are married before their eighteenth birthday. Meeting the challenge of reducing maternal mortality will require education, communication and changes in cultural practices. Within the average Afghan family, there is little knowledge of reproductive health and the impact of sexual behaviour on health.

Despite extreme poverty, ill health, and hunger, Afghans define the lack of security as their greatest problem. Hence, the government of Afghanistan has added this new goal to the eight global MDGs. The main security threat identified by most Afghans is not terrorism or attacks by those fighting the government or its international supporters. The armed opposition is confined to a few border provinces. The main threat Afghans quote is an absence of the rule of law resulting in violent predation by local power holders, criminals, and corrupt officials. Four million Afghans live in communities affected by landmines or unexploded ordnance (UXO), and Afghanistan has the world's highest proportion of handicapped people after Cambodia. Half of the victims of landmines or UXOs are under 18 years old.

Narcotics

Afghanistan's economy is far more dependent on the production, refining, and export of narcotics than any other economy in the world. Afghans receive only a tiny share of the ultimate value of narcotics in retail markets, and many opium farmers are burdened with massive debt, but the little that Afghans do receive forms a substantial part of their impoverished national economy. The UN Office on Drugs and Crime estimates that in 2004-2005 Afghanistan's opium economy earned more than $2.8 billion, three quarters of which went to traffickers, not farmers. This is a fraction of the value of Afghanistan's opium sold on the international market estimated to be worth between $30-60 billion. The income from narcotics exceeds the total official international assistance spent in the country and is more directly accessible to people than most foreign aid. In recent past years the drug economy has grown more rapidly than the legal economy and is estimated to equal 50-60 percent of the legal economy and one-third to 40 percent of the total economy.

At least two million people rely directly on the drug economy for their livelihood, and many more benefit from its indirect effects, such as employment in construction and trade financed by drug profits. Increasing amounts of opium are processed into heroin and other high-value products within Afghanistan with the help of international organized crime, increasing the profits of traffickers, and further corrupting government and law enforcement agencies. Opiates, Afghanistan's only major export, play a significant though as yet un-quantified role in enabling the country to finance the non-drug trade deficit while maintaining price stability and the value of the currency. The government receives customs revenue levied on drug-financed imports. The government has an internationally supported plan for counter-narcotics, but eliminating a third to 40 percent of Afghanistan's economy without endangering security and stability will require massive resources and time.

Disability

Another challenge before the development of the country is disability. In Afghanistan local surveys indicate that probably about 3 percent of the population of 25 million is disabled. This gives a figure of about 700,000 people. War injuries (mainly from mines) and polio account for about half this number. The other half is composed of people with mental retardation, clever palsy, leprosy in certain areas, deafness, blindness, and multiple impairments. As with all disability statistics one must distinguish between incidence (the number who are born or made disabled) and prevalence (the number who survive). 3 percent is an estimate of the prevalence. It would be almost impossible to measure the figure for incidence in the present circumstances. Therefore, as success in Afghanistan rests on addressing poverty and economic depravity, a comprehensive balanced development of the country requires the rehabilitation and reconstruction plan supported by unwavering commitment of the international community which should not ignore to address the challenges such as the disability.

Conclusion

Despite extreme poverty, diseases, and hunger, Afghans define the lack of security as their greatest problem. Hence the Afghan government has added this new goal to the eight global MDGs. The main security threat identified by most Afghans is not terrorism or attacks by those who are fighting against the government and Coalition forces. The armed opposition is confined to a few provinces which are located along the Durand line. The main threat that Afghans face is the weakness of rule of law resulting in violation of law by local power holders, corrupt officials and criminals. Unemployment in Afghanistan is escalating the ongoing conflict, and strengthening the warlords who are threatening rule of law in Afghanistan.

To achieve pro-poor growth while eliminating the criminal economy, we need to focus on particular upon those areas that enhance our current and future productivity, including electricity, roads, irrigation, institutional and human capacity building, creating an enabling environment for private sector development and protecting the rights of the poor. As we target our investments in these areas, we will seek to support likely areas of accelerated economic growth, including rural development (agriculture and rural industries), the management of state assets, mining and extractive industries, and transit.

To overcome these constraints, the Government's key education programmes will (1) expand access to Primary and Secondary education, increase enrollment and retention rates, and strengthen the curriculum and quality of teachers; (2) build a well-managed and internationally recognised system of higher education that responds to Afghanistan's growth and development needs; (3) develop an effective Skills Development system that is responsive to labour market needs.

15

Ownership of Policy-Making in an Aid-Dependent Country: Formulation of Afghanistan National Development Strategy (ANDS): A Case Study

Sayed Muhammad Shah

The policymaking process is messy, but it can be characterised as involving various stages. These include agenda setting, policy formulation and policy implementation. There are various internal and external factors influencing the process throughout, and the result typically manifests in the agenda of the party in power. In Afghanistan, identifying who is actually in power is difficult because the government's autonomy is weakened by its dependency on foreign aid. Sixty two donors[1] *support the Afghan Government with billions of dollars for a part of its recurrent expenditures and for its entire development programmes. These donors have diverse mandates and approaches to the development of various sectors in the country and spend a large portion of development funds directly, without the government's involvement, on specific programmes in their regions of interest. These donors also strive to ensure integration of their priorities in national programmes, making it very difficult for the government to decide on national priority programmes.*

The preparation of the Afghanistan National Development Strategy (ANDS) has been the biggest policymaking and strategy development event in the history of modern Afghanistan since 2001. The last seven years of development efforts in Afghanistan have resulted in important rounds of policy and strategy development. In 2002, a National Development Framework (NDF) was prepared for the Interim Government of Afghanistan and national priority programmes were identified for the emergency period.[2] Based on input from government departments and the direction of the Afghan Assistance Coordination Authority (AACA), the NDF was, according to most accounts, designed and written by foreign experts.[3]

Securing Afghanistan's Future (SAF) emerged after the preparation of the NDF. SAF was written in 2004 by more than 100 international experts from the United Nations (UN) and multilateral development institutions in collaboration with their Afghan colleagues. It put forward a programme of investments designed to lay the foundations for the sustained economic growth needed to support a financially sustainable state capable of undertaking social development and poverty reduction.[4] Both the NDF and SAF documents were developed with limited consultations with Afghans during the formulation process and hence were dubbed non-Afghanised strategies[5].

The Afghanistan Compact (AC) and the Interim Afghanistan National Development Strategy (I-ANDS) process began in early 2005 with a discussion of Afghanistan's Millenium Development Goals (MDGs), which the Government of Afghanistan envisions will improve the well-being of its people. The MDGs, agreed upon by all UN member states, set measurable targets for "enabling more human beings to enjoy the minimum requirements of a dignified life by 2015."[6] Because of its lost decades and the lack of required information, Afghanistan has altered the time frame for achieving its MDG targets to 2020.

The I-ANDS development process was led by a Presidential Oversight Committee (OSC) chaired by Professor Nadiri, then Senior Economic Advisor to the President. Committee members included Senior Advisor to the President and Minister of Commerce; Minister for Foreign Affairs; Minister of Finance; Minister of Economy; National Security Advisor; and Minister of Rural Rehabilitation and Development[7]. Afghanistan Reconstruction and Development Services Director headed the working groups. The OSC worked throughout 2005 and 2006 to develop and refine the contents of I-ANDS and to oversee the process.

Based on the MDGs, the I-ANDS was developed. It contained three pillars, under which eight sub-pillars and six cross-cutting issues articulated policies. The OSC consulted donors, the private sector, non-governmental organisations (NGOs) and civil society representatives through a consultation draft. An External Advisory Group (EAG) of donors provided informal feedback on the I-ANDS. The UN facilitated AC negotiations, and consultations were held between the international community and the Government of Afghanistan to set the benchmarks, which represent consensus on policy priorities between the two. However, some sources said that tea clubs of major ambassadors were responsible for much of the indicator development.

The Afghanistan Compact is a political agreement between the Government of Afghanistan and the international community to work together toward achieving five-year benchmarks. It supports the government's development strategy with each benchmark reflected as a five-year strategic objective of the I-ANDS. The London Conference, held from January 31 to February 1, 2006, brought together 60 delegates from the Government of Afghanistan, the UN and the international community. The delegates met to agree on the AC and I-ANDS with the Government of Afghanistan and subsequently pledged US$10.5 billion in funds to support Afghanistan's reconstruction. The event was a precursor to the development of a full ANDS that would lay out the strategic priorities and mechanisms for achieving the government's overall development vision and would serve as the country's Poverty Reduction Strategy Paper (PRSP).

PRSPs are required by the International Monetary Fund (IMF) and the World Bank before a country can be considered for debt relief within the HIPC (Heavily Indebted Poor Countries) initiative. HIPCs are a group of the 41 least-developed countries with the highest levels of poverty and debt. The IMF and World Bank provide debt relief and low-interest loans to reduce external debt repayments to sustainable levels. To qualify for assistance, the national governments of HIPC countries must meet a range of economic, management and performance targets. In April 2007, Afghanistan became the 41st HIPC via fairly unique circumstances.[8] The Government of Afghanistan had come under pressure from Russia and the IMF to accept a debt of USD 10.6 billion[9] from Russia based on the amount of funds transferred to Afghanistan during the communist regime from 1978 to 1989. However, Afghanistan's status as a HIPC country meant that it would be able to write off the debt. Although the Afghan Parliament reacted strongly against the move, the decision was made on the basis that the country would be more likely to receive support and future funding from donors.

Following the London Conference, the Afghan Government and the international community (donor countries and institutions) agreed to establish the Joint Coordination and Monitoring Board for overall strategic coordination of the implementation of the AC.[10] The JCMB was a high-level decision-making body that focused on resolving strategic problems arising from the implementation of the AC. The JCMB is comprised of seven representatives from the Government of Afghanistan and 21 representatives from the international community. The seven government representatives were members of the Afghanistan National Development Strategy Oversight Committee nominated by the President, Hamid Karzai. They included the Senior Economic Advisor to the President, the Minister of Foreign Affairs, the Minister of Finance, the Minister of Economy, the National Security Advisor, the Minister of Education and the Minister of Justice. The 21 representatives from the international community were the Special Representative of the Secretary General and representatives from the United States, the United Kingdom, Japan, Germany, the European Union, India, Pakistan, Iran, China, Saudi Arabia, Turkey, Russia, the International Security Assistance Force, Coalition Forces, Canada, Netherlands, Italy, France, the World Bank and the Asian Development Bank (ADB).[11] The JCMB had two co-chairs: the Senior Economic Advisor to the President and Chairman of the ANDS OSC; and the Special Representative of the Secretary General, United Nations Assistance Mission in Afghanistan (UNAMA). The first meeting of the JCMB took place on April 30 2006 and involved a review of the Board's role and its scope of responsibilities.

In the post-London Conference period from February 2006 to March 2007, planning were held for the development of the full ANDS document. After the first JCMB meeting in April 2006, the OSC asked the United Nations Development Programme (UNDP) to initiate a multi-donor project to support the formulation of the ANDS. The UNDP subsequently devised a two-year, USD 8.2 million project[12] with funding from the UK's Department for International Development (DFID), the Canadian International Development Agency (CIDA), the UNDP and the Dutch, Norwegian and Italian governments. The purpose of this project was to build a team to coordinate the preparation of ANDS and improve the capacity of team members. From July to September 2006, some 40 team members were recruited, including international and national staff, of which some of the latter had been involved in the formulation of I-ANDS and the AC. This team was called the ANDS Secretariat and was supervised by the ANDS OSC. The JCMB also provided guidance in the preparation of the ANDS.

To support the OSC in their role, the Minister of Finance (MoF) and the ANDS Secretariat officially launched the structure of Consultative Groups (CGs) on 25 May 2006. Based on eight sectors of the ANDS, eight CGs and five cross-cutting thematic groups were formed to coordinate and monitor aid effectiveness and reporting to the OSC. Each CG was co-chaired by the Minister of Finance and a relevant member of the OSC, and its members belonged to relevant government ministries and agencies, donor organisations, UN agencies and civil society. The CGs coordinated and monitored the effective implementation of the AC, assisted ministries in finalising strategies, advised on cross-sectoral priorities, aligned donor funding with strategies, and monitored aid effectiveness within the sector. To support the main functions of the CGs, 22 Technical Working Groups (TWGs) were established. Each of the TWGs was responsible for one or more of the AC benchmarks. Their main responsibilities were collecting and analysing data, developing policies, strategies and development programmes linked to the budget process, ensuring efficiency and monitoring progress toward the implementation of the benchmarks.[13] Its members included representatives from relevant government ministries and agencies, donor organisations, UN agencies and civil society. Within the overall CG structure, Cross-Cutting Consultative Groups (CCCGs) were formed to address cross-cutting themes. The CCCGs had the "dual role of advising CGs and TWGs on cross-cutting themes, as well as reporting to the JCMB through the Oversight Committee on the implementation of cross-cutting policies."[14]

The practical development of the ANDS began in March 2007. The initial deadline for the completion of the ANDS was September 2008, but that time frame was pushed forward by six months to March 2008 at the request of the MoF, which was supported by the IMF. The change was made because the IMF had set a requirement that those HIPC countries that had reached a decision point had to adopt and have implemented their PRSPs for at least one year by March 2009. Once a country had met those criteria, it could reach its completion point, at which time lenders were expected to provide the full debt relief committed at the decision point. It is worth mentioning that, of the 41 countries that have been deemed eligible for HIPC initiative assistance, 23 have already reached their completion points and are currently receiving debt relief from the IMF and other creditors. Ten countries, including Afghanistan, have reached a decision point and are receiving interim HIPC debt relief pending their completion of the full requirements. Eight countries have been deemed potentially eligible for debt relief under the HIPC initiatives but have yet to reach their decision points.[15] In terms of Afghanistan, the deadline change created the first major obstacle in the formation of a credible national development strategy. It accelerated the pace of the ANDS formulation process and diverted the focus away from creating quality work toward simply meeting deadlines.

Ministries' and Agencies' Strategies

The first step in the ANDS development process was the preparation of individual strategies by all government ministries and agencies, which began in February 2007 after the approval of the ANDS work plan in mid-December 2006. In almost all ministries, technical teams were formed to conduct the initial drafting. The teams were comprised of foreign consultants and national ministry staff. The consultants had been contracted by various international organisations to provide technical support to the ministries and assist in the implementation of different programmes. A template was designed by the ANDS Secretariat for the preparation of these strategies with the aim of developing uniformity. The ANDS Secretariat also reviewed and commented on the draft ministries' strategies to aid in their improvement. The strategies were prepared in line with the AC benchmarks. In total, 43 ministry/agency strategies were developed and approved by the ANDS working groups. The ANDS Secretariat claimed strong ownership[16] by the respective ministries and agencies during the strategy development process. Some of the strategies were presented to the Afghanistan Development Forum (ADF) in April 2007 and provided the basis for subnational consultations.

Issues and Analysis

Members of the ministries' drafting team belonged to different organisations with varying agendas, and each would try to ensure that the mandates of their respective organisations were represented in the strategy.[17] The contradiction of interests started a tug-of-war, first among the team members and then between the drafting teams and the ANDS Secretariat. At times, ministries felt their authority challenged as government bodies and sector owners, and they resented the ANDS Secretariat's authoritarian style when their draft reports were returned with specific directions for changes. They also questioned the status of the ANDS Secretariat and whether it was a government body. The ANDS Secretariat was managed through the office of the Chief Economic Advisor to the President but operated under UNDP funding with the presence of numerous foreign consultants.

All ministries were running different programmes to uplift their respective sectors, and some had developed master plans that consisted of several national development programmes (see Case Study 1). Thus, the ministries had already established and were committed to a set of priorities. The AC benchmarks in many cases conflicted with the ministries' programme priorities, making it difficult for drafting teams to reconcile these priorities and satisfy all the stakeholders as well as facilitate better outputs for the sector. The situation further deteriorated when they found that the ANDS Secretariat was inflexible on AC benchmarks, using a directive tone rather than engaging in negotiation (see Case Study 1).

The AC contains 72 development benchmarks incorporating set targets, of which certain benchmarks provided unrealistic and unachievable targets; however, these were immovable and were to be strictly followed. For instance, one of the benchmarks for the Security sector read: "All illegal armed groups will be disbanded by end-2007 in all provinces."[18] Similarly, the benchmarks for Skills Development read: "150,000 men and women will be trained in marketable skills through public and private means by end-2010." Up to the drafting of this report, according to the National Skills Development Programme (NSDP), only 20,000 people had been trained. "We neither have sufficient funds nor human resources and sufficient time to accomplish this target," a senior NSDP staff member said, adding: "Now the MoF has extended programmes up to 2013, but again it is unachievable. Even if we train 150,000 people, the market does not have the capacity to absorb them." Another example is the benchmarks in Urban Development, which said: "By 2010, in line with Afghanistan's MDGs, investment in water supply and sanitation will ensure that 50 percent of households in Kabul and 30 percent of households in other major urban areas will have access to piped water."[19] The working group in this sector in the donors' dialogue on the Urban Development sector strategy said this benchmark was unrealistic and unachievable. OSC Chairman Professor Nadiri[20] said problems with the realising of the benchmarks were due to a lack of information about the sectors that could have been used to inform the assumptions made while they were being set.

From the beginning, the Government of Afghanistan, particularly the ANDS Secretariat, made the claim that ANDS was Afghan-owned, an indigenous development vision that could guide government action in place of strategies that had been prepared outside Afghanistan. However, this claim appeared to be less than genuine in light of interventions by donors. The country's dependence on aid makes the position of its government less influential when dealing with donors on setting national priorities. Afghanistan is funded by 62 donor countries and institutions for its development programmes and recurrent expenditures.

These donors have diverse approaches to the development of various sectors in the country, but all expect their demands to be met by the government (see Sections 7 and 8). Such a situation creates tremendous difficulties for the government, which must wrestle with contradictory demands and eventually compromise on its own priorities. Whether or not it fits into the context of Afghanistan, any idea suggested by an aid organisation is likely to find a place in the country's development strategies.

A further limitation on the effectiveness of the government in determining its own destiny has been the weakness of its own human resources. The shortage of properly qualified staff in government ministries limits the government's capacity to formulate policy and strategy and forces them to rely on technical assistance from foreign consultants. Most ministry staff were trained during the 1970s. Afghanistan's isolation from the rest of the world during the protracted years of civil war left it excluded from modern knowledge and technologies in almost all sectors. Afghanistan's formal education system was not reformed nor its curriculum updated, particularly at the higher education level, during the 30 years of civil war. It has produced a cadre of degree holders with outdated ideas that do not fit the requirements of the modern age. Although much work has been done since 2001 to reform and update the educational system and curriculum, as well as to build the capacity of government staff, neither the education system nor the existing workforce are close to meeting international standards. On the other hand, the attractive salaries and incentives offered by non-governmental organisations have drawn a huge number of professionals, particularly those repatriated from abroad after the *Taliban* regime. In light of its meagre resources, the government sector cannot compete with the salaries offered by international organisations, and thus cannot attract the same calibre of professionals.

While government employees lack up-to-date technical training, foreign consultants who are highly qualified from a technical perspective tend to apply concepts that may not be suitable in the context of Afghanistan. In particular, the ideas of an open-market economy, private sector development and commercialisation have often been promoted by consultants, primarily because there is political concord between the Afghan Government authorities and the international community to embrace such concepts. Consequently, Afghan ministry staff and foreign consultants have had to work together despite a huge gap in ideas and capacity, and with limited opportunities and insufficient time for discussion and the creation of mutual understanding.

Box 1

Case study on ministry strategy formulation in the Ministry of Agriculture, Irrigation and Livestock (MAIL)

This case study identifies some inherent challenges involved in the development of the ministry strategy for the MAIL. This information is based on interviews with members of the working group who drafted the strategy.

MAIL developed a master plan under the Support to Strategic Planning for Sustainable Rural Livelihoods (SSPSRL) project funded by the DFID that started in early 2005. A working group consisting of international advisors and consultants and national ministry staff worked jointly and identified national priorities based on the needs of the agriculture sector in Afghanistan. These priorities were incorporated in the agriculture sector Master Plan (MP), which encompassed seven national programmes. At the time of developing the ANDS ministry strategy, the working group found the AC benchmarks conflicted with MP priorities, which they said resulted in different sector targets. Working group members complained that although the AC benchmarks were not sufficiently realistic, they were non-negotiable and set specific reporting requirements. The MAIL team responsible for the formulation of the ministry strategy began reconciling the MP and the ANDS and decided to meet the benchmarks through the seven programmes of the MP. Eventually, they devised a ministry strategy and sent it to the ANDS Secretariat. However, the Secretariat rejected the document and sent it back to the ministry with directives to report solely according to the AC benchmarks.

With the SSPSRL coordinating the process, the team set about improving the strategy based on the Secretariat's directives and was able to successfully revise the document. Meanwhile, another ministry strategy appeared written by the United States Agency for International Development (USAID) Advisor who was working directly with the office of the Chief Economic Advisor to the President and Chairman of the ANDS Secretariat. It was significantly different from the strategy developed within the ministry, given that USAID had a different approach[21] from other donors for the development of the agriculture sector in Afghanistan. The second strategy surprised members of the drafting team and they protested against it[22], and as a result it was subsequently rejected. However, the matter did not end there; a USAID consultant made another attempt to have the second strategy signed by the Minister by attaching to it the title page of the ministry-led strategy. It was checked before signing and rejected, and the jointly drafted strategy was subsequently signed.

Consultative Process

The ANDS Secretariat described consultations and participation at the centre of the ANDS process and claimed it was the first time in the history of Afghanistan that the government had conducted broad-based consultation with the people.[23] In general, the ANDS consultative process was comprised of two parts: national consultations and subnational consultations.

National Consultations

The national-level consultations were primarily conducted through CG meetings held quarterly, prior to each full JCMB meeting in order to share CG meeting reports with JCMB members. TWG meetings were also held quarterly to enable TWG members to share their reports at CG meetings. The CG meetings were jointly chaired by representatives from the MoF and the relevant ministries. A total of five rounds of CG meetings were held; the first series were held from 6 June 2006 and the final round from January 8-14, 2008. Participants at these meetings included representatives from Afghan Government institutions, civil society organisations, UN agencies and the donor community. The meeting agendas usually included opening remarks by the co-chairs, progress on the sector strategy, implementation and progress of the AC benchmarks, the sectoral budget, open discussions and recommendations, and the achievements of previous JCMB actions and decisions. Other consultative events, such as those organised to consult with youth below the age of 25, were also organised outside of the CG meetings (in the case of youth, these were mainly held at universities).

Subnational Consultations

The ANDS Secretariat also had the mandate to hold consultations at the provincial level. The Secretariat had prepared a consultation plan which it initially intended to facilitate through the offices of provincial governors and Provincial Development Councils (PDCs). However, the weak capacity of provincial administrations necessitated the development of a different approach, and the issue was discussed at the Afghanistan Development Forum[24] in April 2007. At the ADF meeting, some donors proposed the idea of Provincial Development Plans being incorporated into the ANDS process[25]. A draft discussion paper for the ADF on "Provincial Development, Provincial Budgeting and Integration PDPs into ANDS" (April 2007, page 6) states: "At the end of 2006 the PRT's (Provincial Reconstruction Teams) Steering Board approved the PRT

Policy Note which supported the development of the PDPs within the framework of developing the ANDS." The PRTs had already stimulated provinces to work on developing PDPs, and by the time of the ADF meeting in April 2007 about 21 provinces had completed the process of developing PDPs.[26] During this ADF meeting, the PDPs attained lots of emphasis from some donors or PRTs, who argued that the PDPs would create grassroots democracy and gain popular support for the ANDS. They viewed the preparation of the PDPs as the best way to ensure a bottom-up rather than top-down approach in the ANDS process. Certain organisations, including the MoF, the DFID, the World Bank and the ANDS Secretariat opposed the idea of preparing the PDPs as part of the ANDS process[27].

Eventually preparation of the PDPs became part of the ANDS process and the MRRD came forward in the meeting to take responsibility for leading the design and facilitation of subnational consultations and the provincial development planning process through its National Area-Based Development Programme (NABDP) in collaboration with the ANDS Secretariat.

The NABDP had experience developing District Development Assemblies (DDAs) and District Development Plans (DDPs) throughout the country under its Community Development component[28]. Consequently, in consultation with stakeholders, the MRRD and the ANDS Secretariat devised a mechanism and finalised a handbook for subnational consultations and provincial development planning (see Box 2). As mentioned above, some provinces already had PDPs which had been developed before the ANDS. However, they were to be improved because: 1) they had not adequately involved communities; 2) they had not been led by the government; and 3) they were not aligned with the ANDS[29].

The subnational consultations and provincial development planning were completed between June and September 2007 in all of Afghanistan's 34 provinces. The ANDS Secretariat claimed 46 percent attendance by women during the consultations, which was considered a milestone. Consultations were conducted in 13 sectors: Security, Education, Health, Agriculture, Roads, Private Sector Development, Rural Development, Energy and Water, Social Protection, Refugees and Repatriation, Justice, Anti-Corruption and Counter-Narcotics.

The formulation of the PDPs was based on the consolidation of inputs from line ministry strategies; existing PDPs; the priorities of rural communities; the priorities of urban communities, including those set out in Urban Plans; and the priorities of vulnerable social groups such as Kuchis, refugees, returnees and internally displaced persons, and the disabled. Given the concentration of population and the specific issues facing Kabul as the national capital, two separate consultation processes were held and two PDPs were produced for Kabul Province, one covering the urban area and one for the rural districts.

In addition, the Agency Coordinating Body for Afghan Relief (ACBAR) and the Foundation for Culture and Civil Society (FCCS) also consulted the poor at the community level. ACBAR, under its Afghanistan Pilot Participatory Poverty Assessment (APPPA) project,[30] conducted from May 2007 to May 2008, documented the perspectives of the poor regarding poverty for integration into the ANDS. Other NGOs conducted consultations in districts affected by insurgency.

The ANDS secretariat also launched a public awareness campaign, "which aimed to (i) inform the public about the ANDS, (ii) obtain public support for the implementation of the most important ANDS reforms, (iii) manage people's expectations."[31]

Issues and Analysis

The national-level consultations conducted through CG meetings were well organised and allowed stakeholders to express their ideas and concerns over the issues pertaining to the ANDS. These meetings were attended by representatives of government institutions, UN agencies, the donor community and civil society organisations; members of the Afghan Parliament were not invited. The only concern raised in interviews with different sources was the ability of the ANDS Secretariat, as a result of the hasty nature of the process, to analyse the information gathered during these consultations and integrate it into the document.

The subnational consultations and provincial development planning left some stakeholders, particularly donors, quite skeptical because of the poor quality of the outcomes of the consultations and the rushed nature of the process. The PDPs for the 34 provinces were submitted to the ANDS Secretariat at the beginning of October, meaning the consultations and PDPs were completed in four months. An NABDP source said: "The time frame of only four months for countrywide consultations was quite unrealistic. In terms of real planning it was vague, and no mechanism for the systematic use of data existed for provincial planning." The ANDS Secretariat argued that PDPs were not part of subnational consultations before the ADF in April 2007 and that their integration as part of the ANDS process doubled their workload despite previously already having insufficient time to finish the document. Consequently, their primary focus was on the meeting of deadlines and not ensuring the quality of the work. During the planning process for the subnational consultations, the ANDS Secretariat did not involve government ministries[32], which meant that representatives of line ministries who attended the subnational consultation workshops had less orientation and preparation.

One of the basic principles[33] of the formulation of the PDPs was that "these should not lead to the formulation of wish lists but to the preparation of prioritised and fiscally sustainable development plans." However, at the end of the process, the majority of the PDPs appeared no better than wish lists as they did not include budgets or implementation plans. Some sources from donor organisations said the findings of the PDPs were unclear and were not linked to the ANDS. The only mechanism for the implementation of the PDPs was the integration of their priorities into the sector strategies, which remained very vague. In later donor dialogue, donors expressed concerns in this regard. The ANDS Secretariat explained that only those priorities they deemed suitable were integrated into the sector strategies.[34]

The ANDS Secretariat argued that the subnational consultations reduced the distance between the government and the people and that both spoke the same language on national development priorities. However, concerns exist that the process also raised expectations among the populace. "Unfortunately, the PDP process was not explained properly to the people," said a source from the ADB, expressing the fear that the weak service-delivery capacity of the government could increase popular discontent and widen the gap between the government and the people, particularly if it was not addressed through the ANDS implementation. "People have already started asking for what they mentioned as their priority projects in their respective provinces during provincial development planning," he said.

In the donors' dialogue on the first draft of the ANDS in March 2008, the Director of the ANDS Secretariat said they were fully aware of the expectations raised among the communities through sub-national consultations, which was why they held intense discussions with provincial governors and line ministries about integrating the priorities of the PDPs as much as possible into their strategies. He said the government was also reviewing the number of ministries in that regard.

The sub-national consultations were the only forum in which Afghanistan's parliamentarians were consulted. They believe they were deliberately kept away from the other phases of the ANDS process, particularly the national consultations, although as elected representatives of the people they have the right to participate in national priority setting.[35] Based on interviews, it was clear that a fear prevailed in ANDS management circles that the involvement of Parliament could mess up the process, as it had little experience in such matters, and that if the ANDS was taken to the Parliament, it would become politicised and hence be difficult to finalise. As a result, the Parliament of Afghanistan expressed little support for the ANDS upon its completion. On some current affairs programmes aired on Afghan television, the parliamentarians, particularly members of the Economic Commission of the National Assembly, expressed concerns that the National Assembly was not involved in the decision-making process. On the "Guftumaan" programme broadcast on Tolo Television, engineer Abbas Noyan, a member of the Economic Commission of the Parliament, said about the ANDS[36]: "The Parliament summoned the newly appointed Senior Economic Advisor of the President to answer their questions regarding the ANDS and its implementation, but he failed, pretending he had recently taken charge of his office responsibilities and citing his non-involvement in the ANDS process. Some ministers who were members of the Oversight Committee were also questioned in Parliament on the ANDS, but they could not satisfy the parliamentarians. The Parliament is still seeking someone who can answer their questions and remove their concerns about the ANDS implementation, monitoring and evaluation, deadlines, and the prioritisation and sequencing of priorities in the sector strategies."

Box 2

Four core phases of SNC and PDPs: Excerpted from the Subnational Consultation (SNC) and Provincial Development Planning (PDP) Handbook.

1. Preparatory Workshop

A two-day workshop was held in all the provinces in the week before the Subnational Consultation process began with the participation of representatives from rural communities (members of DDAs), urban stakeholders (such as municipal government, city shuras, chambers of commerce, business groups, associations of business owners, women's groups), Kuchi and other vulnerable groups (such as refugees, returnees and disabled people). During the workshop participants would look at the major issues affecting the development of their respective provinces from their perspective and identify priority courses of action.

2. Sub-national Consultation Workshop

The two-and-a-half-day Subnational Consultation workshops were attended by community representatives (who attended the preparatory workshop), line ministry representatives and other groups such as the PRT, UN agencies, donors and NGOs. The participants would be divided into eight groups according to the development sectors identified in the ANDS. In each group the line ministries present their strategy, identifying their goals and the programmes to achieve them. Participants would identify the most important needs and the province's goal for the sector. They would discuss the ministries' strategies and decide how well they responded to the needs and priorities. They would identify elements which were missing and suggest ways to improve the ministries' strategies.

3. Provincial Development Planning Workshop

The Provincial Development Planning workshops ran for two days with the same participants as in SNC workshops. During the workshop, participants would work in the same eight groups as in the SNC workshops. Each group put together a list of priority projects for the sector which should be implemented in the first year. This list of projects for each sector was included in the Provincial Development Plan.

4. Writing up and Reporting

In the final phase of the process, the outputs from the SNC and PDP workshops were combined with information about the province and edited to provide the first three sections of the PDPs.

Sector Strategies

The process of developing ANDS Sector Strategies began in June 2007 with the establishment of Sector Strategy Development Groups (SSDGs). These SSDGs, one for each of the 17 sectors of the ANDS, consisted of deputy ministers, senior foreign advisors, key national staff of the relevant ministries, representatives from the cross-cutting sectors, representatives from the MoF and the Sector Coordinator from the ANDS Secretariat. All were led by their respective line ministries. Meanwhile, UNDP had to provide foreign consultants to be based in the ANDS Secretariat to assist the SSDGs and improve their work, particularly in terms of the English language. The UNDP experienced difficulties in finding consultants[37] for some of the sectors. The ANDS Secretariat felt that time was running out and a lot of work still remained. As a result, it approached USAID for assistance and Bearing Point (USAID) consultants were brought into the process in July 2007. These consultants prepared the template for drafting the sector strategies and enabled the SSDGs to bring uniformity to their work. The ministry/agency strategies, PDPs and donors' comments provided the main inputs for the sector strategies. The first drafts of the sector strategies began by October 2007 and were submitted for donor comments in October and November 2007.

Issues and Analysis

It was the first time in the history of the country that government ministries were given an opportunity to participate in sector-level planning.[38] However, the planning was not an easy task in view of the vast differences among the ministries, their varying mandates, their lack of capacity and insufficient experience, the irrationally short time frames and their general lack of preparedness. "It could have had better results if the ANDS Secretariat had conducted some training on policymaking and planning practices in the ministries before kicking off the development of the strategies," a source from the Food and Agriculture Organization of the United Nations (FAO) said.

Although the ministries were divided into the sectors based on commonality of interest and objectives[39], their individual mandates conflicted with each other at various points. For example, MAIL and the MRRD both work for the rural population and share the overarching goal of poverty reduction. As a result, both were incorporated into the Agriculture and Rural Development (ARD) sector. Similarly, the Ministry of Education (MoE), the Ministry of Higher Education (MoHE) and the Ministry of Labour, Social Affairs, Martyrs and Disabled (MoLSAMD) were grouped into the Education and Skills Development sector because of their common objectives. However, in the ARD sector, both MAIL and the MRRD have different operational structures. MAIL is a single-sector ministry which provides technical and technological services. The MRRD, on the other hand, is a multi-sector ministry with its policy based on five national programmes. It outsources projects as well as undertakes such programmes in rural areas as the construction of clinics, schools, canals, small dams and roads, which other ministries consider within their own mandate. Both ministries also have different fund allocations in their core budgets and a different capacity to spend the allocated funds. while the number of foreign advisors and technical staff is incomparable.

To reach consensus and resolve the conflicting issues, the ministries needed strong inter-ministerial coordination and sufficient time to negotiate. Unfortunately, the hasty nature of the ANDS process did not provide sufficient time for such discussions and the SSDGs were pushed to meet the deadlines. A member of one of the SSDGs from the Ministry of Agriculture, Irrigation and Livestock (MAIL) said: "ANDS gives heart attack; they want everything in two hours."

In addition, UNDP had to place many consultants with the ANDS Secretariat to support the SSDGs and help improve their work. A UNAMA source said a group of 50 consultants on UNDP and Bearing Point contracts worked in the ANDS Secretariat to prepare the ANDS. However, a senior UNDP official said one consultant for each sector worked to assist with the formulation of sector strategies. Some of these consultants, who were initially brought in by UNDP, later switched to Bearing Point.

Although the ANDS Secretariat said the job of the consultants was only to facilitate and edit the language of the SSDG drafts, in reality they provided guidance for the sector strategies and influenced the process[40]. Consultants for some of the sectors changed frequently, causing repeated changes in work formats based on their personal understandings, which not only further complicated the process but also wasted time and resources. A general complaint by the SSDGs in relation to the consultants was their limited familiarity with both Afghanistan and the specific sector, however they still influenced the strategies. A cabinet minister and member of the OSC said in an interview[41]: "The ANDS process is necessary for the country, but constant changes and foreign consultants made it complicated. The Government of Afghanistan was not ready to do it, and anyhow there is always the dilemma about how long should be waited for the government ministries to get the strength and required capacity." A senior foreign advisor and member of the SSDG for the ARD sector[42] expressed the same sentiments: "There was no coordinated approach towards sector strategy development. A person who comes from abroad and has no clue of the sectors writes the strategies built on his personal experience; this is why some of the strategies look like a reporting document."

The quality and shape of each sector strategy depended entirely on the capacity of SSDG members, ANDS internal consultants and the interest of funding organisations in the different sectors. The expatriate consultants were contracted by different organisations for specific programmes in the ministries and were also members of the SSDGs. These consultants wrote their parts of the draft sector strategies, ensuring that they fit the objectives of their respective organisations. For example, the United Nations Educational, Scientific and Cultural Organization (UNESCO) wrote a large part of the Information and Culture strategy and contributed a lot to the content of the Primary Education section of the Education sector.

Donors' Dialogue

All the draft sector strategies, except security, were presented to the donor community for comment in October and November 2007. The donors also commented on other parts of the ANDS document such as Poverty Profiles, the Macro-economic Framework, Implementation and Monitoring, and Aid Effectiveness. UNDP organised and facilitated these donor dialogue sessions in line with the recommendations of the EAG, which was a platform for donors to comment on drafts and the overall ANDS process. The draft national sector strategies, including the strategies addressing cross-cutting issues, were made available to the donors for discussion a few days ahead of the scheduled date, and UNDP also received comments by email before and after the dialogue.

During the dialogue sessions, UNDP noted the donors' comments and the written comments and compiled a 219-page document which was conveyed to the ANDS Secretariat in order to finalise the sector strategies. "In total, 19 separate donor dialogues were held, attended by 417 representatives, generating 157 written comments from 32 various donors and agencies."[43]

Issues and Analysis

The attendance and participation of donors in some sectors remained high. Those sectors included Justice, Governance, Health and Nutrition, Education, Energy, Private Sector Development and Trade, Agriculture and Rural Development, Counter-Narcotics and Gender Equity. Other sectors attracted a medium level of attendance, while a few, such as Culture, Media and Youth, drew very low attendance levels.

The vague mechanism for integrating the cross-cutting issues and priorities of the PDPs caused much concern among the donor community. The cross-cutting issues were seen as the weakest part of the ANDS in the wake of the poor-quality drafts and their insufficient integration into the sectoral strategies. Among the six cross-cutting issues, only Counter-Narcotics satisfied the majority of the donors.

In these dialogues, the donors recognised the lack of coordination among their organisations, and stressed the need for real coordination.

The donors' dialogue culminated in a long document full of conflicting comments[44] that provided the ANDS Secretariat with a reason to ignore the majority of them and integrate only those comments with which they agreed. As a result, the donors were unhappy that their comments were not adequately reflected in the ANDS. Their discontent was evident at a meeting on 10 March 2008 when the first draft of the

ANDS was released and donors were invited to comment. During the meeting, the Director of the ANDS Secretariat said: "Every comment of the donors was read and given enough consideration, but the donors have conflicting views on certain issues such as counter-narcotics and the private sector. The government has to make a decision. We cannot make everybody happy and we cannot make Afghanistan according to the wishes of any specific country." ANDS Director Adeeb Farhadi asked that donors provide harmonisation of specific comments rather than a long list of general comments. He also said that if donors wanted a more perfect document, he would ask the Cabinet Oversight Committee to allow them another four months to work on the document. The co-chair of the event, Marshall Elliot from DFID, said the donors would prepare a Joint Donors' Response (JDR) that would examine some collective issues and aspects of the ANDS.[45]

The ANDS Secretariat was also unhappy[46] with UNDP for not properly consolidating and coordinating the donors' response to the sector strategies. "The UNDP did the job of a secretary and it just put the comments on one and the other and gave it to the ANDS Secretariat," a source from the ANDS Secretariat said.

In April 2008, a JDR to the ANDS entitled *"From Compact to Impact"* was released and presented at the Paris Conference on Afghanistan on 12 June 2008. The paper discussed in detail the issues of ownership, prioritisation, harmonisation, alignment and provincial development plans.

Finalisation of ANDS

The finalisation of the ANDS saw some dramatic ups and downs, and rumours spread that it had been rejected by the IMF. The first draft of the document was produced within a one-month period when OSC Chairman Professor Nadiri was on a trip to the United States. After the submission of the draft document, Professor Nadiri visited the IMF office and was told of the IMF's concerns about the draft ANDS and a letter was formally sent to his office in Kabul.[47] The IMF was not satisfied with certain parts of the draft and wanted changes made, particularly in relation to Private Sector Development. In addition, the country had failed to demonstrate better economic performance under an agreement with the IMF. The MoF had admitted that the Afghan Government had failed to raise the agreed target of USD 715 million in taxes.[48]

This fuelled the rumour that the IMF had rejected the ANDS. The situation compelled President Karzai to step in and ask the ANDS Director to brief him on the issue. He tasked the MoF with finding a solution. In response it formed another drafting team which included some UNDP and USAID staff in an attempt to prepare a workable document before the donors' conference in Paris in June 2008.[49] The Afghan Government feared that the failure to produce an acceptable document would have serious implications for both future international funding and the debt relief it was enjoying under HIPC initiatives. Additionally, it would develop a bad name internationally as about $US9 million[50] in funding had been received to support the drafting of the document.

As the new MoF drafting team began revising the ANDS, Professor Nadiri returned from the US and announced that no other drafting committee would revise the document and that the ANDS would be completed by the ANDS Secretariat. This led to a confrontation over who would finalise the ANDS. In the end, the MoF team gave up in the face of strong pressure and the ANDS was redrafted by the ANDS Secretariat with the required changes.

The document was approved by President Karzai on April 21, 2008 and presented to donors at the International Conference in Support of Afghanistan in Paris on June 12, 2008. At the conference, more than US$20 billion was pledged to finance the implementation of the ANDS during the next two-and-a-half years, including support for the preparation of national elections in 2009 and 2010. This was in addition to the US$10.5 billion funding commitment that Afghanistan received at the London Conference in February 2006, in which it had to generate from US$5-6 billion from its own resources.[51] This represents a total commitment of US$36 billion toward Afghanistan's development. Afghanistan needs US$51 billion for the implementation of the ANDS in the next five years; a commitment the government is expecting[52] to receive from donors for the remaining funds.

Key Findings

Afghan Ownership in Question

The Government of Afghanistan through the ANDS Secretariat claimed ownership of the ANDS development throughout the process. The following realities and challenges surrounding the process weakened that claim: Afghanistan needed a PRSP to qualify for debt relief under the IMF-backed HIPC initiatives, and the ANDS fulfilled this requirement. To qualify for assistance, the Afghan Government had to meet a range of economic, management and performance targets to be ensured by the MoF. The country's centralised system of governance allotted development funds to programmes in different ministries, hence the conditions that the

World Bank and IMF placed on the process and the outcomes of the ANDS clearly reduced the Government of Afghanistan's level of control and ownership.

Afghanistan is the recipient of massive international funds for its development and reconstruction programmes, which are strategised with the broad involvement of foreign stakeholders. Most of the development funds are conditional to specific programmes and regions in accordance with the strategic goals of funding organisations. The Afghan Government had to agree on the conditions and priorities of these funding organisations and integrate them into the ANDS, which weakened the level of its ownership.

The ministries, despite being the owners of their specific sectors and having a broader understanding of the context, remained under intense pressure to follow the AC benchmarks even if their own priorities made more sense. This also put in doubt how the different priorities gathered through the subnational consultations could be included in the strategy. The relatively weak position of the government in determining the content of the ANDS was exacerbated by a lack of professional capacity to draft strategies in government ministries and institutions. The ministries had to rely on the skills of foreign consultants, which increased international involvement in policy design and strategy development.

The shift of initial deadlines for the ANDS from September 2008 to March 2008 by the IMF and the World Bank and the addition of provincial development planning as part of the ANDS process clearly proved a lack of government ownership of the process.

English was the primary language for developing the ANDS and its related documents, which were later translated into the Dari and Pashto languages.

Sacrificing Quality Over Process

The development of PRSPs needs sufficient time and proper time management as it involves many stakeholders and requires extensive consultations. However, in Afghanistan the ANDS Secretariat worked under immense pressure from the IMF through the MoF within an inflexible and tough time frame to meet the deadlines. The ANDS Secretariat stepped up the process which resulted in the sacrifice of work quality.

The subnational consultations and provincial development planning were completed within an irrational time frame of four months, which not only resulted in the production of poor-quality PDPs, but also raised expectations among the communities in the prospect of less orientation to them about ANDS process. Because the PDP priorities will not be costed and the government's structure is too weak at the provincial level to deliver services, there is now an increasing risk of popular discontent and distrust of the government's ability, particularly as communities have already begun asking for the fulfillment of the demands they made through the subnational consultations.

Afghan Government ministries were brought together for the first time to plan at the sector level and needed appropriate time to discuss and build understanding around conflicting issues. The compressed time frame did not provide sufficient time for the SSDGs or for inter-ministerial coordination, and hence strategies were developed through forced compromises rather than through the building of understanding via negotiations.

The creation of the ANDS occurred at multiple levels: through subnational consultations with the general population and provincial development planning; through ministries and multi-ministerial sectors (with significant international involvement); through the ANDS Secretariat and the MoF with technical assistance and management; and through political leadership represented in the OSC and JCMB. These different levels set priorities that varied widely and proved a big challenge in terms of integration, alignment and harmonisation within the ANDS. As mentioned earlier, ignoring the priorities of certain levels or considering them to be of less importance was not an option for the ANDS team. Thus, the only solution for harmonising priorities was further negotiations, which time constraints did not allow.

Lack of Coordination and Other Complexities

A lack of coordination exists at various levels, including among government institutions, between the government and donors and among donor agencies, which has not only hampered the development efforts in Afghanistan but has also complicated the process of national level planning and strategy development.

The Afghan Parliament was involved in identifying priorities only at the subnational level with the participation of its members in the consultative workshop. This limited role led them to feel deliberately excluded from the process. The Parliament of Afghanistan now has a less-supportive stance on the status of the ANDS.

The absence of a clear mechanism for integrating cross-cutting issues and PDP priorities in the sector strategies also caused dissatisfaction among the stakeholders. Thousands of pages of people's comments were generated from subnational consultations, which raised expectations among the communities, but there was no clear method of incorporating those concerns into the ANDS.

Conclusion

The final ANDS is written primarily by foreign experts and manifests the vision of international funding organisations rather than representing a purely indigenous development and poverty reduction plan for Afghanistan. The Afghan Government remained under immense pressure from the IMF, the World Bank, USAID and other major funding organisations to adopt specific policies and meet deadlines that unquestionably stepped up the pace of the process and not only affected the quality of work, but also widened the gap in understanding and weakened consensus among the stakeholders. As well as the government's dependency on foreign aid, which limits its ownership of development policies, the dearth of technical capacity within government institutions to devise policies and strategies also reduced national influence in the decision-making process. A lack of coordination within the donor community and between the government and donors resulted in poor prioritisation and harmonisation of development priorities.

On the other hand, the approval of the ANDS ensured Afghanistan's eligibility for economic incentives under the IMF-backed HIPC initiatives and resulted in the government securing a commitment of more than US$20 billion in foreign aid for the development of the country. In addition, it still has the potential to provide a platform for all stakeholders involved in development to ensure better coordination of development activities and improve the ownership of the Afghan Government. However, the question remains as to whether the ANDS can be successfully implemented and if it can be used to effectively coordinate development efforts and reduce poverty?

The implementation of the ANDS is undoubtedly a big challenge for its implementers, however there are ways forward. AREU's paper on the ANDS content[53] suggests that the broad priorities of the ANDS need sequencing through a regionally responsive implementation plan that is sensitive to the challenges of delivering on development promises in insecure regions and to the potentially negative consequences of marginalising less problematic areas. For the ANDS to succeed in substance, improvements in process are also crucial. To move the ANDS implementation forward, there is a need for greater coordination at all levels, including among the funders of Afghanistan and the Government of Afghanistan. These stakeholders must build greater consensus and support for the development vision foreseen in the ANDS.

Notes and References

1. This figure was quoted by Professor Ishaq Nadiri, ex-Senior Economic Advisor to the President, at a lecture given at the Centre for Policy and Human Development, July 8, 2008.
2. National Development Framework (NDF) draft—for consultation, April 2002.
3. There was a general understanding among those interviewed that the NDF was designed and written by foreign experts, which was emphasised in interviews with senior UNDP employees (04-03-2008) and in an interview with Norwegian Embassy staff, September 2007.
4. Securing Afghanistan's Future: Accomplishments and the Strategic Path Forward, March 17, 2004.
5. The term "non-Afghanised strategy" came into being when ANDS people began calling the ANDS document a completely Afghanised strategy and the NDF and SAF non-Afghanised due to the involvement of numerous foreign experts in their preparation.
6. Summary Report, Millenium Development Goals, Islamic Republic of Afghanistan, Country Report 2005. p. 7.
7. Summary Report, An Interim Strategy for Security, Governance, Economic Growth and Poverty Reduction I-ANDS, February 2006, p. 3.
8. http://www.imf.org/external/np/exr/facts/hipc.htm (20-11-2008)
9. Boone, Jon, "Afghan failure to meet IMF target casts doubt on debt relief." *Financial Times*, April 2, 2008.
10. Joint Coordination and Monitoring Board Terms of Reference, 2006, p. 1.
11. Fact sheet on JCMB, UNAMA, 2006.
12. High-ranking UNDP official pers. comm., August 25, 2008.
13. Consultative Groups Manual, Terms of reference and procedures (page 8, 04 March 2007, p. 8.<http://www.ands.gov.af/ands/Provincial_Consultations/details.asp?id=60&sn=1&psn=0&awareness=0&national=expanded (25-11-2008)>
14. Consultative Groups Manual, Terms of reference and procedures, 04 March 2007, p. 8.
15. IMF website http://www.imf.org/external/np/exr/facts/hipc.htm (20-11-2008)
16. Ownership in this context refers to the level of decision-making in setting national priorities.
17. Sources from government ministries and international organisations, pers. comm., (Between August 2007 to October 2007)
18. Afghanistan Compact document, Annexes I, Benchmarks and Timelines, February 2006, p. 6.
19. Afghanistan Compact document, Annexes I, Benchmarks and Timelines, February 2006, p. 9.

20. Ishaq Nadiri, Lecture on the ANDS, Centre for Policy and Human Development, July 8, 2008.
21. RAMP final report "Rebuilding Agriculture Markets".
22. Member of working group on ministry strategy, pers. comm., (30-11-2007)
23. Progress report of ANDS/PRSP prepared for IMF/WorldBank Board of Directors, 2006/2007, page 15.
24. In January 2002, the Afghan Government agreed to meet with donors annually to review the country's development priorities. The first ADF was held in 2003 and continued until 2007. More information is available at http://www.adf.gov.af/index.asp?page=faqs#watsadf
25. Senior MRRD staff and international and national NABDP staff, pers. comm., September to December 2007.
26. ADF report, Provincial Development, Provincial Budgeting and Integration PDPs into ANDS, April 2007. (page 6)
27. ANDS Director Adeeb Farhadi in a speech marking the occasion of dialogue on the first draft of the ANDS, March 10, 2008 said the ANDS Secretariat and MoF were against the integration of PDPs development as part of the ANDS. Other sources from the MoF, DFID and the World Bank also expressed concerns in this regard, pers. comm., November 2007 to March 2008.
28. More information on NABDP and the role of DDAs is available at the MRRD website: http://www.mrrd.gov.af/nabdp/
29. Subnational Consultation and Provincial Development Planning Handbook, prepared by the ANDS Secretariat and MRRD, revised July 2007, p. 5
30. ACBAR website http://www.acbar.org/ (accessed on 9 October 2008).
31. Progress report of ANDS/PRSP prepared for IMF/World Bank Board of Directors, 2006/2007, p. 16.
32. NABDP source, pers. comm., November 27, 2007.
33. Draft discussion paper for the ADF Provincial Development, Provincial Budgeting and Integration of the Provincial Development Plans into the ANDS, April 2007, p. 7.
34. ANDS Director Adeeb Farhadi in a speech given during donors' dialogue on the first draft of the ANDS, 10 March 2008.
35. Roundtable discussion on the ANDS on Tolo Television's "Guftumaan" programme attended by engineer Abbas Noyan, a member of the Economic Commission of the Afghan Parliament, October 17, 2008.
36. Tolo Television's "Guftumaan" programme, October 17, 2008.
37. International USAID staff, pers. comm., 6 December 2007; senior UNDP staff, pers. comm., September 23, 2008.
38. A senior advisor at the Ministry of Agriculture, Irrigation and Livestock, pers. comm., December 3, 2007.
39. Professor Ishaq Nadiri, ex-Senior Economic Advisor to the President, Centre for Policy and Human Development, July 8, 2008.
40. Members of different Sector Strategy Development Groups, pers. comm., (October to December 2007).

41. Member of the Oversight Committee, pers comm., January 24, 2008.
42. SSDG member and senior foreign advisor, pers. comm., November 28, 2007.
43. Key Issues and Consolidated Comments, from donor dialogues on the Draft Sector Strategies of the ANDS, October-December 2007, p. 4
44. ANDS Director Adeeb Farhadi in a speech given during donors' dialogue on the first draft of the ANDS, March 10, 2008.
45. The researcher was present at the meeting held on 10 March 2008 at the UNDP office, Kabul.
46. ANDS Secretariat staff, pers. comm., May 20, 2008.
47. Senior ANDS Secretariat staff member, pers. comm., May 20, 2008.
48. *Boone, Jon, "Afghan failure to meet IMF target casts doubt on debt relief."* Financial Times, April 2, 2008.
49. Senior staff from the ANDS Secretariat, USAID, UNDP and the MoF, pers. comm., (May to July 2008).
50. Total cost of the UNDP project to support ANDS formulation.
51. Professor Ishaq Nadiri, ex-Senior Economic Advisor to the President, Centre for Policy and Human Development, July 8, 2008.
52. Professor Ishaq Nadiri, ex-Senior Economic Advisor to the President, Centre for Policy and Human Development, July 8, 2008.
53. Paula Kantor and Adam Pain, Delivering on Poverty Reduction: Focusing ANDS Implementation on Pro-Poor Outcomes, January 2009.

16

Mitigating War Effects and Promoting Peace-building through an Effective Education System in Afghanistan: Pitfalls and Development

Alef Shah Zadran

Nearly three decades of turmoil in Afghanistan resulted in tremendous destruction of socio-economic, education and military infrastructure. Internal and external actors tried to put more fuel in this blazing fire. This war deprived a generation of Afghans from the personal benefits of education as well as the benefits that might have accrued to national development. Education provides the underpinning for social and economic development and until education services are restored, there is little hope for significant progress. It is timely therefore for Afghans to come together to develop a vision and goals for an education system that can play a stabilising and peaceful role in the country.

Background of Curriculum, Textbooks and Teacher Training

When Mohammed Daud was the President of Afghanistan in (1973-1978), Ministry of Education (MoE) of Afghanistan had an affiliation with Columbia University of USA. The Curriculum Development and Textbook Writing Directorate of MoE under the supervision of experts form Columbia University developed an updated and timely curriculum and syllabus and on the basis of this syllabus the Afghan experts wrote the textbooks.

Then Saur Revolution occurred. The pro-USSR government of Afghanistan changed the curriculum of the MoE. This curriculum was not in line with the Afghan culture and social values. At the time of *Jihad* (the holy war) the government had not enough power to defend itself. As a result of Red Army invasion, people took refuge in Pakistan, Iran and many other countries of the world. In Pakistan there were about 72 non-government organizations (NGOs) which were supporting Afghan refugees through humanitarian aids. A great number of them were providing education for Afghan refugee children.

The curricula of these NGOs were highly religious, war-like and not according to the psychological and pedagogical principles. The NGOs did not develop a curriculum framework to contain a syllabus having vertical and horizontal sequences as well as rationale and objectives. If an education system does not have necessary elements in its system how can it develop appropriate textbooks for their schools and how can it teach the students.

Those Afghan refugee children who were attending Pakistani schools were learning natural and social sciences and they were improving their technological knowledge and skills, but loosing their culture and languages. The refugee children in Iran were using the textbooks which were used in Iranian schools. Iranian culture and language is different from the Afghans. The situation inside Afghanistan was not also very promising in this respect. The children, who were enrolled in schools inside the country, were utilizing the instructional materials developed in Peshawar for refugee children.

Afghanistan's curriculum in the past was socially, educationally and economically unrepresentative of the needs of the Afghan nation. During 1970s and the ensuing war among competing groups throughout the country, each group developed their own curricula that often promoted various political ideologies and dialogues rather than academic content. In 2002, the Department of Curriculum Development and Textbook Writing developed a new Curriculum framework for general education under the MoE. The focus of this framework was the development of a standard curriculum to be used thought the country. While the updating and revision of textbooks for primary education (grade 1-6) was nearly complete, more effort was required to upgrade the textbooks and curriculum for secondary education. In addition, the curriculum was overburdened and does not reflect the actual learning interest of the students and teaching capacities of the teachers. The contents of the textbooks need to ensure that it is relevant to the histories and cultural values of all the people of Afghanistan as well as to ensure that it can respond more effectively to the economic and technological development needs of the country. In addition to this, more effort needs to be placed on providing good quality learning materials for children with special learning needs for accelerated learning classes and for pre-primary education.

The development of a quality curriculum that responds to the real education needs of Afghanistan is a critical element in building the human capital of the country and in developing the knowledge, skills, values and attitudes that the nation wants its children to embrace. On the basis of this urgent need, USAID in 2005 asked its partner, Afghanistan Primary Education Project (APEP) manager to hold a meeting with high level representatives from the Ministry of Higher Education, Ministry of Education, USAID and APEP to identify two urgent projects for the MoE. This assignment was given to me, Prof Dr. Alef-Shah Zadran, APEP Accelerating Learning Programme Manager. After a tough and lengthy discussion as urgent needs of the Ministry of Education, the Chairperson proposed two very important and urgent projects for MoE. One was curriculum development and the other teacher training. These proposals were highly appreciated and accepted by all participants present in the meeting. USAID representatives took the proposals to their office and worked with MoE together on them extensively and finally both proposals were approved by the MoE and USAID. These two projects were supported financially by DANADA, JIKA, USAID and World Bank.

Context of Secondary Education Curriculum Development

Six years ago MoE developed a Curriculum Framework for primary and secondary education that was approved by the Government of Afghanistan in July 2003.

In following years the new Curriculum Framework was implemented in primary education (grades 1 to 6). Syllabi and textbooks for primary education were produced and gradually introduced to schools all over the country. The school year 2007/2008 completed the cycle of curriculum change and improvement for all primary grades and subjects.

Changes in primary education reached completion of one full cycle in 2007. It was imperative that curriculum provisions for secondary education should also be revised and improved, and that new Framework for Secondary Education should be issued to reflect the new conditions, challenges and opportunities that education stakeholders and beneficiaries were facing in Afghanistan.

An international workshop was held in Kabul from August 26 to September 7, 2006 at Ottawa Hotel that aimed at setting the grounds for secondary curriculum reform. The workshop was organized jointly by the Ministry of Education and UNESCO (UNESCO Office Afghanistan and IBE UNESCO/The International Bureau of Education). Almost 60 participants (representatives of the Curriculum and Textbook Directorate/

MoE, professors of tertiary education and others) interacted with international colleagues and many other guests from the Ministry of Education, MOHE and the Afghanistan Parliament. While attempting to set coherent foundations for secondary education in Afghanistan, the participants identified several important issues that could address public consultations more thoroughly as to inform education policy decisions to be taken by the Ministry of Education.

His Excellency, Mr. Haneef Atmar, ex-minister of Education, who interacted with the participants in the workshop extensively, reiterated that curriculum reforms were at the heart of improving the quality of learning in Afghanistan as the basis for societal changes leading to progress and consolidation of a peaceful, open and tolerant society whose individuals and communities participate constructively in the today's and tomorrow's global interdependencies.

Principles of Developing the New Secondary Curriculum

The new curriculum development for secondary education capitalises on achievements in primary education curriculum and textbook development and addresses characteristics of lower and secondary education, as follows:

Progress in Continuity

The secondary education curriculum consolidates student achievements in primary education, especially the basic and key skills, such as communication (reading, writing, oral skills) and numeracy. At the same time, it constitutes the basis for broadening the students' horizon and expands their competencies in connection with exploring in more depth different learning areas and subjects of the curriculum. In new secondary education curriculum knowledge and skills become more complex and specialised with a view of preparing the young for further studies and/or professional life.

Unity and Coherence

The new curriculum is based on common quality standards for all students such as emphasis on learner-centeredness and access of students to new developments in science and relevant areas of human action. It is a unitary curriculum for all students of Afghanistan and aims to strengthen national unity and solidarity based on common requirements, approaches and learning outcomes. As in the case of primary curriculum, secondary curriculum development preserves an interest in ensuring vertical and horizontal coherence and consistency of approaches throughout lower and secondary stages. This curriculum meets our country's needs and international requirements.

Openness and Flexibility

While catering for national unity and coherence, the secondary curriculum allows also for openness and flexibility. Students are provided with elective subjects though which they can envisage their local conditions, interests and needs in closer connection to conditions and perspectives of their local community. At the same time, textbook and other learning materials address different learning styles and provide for remedial action with a view to overcome leaning styles and provide for remedial action with a view to overcome learning difficulties of all kind.

Integrative Learning and Connections with Daily Life Situations

The secondary curriculum, while emphasising academic aspects of learning in more depth, caters also for integrated learning of specific ways. The new secondary curriculum introduces combination of subjects in areas such as sciences and social studies (lower secondary education). In addition, syllabuses and textbooks will highlight connections between different learning areas and subject and their relevance for daily life. All subjects address vocational aspects and skills as a means to prepare students for active citizenry and responsible participation in community matters, such as community service.

Cultural Awareness and Constructive Management of Diversity

The secondary curriculum aims at providing access of students to various aspects of Afghanistan cultures and traditions while developing a sense of respect for their heritage along with respect for, and interest in other cultures. Students are acquainted with Islamic values, traditions and ways of life. They are educated to appreciate the benefits of cultural diversity and manage differences peacefully and constructively.

Balance of Tradition and Innovation

The secondary curriculum caters for a good balance between tradition and innovation, and between local and international aspects and approaches. While learning about their traditions and past, as well as about their Islamic culture, students, both boys and girls, also have access to developments in the today's world in different relevant areas of human knowledge and action. Special emphasis is given to modern science and technology and to life long learning dimensions, such as learning to learn.

Education Policy Provisions for Secondary Education

Education content and methods ought to be underlined by sound policy provisions reflecting a consensual vision of education stakeholders and beneficiaries with regard to what should the students learn, why and how. Following were identified as important policy statements that education specialists should consider in the process of changing and improving the secondary education curriculum:

- Education in Afghanistan aims at developing in all citizens, males and females, children and young, a deep belief in Islam and loyalty to their country and countrymen based on cultivating Islamic values and a sense of national unity and living peacefully together.
- Education is eyed as an important resource for strengthening national unity and solidarity, patriotism and dedication of all citizens for defending national sovereignty, traditions and cultural values.
- Quality learning and education ought to feed altruist attitudes and refusal of discriminations of all kinds.
- The education system of Afghanistan has to be rebuilt in such a way that it connects to best practices and developments in the today's world. In reshaping secondary education, successful experiences of neighboring and other countries should be considered.
- Learners ought to develop interest in sciences and manifest respect and admiration for scientists. They should be able to make reasonable connections between causes and effects, and be aware of consequences (including ethical ones) human activities (including science and technology) may have on the natural and manmade environment.
- The education system of Afghanistan comprises of compulsory education (grades 1 to 9) and post-compulsory (grades 10 to 12). The first six years of compulsory education represent the primary stage, which is divided in two cycles (first cycle: grades 1 to 3; second cycle: grades 4 to 6). Grades 7 to 9 constitute lower secondary education—yet as part of compulsory education they complete the 9 years pertaining to basic education. Grades 10 to 12 pertain to upper secondary education (Islamic education; General education; Vocational education and Teacher training schools).

Structure of the Education System of Afghanistan

Primary education, lower and upper secondary education are free of charge and open to all students regardless of their ethnic affiliation, language, religion, sex, descent and social position.

- The education system is seeking for balance between different cycles/stages and grades, as well as between different streams (general, vocational and religious schools) and branches.
- Religious schools (madras's), general, vocational and teacher training schools benefit of equal attention from the ministry of Education and their facilities (in Kabul and provinces) should be improved substantially so that they can offer students a safe, civilized and motivation learning environment.
- Students should be instructed in the languages mentioned in the Afghanistan constitution and a good balance should be provided between mother tongue instruction and the learning of other mother tongues should be made possible through the curriculum in compliance with conditions and need of different regions.
- Special education provisions ought to be provided fro learners with disabilities, travelers and migrants (IDP and refuges/ returnees). Special attention has to be also given to the education of girls and women who ought to be encouraged attending formal education in both Kabul and the provinces.
- The academic level and professional skills of teachers ought to be improved considerably in line with improving livelihood for teachers in both rural and urban areas.
- The new secondary curriculum should support struggling against illiteracy and against inequalities and discriminations of all kind especially disparities boys' conditions.
- In its efforts to reconstruct secondary education in the country, the Ministry of Education relies on the altruistic participation and support of many countries, international organizations, non governmental organizations and other stakeholders. It aims at developing and improving further its managerial and administrative capacities along with improving and disseminating/implementing effectively transparent and coherent legal provisions for the education system.

The Scope of Secondary Education

Secondary education is divided in two stages:

(a) Lower secondary education/LS (Grades 7 to 9) constitutes the final stage of compulsory and basic education. Access to LS education is provided to all students without restrictions for it aims at accomplishing basic education goals for bout boys and girls, in the capital and the provinces. Lower secondary education is actually an upper-primary stage: students are offered a chance to develop and improve basic skills and key competencies, such as reading, writing and numeracy while starting exploring different areas of knowledge and human action in more depth and in a more systematic way, based on contents and methods pertaining to different learning areas/subjects of the curriculum. Lower secondary education has also an orientation function for students to learn about their strengths and weaknesses, their talents and interests in order to make informed choices regarding further studied and career paths. Streaming of students into religious schools (madrasas) should start after grade 9, and not after grade 6 as it was the case in past.

(b) Upper secondary education (Grades 10 to 12): Upper secondary education is streamed at present into (i) general/academic schools; (ii) vocational and technical schools; (iii) religious/Islamic schools (madrasas); and (IV) teacher training schools.

Upper secondary education is free of charge, but it is post compulsory. That means access of students to upper secondary is provided from those who are interested and able to pursue their studies in view of tertiary education and/or integration in the labour market. Access to upper secondary education takes into consideration the results of students in lower secondary education, their interests and talents, as well as society needs.

Upper secondary education opens doors for specialisation in different areas of knowledge and human action while also catering further for the overall development of students' personality and for the refinement of broad competencies in learners, such as communication, problem solving, social, emotional, spiritual and motor competencies.

General Aims of Secondary Education

Secondary education paves the way for further studies and integration of young in the labour market. Lower secondary education aims at accomplishing compulsory/basic education of 9 years as a basis for enhancing quality education for all. At the same time, it ought to provide access into upper secondary education to a larger number of young thus augmenting access and participation rates in upper secondary education aims at equipping young with knowledge and skills contributing to personal development and successful participation in public, professional and private lives.

The general aims of secondary education comply with general aims of education in Afghanistan, and they are as follows:

- To educate young in the spirit of Islam and support their development as true Muslims;
- To foster national identity and the sense of solidarity in the service of the Afghan nation's advancement;
- To educate civilized and functional persons able to participate constructively in today's interactions at local, regional, national and international levels;
- To help learners acquire and develop knowledge, skills and attitudes in compliance with Afghan religious and national values, and with international standards of excellence in all relevant areas of today's knowledge and human action;
- To equip students with knowledge, skills and attitudes that are required in the labour market and advise them with regard to career opportunities and choices;
- To cultivate in learners the values of peace, security, harmony and happiness at both individual/family and community levels.

In lower secondary education, special emphasis ought to be put on the following:

- To build on primary education achievements in the context of safe, friendly and effective educational environments;
- To develop further key competencies, such as communication in official languages of Afghanistan, local languages and international modern languages (listening, speaking, reading and writing), information processing skills; organisational skills (including usage of time); numeracy and scientific literacy skills;
- To enhance students' participation in the learning of different specific areas/subjects of the curriculum, such as Islamic

studies, mathematics, sciences, technology, social studies, language education (grammar, literature) and art education;

- To deepen students' understanding of religious and moral values and their observance of Islamic traditions and rules;
- To support students' personal development through emphasising aspects such as belief in God, self-respect and respect of the others; altruistic attitudes and honesty;
- To foster students' mental/intellectual, physical and social and emotional development through linking theoretical knowledge with daily life experiences and practical skills;
- To develop positive values and attitudes in students, such as patriotism, friendship, preservation of a safe and healthy environment, interest in working with others and sharing by pursuing common goals, rejection of any kind of discrimination and of means of war and destruction (i.e. drugs; violent acts; hatred);
- To guide students identify their strengths and weaknesses, their talents and interests with a view to make informed study and career choices.

In upper secondary education, learning outcomes of previous stages ought to be consolidated and new horizons have to be explored with students in order to prepare them for tertiary education and the labour market.

Curriculum Content and Structure

Curriculum areas and subject; Timetables (Grades 7 to 12)

The plan of study for lower and upper secondary education encompasses eight broad learning areas:

- Islamic studies
- Language education
- Mathematics
- Sciences
- Social studies
- Arts and culture
- Technologies
- Physical education/PE

The eight learning areas are essential for a unitary, comprehensive and balanced education in Afghanistan. Schools must ensure that all students have access to subjects in all eight areas during the twelve (respectively nine) years of schooling. The curriculum content and structure provide common requirements while catering also for flexible solutions addressing the students' learning styles, needs and interests, as well as local conditions and priorities i.e. agriculture.

Cross-cutting objectives and dimensions ought to be observed in all subjects, such as:

- Psycho-social training and guidance for students, especially with a view to help them overcome traumas and develop their personal and social skills;
- Language education and communication: all students should master communication skills in their mother tongue and the official languages of the country, as well as in modern foreign languages;
- Awareness of Afghanistan's culture(s) and traditions; interest in, and respect for other cultures and for constructive management of diversity;
- Integration of vocational aspects in all learning areas and subjects in order to prepare students for integration to the labour market;
- Participation in community life and in community service as a basis for fostering active, competent and responsible citizenry.

Curriculum Framework: Implication for Syllabi Development

On the basis of this curriculum framework, MoE made a plan to prepare syllabi for lower and upper secondary education. To achieve this end a group of 40 persons, mostly senior officials of MoE were assigned to participate in an international workshop in Amman, the capital of Jordan. This writer was included in this delegation which took place for a month from November 18, 2006 to December 14, 2006. In Amman, the professors of different Universities of Jordan were working with the Afghan delegations together to work out syllabi for all subjects of Afghan schools. The Jordanian professors are skillful and professional individuals in the area of developing curriculum and making syllabi. This delegation carried out their task with another group of specialists from NSW Australia, University of Massachusetts and Delaware of USA.

On the basis of the curriculum framework which was made before syllabuses were developed for lower secondary (grade 7-9) and upper second day (grade 10-12). Curriculum framework: implications for syllabus development included the following areas:

- Cross-cutting issues such as communication, social skills, environment education, gender issues, health and HIV/AIDS education, traditions and culture and so on.
- Balancing tradition and innovation syllabus template included the following areas: introduction, rationale for the subject, learning objectives
- Mapping of subject/content and learning outcomes (scope and sequence) for different grades (strands/topics, outcomes, activities and methods of assessments)
- Other information, such as student homework

An example of the form of syllabus is as follow:

Table of Scope and Sequence for Grade 10, 3 Hours per Week

Strand	*Topics*	*Subtopics*	*Knowledge*	*Skills*
Part: 1 History	Unit-1 Islam and Afghan	• Situation of Arab peninsula before Islam • Mohammed's life and his personality • Prophet in Madena • Politics, culture and economy during the Prophet's time	• To become acquainted briefly with the situation of Arab Peninsula before Islam • To know Mohammed's personality • To become familiar with Mohammed's l ife in Mecca • To become familiar with political, cultural and economic situations of Muslims during Mohammad's time.	• To be able to analyze briefly Arab's situations before Islam. • To explain Mohammed's life and personality

Textbook Development

A textbook as defined in a lexicographical note is a book that contains detailed information about a subject for pupils/students who are studying that subject, e.g. a science textbook of chemistry. For many people the term "textbook" refers to "learning materials used in the classroom". This is the replacement of the term "school book", which is also in vogue in some countries.

Textbooks are a tool for learning. These also explain the specific role of textbooks as nucleus of all learning activities related to a particular curriculum or syllabus. In a technical term a textbook is a teaching tool to help student to acquire some learning. All other pedagogical activities revolve around the material that reflects curriculum, the outline of study and the syllabi.

Textbook development as a field of study has quite been considered as part of pedagogy because it is the end result of the curriculum development. A textbook is necessary tool between a teacher and taught. It mediates transfer of knowledge, believes, behavioural aspects and skills. As such it focuses on basic cognitive elements and techniques to develop or inculcate a complete body of knowledge and has its own course to run.

There is a big history of text book improvement and this history leads to a textbook war in the west. Some say that a textbook can not translate knowledge curriculum to its entire satisfaction, as a textbook is just a reading material and the knowledge is not transferred through this medium of skill only. The others declare that they can improve textbooks to impart skills and changed behaviours.

Teacher Training Programme

We should Reach Out to Afghanistan's 183,000 Teachers

Teacher training has a long history in Afghanistan. During King Mohammad Zahir Shah and Precedent Mohammad Dawad rule Ministry of Education had a reasonable teacher training and teacher education programme. At that time teacher training programme, had a form of in-service training. During the rule of these leaders the Ministry of Education of Afghanistan were inviting the teachers form all over the country to Kabul city, the capital of the country. These teachers were given knowledge and skills in their area of study as these teachers were taking psychology and pedagogy courses at will. The teachers were invited to Kabul during their vacation time in the winters. They were living in Teacher Training College dormitory, near Kabul University. The training programmes were for two-three months. Professors form Kabul University and other scholars (Afghans and foreigners) were teaching the teachers. It was a centralised type of in-service teacher training programme. It was neither efficient nor effective.

The Present Challenges

Education in Afghanistan is seriously hampered by a shortage of qualified teachers. Afghanistan has only about 183,000 teachers for 7.2 Million students, making a classroom ratio of about 53 students per teacher. In some communities, as many as 70 (or more) students are sitting in a single classroom.[8]

Abut 6 per cent of our teachers have a degree of beyond high school. About 183,000 teachers need upgrading. Over 80 per cent of teachers teach in rural, remote areas. Teachers receive $55 to $65 per month (In April 2009 the teachers may get a salary raise). Teacher education/training needs a revised certification system based on standard and competences.

The Response

In collaboration with several donors, USAID, Afghanistan primary Education Programme (APEP) helped initiate the Teacher Education Programme (TEP) identified inadequate training as a main constraint to quality of education and in 2003 set up a programme of in-service teacher training to provide relevant knowledge, skills and change of attitudes. TEP immediate goal was to develop urgently needed in-service teacher training. Initially it was planned that over a ten year period, in a collaborative effort between the Ministry of Education and the Ministry of Higher Education, TEP will address four major issues:

1. Comprehensive reform of Afghanistan's teacher education to promote the professional development of teachers.
2. Pre-service teacher training (PRESET).
3. In-service teacher training (INSET).
4. Institutional development to support teacher education.

To address these four issues our previous old system of teacher training was neither efficient nor effective. A very new and famous teacher training model was selected for this purpose. This teacher training model is called Ugandaian Model. This model is consisted of the following components.

1. A Nationwide In-service Training;
2. A design team and core trainers who produce training package;
3. Core trainers who train master trainers;
4. Master trainers who train teachers' educators in provinces;
5. Teacher trainers form resource teams (TRTS), who provide training, a follow-up to teachers at sub-provincial level.

Professional Standards for Primary and Secondary Teachers (6)

Dr. Edna Mitchell of APEP, TEP Primary Standards Committee and MOHE made ten standards for teachers in January 2005 to teach their students. Basically, the first eight standards were made for primary level and then considering secondary level, two more standards were added to them. These professional standards each have three main purposes including knowledge, skills and attitude:

Quality is Given First Priority

Ministry of education gives first priority to quality teacher training now. Teacher training programme needs to be:

1. Standard-based, linked to new curriculum and textbooks which are prepared already or under.
2. Preparations based on a unified curriculum (regardless of where trained).
3. Learner-centered value-appropriate.

Also, Teacher Training System Needs to:

1. Certify
2. Continue the updating and upgrading begun

Based on the new standards, the continuing in-service programme will include these topics: Child psychology, pedagogy, classroom organization, new textbook development, material development, assessment/evaluation, planning, school management and community involvement. The purpose of MoE is to make in-service training nationwide and out reach to remote rural areas and the grassroots where real needs exist.

Summary and Conclusion

We tried to conduct a situation analysis of curriculum, syllabus and teacher training, in past and present. We explained that our curriculum syllabus, and teacher education were not meeting our country and children needs and they were in line with is the present requirements. Then we explained our new curriculum which based on the needs of our county and children. We have developed our curriculum and our syllabi on the basis our international standards and requirements. On the basis of our new curriculum we developed our syllabi. In our new syllabi we took into consideration vertical and horizontal sequences and objectives for each subject. We discussed that on the basis of our new curriculum we prepared textbooks for primary schools. Most of the textbooks for secondary schools are written, printed and distributed to students and the remainder of them will be written, published and distributed during the coming academic year.

We discussed the issues of in-serine training in detail. We explained that our previous teacher training programme was neither efficient nor effective. We are utilizing Ugandian teacher training model now. Based on this model we have design team and core trainers to produce training packages. We have core trainers to train master trainers, we have master trainers to train teacher educators in provinces, we have teacher educators to form resource team in order to provide teacher training and follow-up to teacher at sub-provincial level. We said that our present teacher training programme is standard based, inked to the new curriculum and textbooks, based on a unified curriculum, student-centered, relevant and value-appropriate.

Recommendations

1. Gender issues, gender problem and gender equity and equality should be taken into consideration when the authors are written the new textbooks and teacher guides. It is a very serious and professional task. Our friendly country people, the Indians, experience in this regard is very important for the MoE.
2. At this moment of our history, peace-building and cultivation of peace concept in the minds of our people and our children is very important and essential. We have to reflect these concepts in the textbooks for our children. Moreover, reconciliation is another very important concept that should be reflected in our textbook and in our teacher training programmes to enable our teachers to teach our children. Very competent and professional textbook writers and experienced master trainers and teacher trainers are required to carry out these very important tasks.
3. Democracy is a new born baby in Afghanistan. In the curriculum of MoE there is an area called culture, democracy, human-rights and art. India as a model of democracy in the world can help us in this respect. How to achieve this goal, the afghan and Indian scholars and educators should sit together and thank about a project regarding this very important subject.

Note and References

1. T. Gretee, *Curriculum Development and learning Material.* A paper prepared by a committee in ACBR, 2003.
2. Attash Durani, *et al. Textbook Development.* Islamabad: Allama Iqbal Open University, 2008.
3. Dakmara Georgescu, Secondary *Curriculum Framework (Grade 7 to 12) What Should Students Learn and How?* An International Workshop in Ottawa Hotel, Kabul, 2006.
4. Dakmara Georgescu, Curriculum Framework: Implication for Syllabus Development. An International Workshop 18.11.2006-14.12.2006, All Fanar Hotel, Amman, 2006.
5. Mary Ellen Lepionk, *Writing and Developing your College Textbook.* 2nd ed. Gloucester: At lantic path publisher Com, 2008.
6. Edna Michell. *Proffessional Standards for Secondary Teachers.* Ministry of Higher Education Kabul, Afghanistan, 2005.
7. Ministry of Education. *Teacher Education Programme: A Multi-Stakeholder Collaboration for Afghanistan.* An International Workshop for Teacher Training Programme, 2005.
8. TEP was and still is a joint program of the Ministries of Education and Higher Education, implemented with the technical and financial support of five international partners. UNICEF, USAID, DANADA, JICA, and the world Bank.

17

The Involvement of *Jirga* System and Role of Community Based Councils in Reconstruction of Afghanistan

Farhat Akram

Introduction

Almost three decades of conflict and civil war have caused massive disillusionment, disruption and disintegration of Afghan state and society thus representing a classic example of challenges and dilemmas facing international community in the so-called 'new world disorder'. To help resolve the problems faced by the "land of unruly" what is required as opposed to these 3Ds (i.e. disillusionment, disruption and disintegration), 3Rs: reform, re-engagement and reconstruction.[1] While various reforms and reconstruction efforts launched since end of the *Taliban* regime were in order to create a sound base for democracy, good governance and economic development in Afghanistan, it nevertheless remained short of the desired objectives. This is because they were unable to create an effective linkage between international developmental efforts and local informal traditional institutions. By reviving developmental role of village and area councils, as effective linkage, could become an effective policy option in order to jumpstart development and reconstruction efforts. The participatory approach by international community for reconstruction and development in Afghanistan has now reached a "stand off" point between what the international community wished to see, in terms of their liberal ethos and what the Afghans were trying to carve out for themselves, "to cajole and adapt to their circumstances, culture and history".[2]

In order to understand the essence of the Afghan conflict and to arrive at a probable solution for chaotic conditions, it is necessary to discover the missing link that would reconcile liberal institutions of international community with popular local traditional tribal institutions. This paper tries to underline the fact that any nation-building or reconstruction efforts may not succeed if it ignores existing traditions, cultural values and symbols. Most of these developmental efforts can be effectively created when constructed on the concept of enhancing local capacity through inclusive and intense engagement of national and sub-national stake holders. In other words, in order to have a trickle-down development approach at grassroots level, existing customs, values, traditions and local power structures in a tribal and traditional Afghan society cannot be minimised. The post-Bonn era provided the Afghans an opportunity to rebuild their war-torn country. The Afghan Constitution of 2004 provided a "bottom up" approach for active grassroots level participation of native population in the rebuilding process. In formulating comprehensive participatory frameworks, the international community neglected the traditional aspect of Afghan society where local governance institutions are more respected and considered legitimate than the newly installed councils for development. The rich tradition in Afghan society and the resilience[3] they have demonstrated during decades of conflict are yet to be fully comprehended and reconciled to the international community given their uneasiness with traditional and informal institutions. Reviving the developmental role of village and area councils, while creating an indigenous and effective leadership, could turn out to be an effective policy option to expedite development and reconstruction.

The paper intends to study the linkages between village councils, such as the *Jirga* and various participatory models of the International community such as National Solidarity Programme (NSP). In addition, it brings out various areas of convergence and divergence of these community based organisations and traditional councils. Finally, it exposes various limitations and challenges faced by these programmes.

I. Setting the Historical Context

Afghanistan and its civil society have been devastated and continued facing enormous socio-economic challenges wrought by wars and interventions and till today compounded by drought, poverty and Internally displaced persons (IDPs). The fighting against foreign invaders and civil war transformed the traditional fabric of the state, embedded multilayered power structures and disrupted the evolution process that had first begun in the eighteenth century. Afghan history depicts that before the Communist coup, the Afghans managed to establish effective local governance with a fair level of connection with strong centre due to adoption of 1964 constitution. This introduced a democratic state than the previous ones. But the democratic practice introduced remained as "democracy from the above"[4] as with minimal level of participation of local communities[5] elections were elections of personalities.[6] The uneasy relations continued between the core and periphery[7] of the Afghan society even after the Communist coup in 1978[8]. During the 1980s, most of the country drifted under a combination of traditional local institutions and remnants of pre-communists administration and overlaid by Mujahideen commanders (warlords) with the local population having least involvement in the government.

After the Soviet Union left Afghanistan 1989, a vacuum was created but swiftly filled by the Mujahideen forces after a brief period of peace, civil war broke among different factions resulting in damage to society and state structure at local district and community levels. These local commanders became oppressive to such an extent that their rule led to huge exodus of refugees to neighbouring countries. The *Taliban* emerged as a new force out of the deprecation of these commanders and were supported by the locals at various levels. They fanned out throughout the length and breadth of the country and established their form of governance based on self-interpreted governance principles of structured on Islamic jurisprudence. They stripped powers of the Centre and ruled through the network of local appointees through force and coercion. The US invasion of 2001 abruptly overthrew the *Taliban* regime with the local support. The vacuum was soon swiftly filled by the warlords establishing their power centres at the local level.

Post 9/11 and more precisely post-Bonn environment enabled Afghan people to venture forth and become custodian of their fate. Once labeled as a "Rentier state" by scholars[9] Afghanistan required assistance from outside to help rebuild a stable, democratic and prosperous country that would contribute to regional and global security. Various national level governance models[10] were drafted and implemented along with the ratification of a new Constitution, establishment of a new parliament, followed by election of the *Wolesi Jirga* (Lower House of Parliament). However what was lacking has still remained missing since 2002, an effective implementation of governance models which lacked efficacy in execution at local levels. This distrust and conflict between the centre and the periphery has exacerbated and continued even today. The traditional local distrust with the government interference strongly conflicted with the need for state building and state managed assistance to address reconstruction and development needs.[11]

The post-Bonn approach aimed at bringing the conflict to an end reconciling with the different warring factions which had allowed warlords to assume a preponderant role in governance. Provision of March 2007 of *Wolesi Jirga* whereby all alleged war criminals among the parliamentarians were provided amnesty reflected attitude of compromise by the incumbent Karzai government. Increasing poverty, proliferation of opium trade and resistance to change, are few of the challenges that were being faced by the Afghan state. These challenges may seem unprecedented. Yet the international community, peace and reconstruction efforts could be strengthened by merging them with local traditional institutions widely supported by the local Afghan population.

Table 1: Afghanistan Economic and Social Statistics[12]

Population:	*31 million*
Ethnic Groups:	Pashtun 42%; Tajik 27%; Uzbek 9%; Hazara 9%; Aimak 4%; Turkmen 3%; Baluch 2%; other4%
Religions:	Sunni Muslim (Hanafi school) 80%; Shiite Muslim (Hazaras, Qizilbash, and Isma'ilis) 19%; other 1%
Size of Religious Minorities	Christians-estimated 500-8,000 persons; Sikh and Hindu-3,000 persons; Bahai's-400 (declared blasphemous in May 2007); Jews-1 person; Buddhist-unknown, but small numbers, mostly foreigners. No Christian or Jewish schools. One church, open only to expatriates.
Literacy Rate:	28% of population over 15 years of age
GDP:	$10.2 billion est. for 2008. $7.5 billion in 2007.
Value of opium production in 2008 est:	732 million (7% of GDP), down from 13% of GDP for 2007 (Aug. 2008 UNODC report.
GDP Per Capita:	$300/yr; ($800 purchasing power parity). Up from $150 year per capita when Taliban was in power GDP Real Growth: 12% (2007)
Unemployment Rate:	40%
Children in School/Schools Built:	5.7 million, of which 35% are girls. Up from 900,000 in school during Taliban era. 8,000 schools built; 140,000 teachers hired since Taliban era.
Afghans With Access to Health Coverage:	85% with basic health services access-compared to 8% during Taliban era, although access is more limited in restive areas. Infant mortality has dropped 18% since Taliban to 135 per 1,000 live births. 680 clinics built with U.S. funds since Taliban

Population:	*31 million*
Roads Built:	About 5,000 miles post-Taliban, including ring road around the country. Now possible to drive from Kabul to western border in one day.
Judges Trained:	950 since fall of Taliban
Access to Electricity:	15%-20% of the population.
Revenues:	About $1 billion in 2008; $715 million in 2007; $550 million 2006
Expenditures:	About $1.5 billion in 2008; $1.2 billion in 2007; 900 million in 2006. Afghan government to Contribute $6.8 billion during 2008-2013 for $50 billion Afghan National Development Strategy; the remainder to come from international donors.
External Debt:	$8 billion bilateral, plus $500 million multilateral. U.S. forgave $108 million in debt to U.S. in 2006
Foreign Exchange:	$3 billion (Karzai interview September 2008), Foreign Investment $500 billion est. for 2007; about $1 billion for 2006
Major Legal Exports:	fruits, raisins, pomegranate juice (Anar), nuts, carpets, semi-precious gems, hides Oil Production: negligible
Oil Proven Reserves:	3.6 billion barrels of oil, 36.5 trillion cubic feet of gas, according to Afghan government on March 15, 2006
Major Imports:	food, petroleum, capital goods, textiles
Import Partners:	Pakistan 38.6%; U.S. 9.5%; Germany 5.5%; India 5.2%; Turkey 4.1%; Turkmenistan 4.1%, Number of Cell phones 5.3 million

Traditional/Customary Councils: *Jirga* and *Shura*

Jirga[13]*/Shura and Maraka*[14] are traditional local councils that have been predominantly practiced throughout history by the Afghan people. Mountstrutat Elphinstone, British statesman and historian, described *Jirga* as the "internal government of the Pashtun tribe".[15] At the local level these customary system of "self-governance" continues to exist and functions, even during the worst of times, in tribal Pushtun areas. According to Pushto descriptive dictionary, "*Jirga* is an original Pushto word, which in its common usage refers to the gathering of a few, or a large number of people; and meant consultation.[16] Some scholars believe that it has a Turkish origin and is derived from the word '*Jirg*', which means a 'wrestling ring', or a circle. But more specifically, it has been defined in terms of gathering of the people. These social structures have evolved through time and traversed through diverse discourses many changes and adjusting.

Jirga/Shura structures are actually egalitarian bodies where every member has a voice, representing his lineage (*Qaum*) or its constituent households. However, in practice this egalitarian principle is compromised by the social inequality found throughout the rural Afghan areas. The *Jirga/Shura*[17] (*Maraka*[18]) councils function mainly to resolve the emerging conflicts thus playing an important role in maintaining social order and not geared for everyday governance.[19] What is often misunderstood about traditional village councils is that they usually meet when there is a problem. But they may also be convened for other purposes related to collective action such as common defence or development projects.

Traditional local Pushtun institutions of governance have proven resilience and stability by their sheer capacity to continue to exist. Part of the reason for their continuity is because of the local paradigm or world view of the community.[20] The relations between the centre and the local power structures remained non-interfering through most part of the Afghan history. This practice over the years resulted in development of local communities in traditional ways. As Oliver Roy puts it "Traditional political forces have a need for a distant and benevolent state, whose experience they do not challenge"[21] Afghanistan is trying to reconstruct this 'fragile equilibrium" between the centre and periphery and Roy is of the opinion that currently "there is no...ideological force committed to replace the present regime".[22]

Table 2: Examples of Community Traditional Governance Actors and Structures[23]

Actor/Structure	*Other Names*	*Function/Meaning*
Ashar		*Communal Labour*
Commander	*Qumandan*	Local leader with armed followers who draws authority from defence of community or participation in Jihad or control of armed men.
Jirga		Conflict resolving council arise, conflicts range from disputes to maintenance of communal property
Khan	*Zimindar, Beg, Arbab, Sardar, Nawab,*	Large landowners who controls resources in the community; may provide jobs to labourers and land to sharecroppers; may also arbitrate conflicts.
Malik	*Arbab, Qaryadar*	Representative between community and central power/government. Can resolve disputes; maintains communal property.

Actor/Structure	*Other Names*	*Function/Meaning*
Ashar		*Communal Labour*
Commander	*Qumandan*	Local leader with armed followers who draws authority from defence of community or participation in Jihad or control of armed men.
Jirga		Conflict resolving council arise, conflicts range from disputes to maintenance of communal property
Khan	*Zimindar, Beg, Arbab, Sardar, Nawab,*	Large landowners who controls resources in the community; may provide jobs to labourers and land to sharecroppers; may also arbitrate conflicts.
Malik	*Arbab, Qaryadar*	Representative between community and central power/government. Can resolve disputes; maintains communal property.

Limitation of Traditional Councils (TCs)

Traditional *Jirgas* and *Shuras* play significant role in communities but possess several limitations in terms of providing critical base for democratic reforms at local level.

Elitist in Principal: They are Malik-based systems where local elite hold traditional power centre.

- *Undemocratic*: *Jirga* seems to be a democratic institution but it is minus involving women in decision making process except in very unusual circumstances, as for example, when they may act on behalf of a deceased husband.
- *Lack of Women's Role:* To address gender inequalities these *Shuras* are inappropriate as they are locked in their own dogmas and notions. Even the Afghan constitution of 1964, a limited number of women were allowed to participate in the parliamentary bodies. But the new Constitution of 2004 states that fifty percent of the members of the district and provincial councils would be women.[24] The programmes like that of NSP where new CDCs are formed required extensive women participation throughout the country.[25]
- *Rigid in Rules and Principles:* These traditional models have own set of regulations to implement traditional law (*Pashtunwali*) that are opposed to state laws much as punishment to criminals and ensuring law and order situation.

Frameworks for Effective Local Level Reconstruction

Since the end of the *Taliban* rule and after the Bonn process various significant frameworks for reconstruction were introduced. All of them were framed to set the stage to reconstruct the destroyed Afghan state structure. The Afghan government is working with international partners to address the country's immediate and long-term needs through these major policy frameworks. These policy structures promote participatory approach as Afghanistan National Development framework recognises that

> People in general and the poor in particular are not passive recipient of development but active engines of change. Sustainable development requires citizens' participation and adopting of methods of governance that enables the people to take decisions on issues that affect them and their immediate surroundings.

Afghan Constitution 2004[26] and CDCs

The Afghan Constitution of 2004 is decentralised in letter and spirit and provides effective provisions for local level participation and calls for the administration to increase participation. Moreover, it provides a structure for participation in local governance with councils to be elected to the provincial, district, village and municipal levels.

Provisions in Constitution

Article 84[27]**:** The article outlines the role of district and provincial councils in electing member of the Meshrano Jirga.

Article 138[28] *and 139*[29] describe the formation, terms and roles of Provincial Councils, stipulating that the provincial council "takes part in securing the development targets of the state and improving its affairs in a way stated in the law, and gives advice on important issues falling within the domain of the province"

Article 140[30] calls for the formation of councils at the district and village levels with the intent to "organise activities.... and provide [people] with opportunity to actively participate in the local administration." It is also mentioned in this article that "the participation of nomads in these councils is regulated by law"[31]. Constitution did not provide the really function of mayors and municipal councils.

Table 3: Key Legal Documents Related to Local Governance in Afghanistan[32]

Legal Documents	*Key Provisions of Local Level Governance.*
The Constitution of Islamic Republic of Afghanistan 2004	Provision for elected councils at village, district, municipality, and provincial levels.
Provincial Council Law of November 2005 (amended March 2007)	Describes Provincial Councils functions, including providing consultation (2005) and oversight without veto (2007) to provincial administration.
The Local Administration Law of 2000 (passed by Taliban in 1421)	Defines the Ministry of Interior's provincial and district structure
The Ministry of Rural Rehabilitation and Development (MRRD) of July 2005	Provides the guidelines regarding the establishment of the District Development assembly and the District Development Plan Linking these to provincial planning
Cabinet decision of November 2005	Establishes the Provincial Development Committees.
Decree of November 2006 establishing Community Development Councils (CDCs) bylaws	Institutionalise CDC as a local government unit at the village level
The Municipal Law of 1957	Provides for the election of municipal assembly, municipal council and deputy mayors

Although provincial council law in the Afghan constitution outlines the structures and authorities of provincial councils (PCs) the relationship of the PCs to provincial administration, village level communities, traditional governance and adjudication bodies (*Shuras and Jirga*), lower level district councils, the National Assembly and the Government in Kabul remained undefined.

Key Policy Documents Since Bonn Process

After the Bonn Process guided by the Afghanistan Millennium Development Goals (AMDGs)[33] major policy documents were prepared to lay the foundation for decentralisation and reconstruction at grass root level. In this regard, three key policy documents include:

National Development Framework (ANDF)—2002[34]

- Afghanistan Interim National Development Strategy (I-ANDS)—January 2006[35]
- Afghanistan Compact[36]

Adherence to AMDGs, I-ANDs, and Afghanistan Compact is coordinated and managed by twelve primary mechanisms known as National Priority Programmes (NPPs).[37] Three of these NPPs, i.e. the Afghanistan Stabilisation Programme (ASP), the National Solidarity Programme (NSP) and the National Urban Programme (NUP) are directly related to the local government and capacity building.

Afghan Stabilisation Programme (ASP) involves local administration, both infrastructure and personnel, at district and provincial level.[38]

- National Urban Programme (NUP) aims at urban infrastructure, urban services, and administration.
- National Solidarity Programme (NSP) deals with local governance at villages level, electing village Community Development Councils (CDCs).

Development and reconstruction in Afghanistan is primarily carried out two instruments: the Afghan Budget and Afghanistan Reconstruction Trust Fund (ARTF)[39] of May 2002. The ARTF supports investment projects, capacity-building, feasibility studies, technical assistance and the return of expatriate Afghans. These development frameworks make reference to establishment and improvement in structures that contribute to overall development but little attention has been paid about improvement and proper implementation of these structures. Unfortunately, implementation has remained relatively ineffective at the sub-national level because there is not a coherent and common vision for a sub-national government structures and how new institutions will integrate into the existing complex formal and informal local governance.

Table 4: Administrative and Political Structures: Traditional and Non-traditional (Governmental Level)

Non-Traditional		*Traditional and local*
Central Government	• President, • Ministries	• Parliament/*Loya Jirga*
Provincial Government	• Governor • Ministry Departments • Chief of Police	• Provincial Council • Provincial Development Committee • Sectoral Council
District Government	• *Woluswal* (District Governor) • Ministry Departments • Chief of Police	• Traditional *Jirga/Shura* • District Development Assembly

	Non-Traditional	*Traditional and local*
Municipal Government	• Mayors	• Elections have not taken place
Village Government	• Schools • Health Clinics	• Traditional *Jirga/Shura* • Community Development Councils • Sectoral Councils • *Malik/Arbab* (traditional economically powerful village leaders) • *Mirab* (village water controller) • *Khans/Nawabs*

National Solidarity Programme (NSP) and Community Development Councils (CDCs)

National Solidarity Programme (NSP) (Dari: *Hambastagi-e-melli* while in Pashto: *Milia Paiwastoon*) is a national level rural reconstruction and development project created and implemented in 2003 by the Ministry of Rural Rehabilitation and Development led by the Transitional Islamic Government of Afghanistan (TISA) It was defined by NDF and is one of the still functioning original element of the National Priority Programmes (NPP). Through the promotion of good local governance, the NSP main objective is to alleviate empower rural communities to make decisions affecting their own lives. Keeping in view this context, NSP was launched as one of the twelve NPPs throughout the country. The original NSP was followed by a second phase (referred to as NSP II) launched in April 2007. NSP II extended the programme to communities that were not covered by the first phase and has a three-year mandate instead of two years.

Programme Objective and Functions

This programme aims at conscious efforts to effect self governance through two main objectives via NSP's four core elements.[40] These objectives are:

(i) To establish a framework for village-level consultative decision-making and representative local leadership as a basis for interaction within and between communities on the one hand and the government and aid agencies on the other;

(ii) To promote local-level reconstruction, development and capacity building, that would lead to a decrease in poverty levels.[41]

The NSP interacts at basic and core level of traditional power structures. The programme can be seen as restructuring and realigning the traditional structures that can re-establish the "fragile equilibrium" of a sustainable Afghan State. According to a source,[42] Amir Abdur Rahman did exactly this re-shaping and re-aligning of "tribal aristocracy and religious establishment" to bring about the first semblance of a stable Afghan state that lasted till 1978. The programme is trying to break the old dogmas and taboos associated with historical norms and practices that concern the participation and inclusion of local communities in a traditional, hierarchical and centralised state system, as well as norms and values with regard to women's participation in community affairs.[43]

The programme is implemented with the help of NSP Facilitating Partners—UN Habitat and twenty eight international and local NGOs. The core function of NSP activity is human capital development, involving administrative training for Community Development Council members as well as literacy and improved livelihood involving women at the primary participants. With the core objective of creating empowered rural communities collectively so as to increase human capacity, the programme is inclusive, supporting entire communities including the poorest and vulnerable people. The programme approaches the community level governance so that local people manage the sub-projects that improve access of the people to development.

Methods of Execution of NSP

The CDCs are the basic units of NSP. These are the organisations elected to form a base on participatory philosophy of development which emphasises working with local institutions. CDC is to identify project needs in close cooperation and consultation with the community members by whom it was elected, to priority projects, and to prepare and submit proposals for projects to MRRD. The responsibility for overall management and supervision lies with the Ministry of Rural Rehabilitation and Development after the release of block grant[44] CDCs manage the approved projects with community contributions and is facilitated at village level through NGOs, the Facilitating partners (FPs).

Gender and NSP

Participation of women in development activities is of high priority in the NSP approach for community development but generally it has remained the most sensitive and difficult problem faced by the FPs and NGOs.[45] The participation of women in post-conflict society like Afghanistan is necessary in view of the huge task of reconstruction and development of the country, and women's contribution as a resource require participation in planning and decision making. It is believed that the participation of women in the reconstruction and development of Afghan society has been effected by the norms and values as participatory approach challenge the central concept of *Purdah*. In a sharp contrast to the "conservative" colour of Afghan society the NSP tried to validate the democratic activity by consciously making the 80 per cent[46] of the voters for an election to assure women participation in certain CDCs. Without the participation of women in the NSP, the dream for empowerment of citizens will only include half the population of Afghanistan. Women's participation in decisions making in various spheres of social, economic and political processes could change the historical gender difference that has existed for long. Though not denying the fact that the CDCs would provide avenue where women may influence, participate and have their voices heard the pre-history gender dogmas would be hard to change easily.

Elections by NSP

These CDCs are formed through election process, a sharp contrast to what we have observed in village *Shura* and *Jirga* councils. These are also not gender discriminative and both male and female may become part of the council with the help of adult franchise. Various evaluation units and agencies have conducted surveys of the CDCs and found them very effective[47] but at the ground level, only 60 per cent of them meet the governance objectives of the programme. Elections for CDCs are the central element of NSP, both with regard to community participation in reconstruction and development, and as a catalyst for inclusive learning about democracy.

Elections are conducted according to a specified set of rules which require that:

Everybody in the community is entitled to vote in government elections;

- Each person has one vote;
- Both men and women are eligible to vote and to be members of CDCs;
- Candidate and electioneering is prohibited; and
- At least forty per cent of eligible voters have to vote for an election to be valid.[48]

Non Governmental Organisations: Facilitating Partners (FPs)

Facilitating partners (FPs) are the clusters of NGOs that are involved in the NSP. They provide the block grants; use various approaches to reach out to the communities. According to the information[49] NSP has contracted with 29 FPs and one UN Agency (UN-Habitat) to work directly with targeted communities to implement NSP activities at the local level. More than 4,000 FP staff support programme implementation. Specific activities undertaken by FPs include:

- Educating communities on NSP policies and procedures;
- Facilitating fair and open elections of Community Development Councils (CDCs);
- Providing technical assistance to help CDCs prepare a Community Development Plan, develop subproject proposals, and promote values of transparency and inclusiveness;
- Providing other assistance during project implementation;
- Training CDC members in management skills; and
- Conducting monitoring and reporting.

Challenges Faced by NSP Based CDCs

NSP has started without having the fair level of base where such kind of "out of the box" projects acquire the status of a success. Absence of effective civil society, literacy, development, security, effective economic base and fair level of understanding of such programmes (among government sectors and masses) would result into certain level of failures and challenges exacerbate and become insurmountable. Underlining democratic notion of NSP has to be adapted according to the particular needs of the communities and not the communities work to an ideal type of the system provided by the international community. Facilitating partners supporting the NSP project highlighted various areas of challenges these CDCs face at the ground level. These include the process to negotiate with the local power holders, issue of gender where women are the harbingers of change and to assure there active participation in the programme, to find legitimacy and authority at the grassroots level except having the support of the government and FPs, and how the programme may well be sustained and continued in the absence of FPs.[50]

Introduction of NSP in the local communities have caused various traditional power structures feel threatened and marginalised and have thus caused the deepening of the divide and conflict. This is because of the fact that CDCs of NSP are gaining power in realms beyond development, which include community conflict resolution role of traditional councils and political representation on district, regional and provincial councils. The decades of disruption and conflict caused multilayered power structures to compete for governmental and communal legitimacy where NSP adds the CDCs to the mix. NSP may be seen as re-aligning of the local power structures that already exist in Afghan communities, NSP also introduced values that are contrary to local culture such as women's participation, and elections.

Difference Between Traditional Village *Jirga* and NSP initiated CDCs

From various reports[51] it was evaluated and found that the CDCs are perceived and accepted by the communities as facilitating tools for the reconstruction and development. It has also been found out that the perception about the government by the local communities which includes villages *Shura/Jirgas*, is that it is an "excretive (separate) one way system" and the relationship exists on "factional elitist politics" where *Malik* act as the middle man in this top down government.[52] The legitimacy and legality provided to the CDCs under NSP by the MRRD and Government of Afghanistan, provides installed structures with some credibility so as to become acceptable to the locals. This is one of the major factors that make a distinct characteristic of the traditional customary governance structures (*Jirga/Shura*) and Community Development Councils as formal democratically elected decision making body a perceived by the people.

It was also found out[53] that communities from all the provinces that were involved in NSP initially were reluctant to engage in the project. This perception was due to their historically negative experience of unfulfilled government promises, and fear of change induced by foreigners, including the fear of threats to traditional norms and values by western culture. Along with this the CDCs need time for consolidation in the communities, in order to become fully recognised as new local-level formal institution working in parallel to the local traditional governance structures.

Following table enlists the differences that exist between *Jirga/Shura* and the CDCs initiated by the NSP.

Table 5: Traditional Village *Jirga* versus Community Development Councils

	Traditional Shura	*Community Development Council/Formal*
Membership	*Open*	*Fixed*
Legality/support	Informal customary structure of local level governance	A decision making body supported by MRRD, FPs, NGOs and the Government
Member characteristics	Age Religious competence Economic power/social power Contact with authorities	Development vision Modern education Representative of whole population Contact with agencies
Objectives	Problem-solving and conflict Resolution	Planning, implementation and running of community projects
Function	Reactive	Proactive
Structures	Loosely structured with elders and experienced at the centre	Formal posts: • Chairman/Chairperson (*Rais*) • Deputy chairman • Secretary or clerk (*munchi*) • Accountant.
Method of voting	Discussion/hand raising/non-democratic	Secret ballots/Elections
Gender	Restricted to Men only	Men/women both can participate

Above list clearly depicts the deep divide between the two structures working in parallel to each other. Key concept here is that to link customary/traditional councils with formal governance structures in a way that both work in coordination with each without having any enduring conflict that further divides the already divided society. Both have their own positive and negative characteristics which can equally be fruitful.

Concluding Reflections

The key concept of the paper revolves around the argument is that any reconstruction or reform effort in Afghanistan will not be successful unless and until the local traditional values are not incorporated along with the modern liberal development initiatives. The underlying idea is that integrated efforts in Afghanistan, culture of the particular region and local value structures cannot be ignored. There is a growing need of "Afghanisation" of reconstruction efforts where by the natives become the custodian of their own destiny. It is believed that when reform missions establish there presence in the conflict zones then they come into direct interaction with the local population in various important ways like that of socio-economic and cultural levels. Among the local population, the perception exists that whatever the reconstruction efforts or reform efforts are either of western style or of not, have the profound local colour that may help the population to identify themselves with the particular programme or any project. It has often been perceived by the population that these reform missions lack the basic understanding of the core values of structures that were being practiced by Afghans throughout their history. The imposition of western style formal and informal systems show even lack of sensitivity to the local society's own legal, political and conflict management traditions and elevates a specific normative ideal over exchange-based understandings that have more traction in and relevance to the affected society. Afghan Ministry for Reconstruction and Rural Development supported one of the National Priority Programme, illustrated as NSP, is functioning along with the traditional governance structures. The key concept of this programme is that local governance based on formal governance model is ineffective when it is not mediated through cultural practices and power relationships that are meaningful to the community. Traditional governance structures are the networks that are significant vehicles for political actions. Challenges are unprecedented to these grassroots level initiatives but it is significant that since the Afghans are custodians of their own destiny, they must share the large part of the efforts instead of solely relying on the efforts made and coordinated by the International Community.

Since grassroots level reconstruction efforts face various challenges and at the same time provide opportunities to reflect and find out a concrete way forward to minimise the intensity of the conflict.

Traditional local power stake holders still hold key decision making and implementing positions at village and municipal levels. There supporting structures like *Jirgas/Shuras* are acceptable and have fair level of legitimacy among the local population. It is suggested that if these formal institutions are bridged with traditional institutions successfully, then it will form communally acceptable governance structures at the local level. Hence, without threatening the local power structures, involving them as significant vehicles for change would be more fruitful. Although NSP is formulated on the basis of traditional form of governance in Afghanistan but the new CDCs members are not the traditional leaders. They need to reconnect with the mainstream in order to have a deep insight from these powerful locals. This would not only reduce their sense of threat, this practice would also provide an essential link between the government and the community.

- Illiteracy and lack of adequate effective knowledge at higher and local levels about various development initiatives is one of the major challenges that the international reconstruction efforts face at the moment. For example, governance objectives and accomplishments of NSP and CDCs were unknown to large number of government officials and only a few knew about the provisions that make CDCs more permanent institution. CDCs bylaws were signed in November 2006.[54] It is very important that information and insight are collected and shared among the government and donors on regular basis in order to have a complete picture of what are the policy developments, opportunity to learn and understand during the programme adjustment.
- At the community level, CDCs must define their relationship with the traditional institutions, including the *Jirgas/Shuras*, which people currently turn to for resolution of problems. Given the complex political terrain at the local levels, any recommendations for new institutions or structures must take into account how the structures will integrate with local organisations. Before initiating such structures at the local level, it would be necessary for the governance bodies at the higher level to consider the needs of local populations and what sorts of governance gap exist.
- An Afghan formulation of a coherent policy and strategy for sub-national governance, and its effective communication and implementation is required. The lack of attention to a strategy of reform of governance structures at sub-national levels like that of municipal, district and at the village level has resulted in confusion and uncoordinated initiatives. Provincial Councils were elected in 2005 because they were needed to form the National Assembly; but before any serious deliberation or laws

were written to define their roles and authority. CDCs were formed in many villages but some parts of government have seen these as governance institutions and others view these as part of particular rural development programmes.

- Lack of effective planning and absence of human resource capacity are the two major cross cutting issues that have limited the effective development of these sub-national governance structures. The weak conceptual approach to planning with minimum resources has only produced a long list of projects with no prioritisation, no indication of consultation and no technical and budget analysis thus these projects are frustrating the donors and the masses as there exists minimal relative response to these initiatives. More focus on budgeting and budget execution both at horizontal and vertical levels would pay much higher returns. While regarding the limited human resource capacity, a human resource strategy based on reform of administration, existing governance structures is needed in order to have effective execution of projects at various levels. The Public Administration Reform (PAR) and Priority Reform and Reconstruction (PRR) process remain on cards but have barely begun to be implemented.

Notes and References

1. Antonio Donini, "Local Perceptions of Assistance to Afghanistan", *International Peacekeeping*, Vol. 14, No. 1, January 2007, p. 169.
2. Tadjbakhsh Shahrbanou and Michael Schoiswohi, "Playing with Fire? The International Community's Democratization Experiment in Afghanistan," *International Peacekeeping*, Vol. 15, No. 2, April, 2008, p. 258.
3. See Masooud Karokhail and Susanne Schmeidl, "Integration of Traditional Structures into the State-Building Process: Lessons Learned from the Tribal Liaison Office in Loya Paktika", in *Promoting Democracy Under Conditions of State Fragility—Issue1: Afghanistan*, Berlin, Heinrich Boll Foundation, 2006, pp. 59-81, http://www.tlo-afghanistan.org/fileadmin/pdf/SchAfgahnEn.pdf.
4. Shahrbanou, and Schoiswohi, "Playing with Fire?", p. 255.
5. Inger Woesen, "From the Subjects to Citizens: Local Participation in the NSP," Working *Paper Series*, Afghanistan Research and Evaluation Unit, August 2004, p. 5.
6. L. Dupree, *Afghanistan*, London, Oxford University Press 1980, pp. 587-589.
7. See, Dupree, 1980; Grevemeyer,1987; A, Christensen, "Aiding Afghanistan: The Background and Prospects for Reconstruction in a Fragmented Society"

NIAS (Nordic Institute of Asian Studies) Reports, No. 6, Copenhagen,1995; Barnett Rubin and H. Malikyar, *The Politics of Center Periphery Relations in Afghanistan* (Washington, DC: World Bank, 2003) and various others for discussions of the relations between centre and periphery in Afghanistan.

8. The Democratic Republic of Afghanistan (DRA) was established with Soviet support in April 1978 and dissolved after the Soviet withdrawal in 1989, the collapse of the Soviet Union, and the fall of the DRA government to the Mujahideen *Talibans* in 1992.
9. Works like Antonio Giustozzi, *War, Politics and Society in Afghanistan,* London: Hurst and Co., 2000; Nazify M. Sharani, "State Building and Social Fragmentation in Afghanistan: A Historical Perspective" Richard S. Newell, "*The Prospects for State Building in Afghanistan.*" in *The State, Religion, and Ethnic Politics. Afghanistan, Iran and Pakistan: Contemporary issues in the Middle East*, Syracuse: Syracuse University Press, 1986; Angelo Rasanayagam, *Afghanistan. A Modern History: Monarchy, Despotism or Democracy? The Problems of Governance in the Muslim Tradition (New* York, 2003); the concept of Afghanistan as a rentier state is based on the analytical framework provided by, *Barnett Rubin, The Fragmentation of Afghanistan (Michigan*, 1995). New Haven and London: Yale University Press 1995.
11. Woesen, "From the Subjects to Citizens," p. 6.
12. *CIA World Fact book*, January 2008, Embassy of Afghanistan in Washington, DC; President Bush speech on February 15, 2007; *International Religious Freedom Report*, September 19, 2008; Afghan National Development Strategy.
13. For extensive study of the traditional institution of *Jirga* see Watkins 1963; Dupree 1969; Ghobar 1978; Male 1982; Bhabani 1985; Roy 1986; Ma'aroof 1987; Barth 1987; Carter and Connor 1989; Elphinstone 1992; Olesen 1995; Kakar 1995; Rubin 1995; Glatzer 1998; Giustozzi 2000; Rafi 2002; Wardak 2003; Khuram 2004; for a critical study of *Jirga* System see M. Elphinstone, *An Account of the Kingdom of Kabul,* Karachi: Oxford University Press,1972 (1815).
14. *Marka* involve very similar processes as that of *Jir*ga and both share the similar fundamental values. Therefore, the concepts are often are used interchangeably. However, the fact that *Jirga* deals with serious and important conflicts while *Maraka* deals with lesser significant issue which is relatively less serious at the local village level. It is loosely structured as compare to *Jirga* and its related rituals are not as elaborate as those of a tribal *Jirga* are. See for further explanation, Ali Wardak, "*Jirga*: Power and Traditional Conflict Resolution in Afghanistan" in John Jonathan Walter (ed.), *Law after Ground* Zero, London: Cavendish, 2002b.
15. Elphinstone, *An Account of the Kingdom of Cabul*, 215.
16. Cited in Ali Wardak, "*Jirga*".
17. *Shura* is Arabic word for "consultation". It is the method adopted by the pre Islamic Arab tribes and selected leaders to decide over the major issues related

to political decisions making. In Afghan context the institution of *Shura* used to resolve disputes related to business matters, property and family matters. In the war against the invading forces in early 80s, *Shura* was legitimised and was being used by the then Mujahdeen Commanders.

18. Difference of these two can be guessed from the definitions; *Jirga* is a Pashtun word, and comes from the Turkish for "Circle" *Jirg*. Both *Jirga* and *Maraka* are often used interchangeably. However, the difference between the two lies in the fact that Jirga deals with serious and important conflicts within the tribe, or between the tribes, operates at higher level of tribal formation and is more structured. While *Maraka* deals with civil and relatively less serious issues and loosely structured rituals. See Ali Wardak, "Building a Post War Justice System in Afghanistan", vol. 41, no. 4, May 2004, www. institute-for-afghanstudies.org/Contributions/Projects/AliWardak/Law%20and%20Social%20Change%204.doc
19. *Ibid.*
20. Cited in Palwasha Kakar, "Fine-Tuning the NSP: Discussions of Problems and Solutions With Facilitating Partners" *Working Paper Series*, Afghan Research and Evaluation Unit (AREU), 11 quoting T. Hoahe, "Clash of Paradigms in East Timor," *Contemporary South Asia*, Vol. 24, No. 3 (2002):570.
21. Oliver Roy, Afghanistan: Internal Politics and Socio-Economic Dynamics and Groupings, UNHCR—Write Net Paper, 2, http://www.unhcr.org/home/RSDCOI/3e9ae5535.pdf.
22. *Ibid.*
23. Cited in Hamish Nixon, "The Changing Face of Local Governance: Community Development Councils in Afghanistan", *Working Paper Series*, Afghanistan Research and Evaluation Unit (AREU), Kabul, 2008.
24. The Constitution of Afghanistan 2004, Article Eighty Four Chapter 5, Article 4.
25. Elections o f Community Development Councils (CDCs) resulted in non-election of traditional power brokers such as Maliks; Kakar, "Fine-Tuning the NSP" 13.
26. The Constitution of Afghanistan 2004, http://www.president.gov.af/english/constitution.mspx
27. *Ibid*, Article 84, Chapter Five.
28. *Ibid*, Article 138, Chapter Eight
29. *Ibid*, Article 139.
30. *Ibid*, Article 140.
31. *Ibid*, section 4.
32. "An Assessment of Sub-National Governance in Afghanistan" 2007, Asia Foundation.
33. In 2004, Afghanistan's transitional government declared its intention to achieve the Millennium Development Goals (MDGs) established at the 2000 UN Millennium Summit. MDGs are intended to act as a framework to guide the development of national policies and reconstruction priorities around

the world, with benchmarks set for 2015 and 2020. The MDGs are incorporated into the Afghanistan National Development Strategy and the Afghanistan Compact The eight MDGs are: 1. Eradicate extreme poverty and unger; 2. Achieve universal primary education; 3. Promote gender equality and empower women; 4. Reduce child mortality; 5. Improve maternal health;6. Combat HIV/AIDS, malaria and other diseases; 7. Ensure environmental sustainability; and8. Develop a global partnership for development. To this list, the Afghan government has added a ninth goal for its own development initiatives: enhancing security. In June 2005, the Afghan government held a conference in Kabul to discuss how to meet the MDG benchmarks and determine MDG progress. The meeting resulted in the "Afghanistan's 2020 Vision" report, in which most of the 2015 targets were revised to be met by 2020, recognising capacity constraints and security impediments on the country's development. "Millennium Development Goals (MDGs)", www.un.org/millenniumgoals.

34. The National Development Framework, April 2002, http://www.adf.gov.af/index.asp?page=faqs.
35. Afghanistan National Development Strategy (ANDS), www.ands.gov.af.
36. Full text of Afghan Compact see "The A to Z Guide to Afghanistan Assistance—Seventh Edition" Afghanistan Research and Evaluation Unit, 2009, 114-129.
37. The 12 National Priority Programmes (NPPs)—www.af/npp
38. Details about Afghan Stabilisation Programme (ASP), see, http://www.asp.gov.af/Default.asp?button=12.
39. Details about Afghanistan Reconstruction Trust Fund (ARTF), see, www.worldbank.org/artf.
40. The NSP seeks to attain these objectives through four core programme elements: 1) facilitating the creation of Community Development Councils (CDCs), representative decision-making bodies elected by secret ballot in fair and open elections involving both male and female community members;2) helping the CDCs produce a Community Development Plan (CDP), which outlines development priorities and proposes reconstruction projects;
    3) providing direct block grant transfers to fund CDP priorities; and 4) linking CDCs to government agencies, NGOs, and donors to improve access to services and resources; For more details see National Solidarity Programme official website www.nspafghanistan.org.
41. National Solidarity Programme official website, www.nspafghanistan.org
42. Cited in Kakar, "Fine-Tuning the NSP"11 quoting A. Ghani, "Islam and State Building in Afghanistan," *Modern Asian Studies*, Vol. 12, No. 2, 1978, p. 271.
43. Woesen, "From the Subjects to Citizens," 60.
44. Block grant: The grant provided by NSP to eligible communities, used to fund approved subprojects. It is calculated based on AFA 10,000 (approximately US$ 200) per family (subject to a maximum of AFA

3,000,000, i.e. approximately US$ 60,000 per community). Communities may elect to combine part or all of their block grant entitlements with those of other neighbouring communities to finance one or more joint-CDC subproject(s). see, http://www.nspafghanistan.org/about_nsp/nsp_definitions.shtm#BlockGrant.

45. Woesen, "From the Subjects to Citizens."
46. *Ibid.*
47. *Ibid.*
48. NSP official website, www.nspafghanistan.org
49. *ibid.*
50. For further details, *Ibid.*
51. Woesen, "From the Subjects to Citizens," and Kakar, "Fine-Tuning the NSP".
52. *Ibid.*
53. *Ibid*, 57-60.
54. Key findings of Asia Foundation report on "An Assessment of Sub-National Governance in Afghanistan" April 2007,

Contributors

Abdul Rahman Ulfat Mahmoodi, Relief, Recovery, Reconstruction, Institutional Development and Governance Officer, United Nation Assistance Mission for Afghanistan (UNAMA), Kabul.

Alef Shah Zadran, Senior Professor, Faculty of Social Sciences, Kabul University.

Aunohita Mojumdar, Freelance Journalist, Kabul.

Binoda Kumar Mishra, Fellow, Maulana Abul Kalam Azad Institute of Asian Studies (MAKAIAS), Kolkata.

Farhat Akram, Assistant Research Officer, Islamabad Policy Research Institute (IPRI), Islamabad.

Gulshan Sachdeva, Associate Professor, School of International Studies, Jawaharlal Nehru University (JNU), New Delhi.

Jagmohan Meher, Associate Professor in Political Science, National Defence Academy, Khadakwasla, Pune.

Jamal Syed Rehman, Advisor to the Chief of staff of Office of the President of Islamic Republic of Afghanistan on Foreign and Culture Affairs, Kabul.

Mondira Dutta, Associate Professor, School of International Studies, JNU, New Delhi.

Noorullah Elham, Senior Communications Assistant, Afghan Research and Evaluation Unit (AREU), Kabul.

PL Dash, Professor of Eurasian Studies, Centre for Central Eurasian Studies, University of Mumbai, Mumbai.

Sanaullah Tasal, Head, South Asian Affairs, Regional Studies Center of Afghanistan and Director, BCPCR Center.

Sanjeev Bhadauria, Associate Professor, Dept. of Defence and Strategic Studies, Allahabad Central University.

Sayed Muhammad Shah, Senior Policy and Communications Officer, Afghan Research and Evaluation Unit, Kabul.

Shahmahmood Miakhel, Country Director, United States Institute of Peace (USIP), Kabul and former Governance Officer, UNAMA, Kabul and Former Dy. Minister of Interior, Afghanistan.

Shakti Sinha, Former Officer, UNAMA, Kabul and former Research Fellow at the Institute of South Asian Studies, National University of Singapore.

Sreemati Ganguli, Fellow, MAKAIAS, Kolkata.

Vishal Chandra, Associate Fellow, Institute for Defence Studies and Analyses (IDSA), New Delhi.

Index